This book addresses some basic questions about intrinsic value: What is it? What has it? What justifies our beliefs about it? In the first six chapters the author defends the existence of a plurality of intrinsic goods, the thesis of organic unities, the view that some goods are "higher" than others, and the view that intrinsic value can be explicated in terms of "fitting" emotional attitudes. The final three chapters explore the justification of our beliefs about intrinsic value, including coherence theories and the idea that some value beliefs are warranted on the basis of emotional experience. Professor Lemos defends the view that some value beliefs enjoy "modest" a priori justification.

The book is intended primarily for professional philosophers and their advanced students working in ethics, value theory, and epistemology.

CAMBRIDGE STUDIES IN PHILOSOPHY

Intrinsic Value

CAMBRIDGE STUDIES IN PHILOSOPHY

General editor ERNEST SOSA

Advisory editors JONATHAN DANCY
GILBERT HARMAN, FRANK JACKSON
WILLIAM G. LYCAN, SYDNEY SHOEMAKER, JUDITH
THOMSON

Intrinsic Value

Concept and Warrant

Noah M. Lemos
DePauw University

CAMBRIDGE
UNIVERSITY PRESS

Published by the Press Syndicate of the University of Cambridge
The Pitt Building, Trumpington Street, Cambridge CB2 1RP
40 West 20th Street, New York, NY 10011-4211, USA
10 Stamford Road, Oakleigh, Melbourne 3166, Australia

First published 1994

Printed in the United States of America

Library of Congress Cataloging-in-Publication Data
Lemos, Noah Marcelino, 1956–
Intrinsic value : concept and warrant / Noah M. Lemos.
p. cm. – (Cambridge studies in philosophy)
ISBN 0-521-46207-X
1. Values.   I. Title.   II. Series.
BD232.L397   1994
121'.8 – dc20   93-48142
                                          CIP

A catalog record for this book is available from the British Library.

ISBN 0-521-46207-X hardback

To My Parents,
Mamie Lou and Ramon

Contents

Preface

The topic of intrinsic value is of fundamental importance for ethical theory. Many major moral theories recognize at least some prima facie duty to promote what is intrinsically valuable or good or to choose actions whose total consequences are intrinsically better than the total consequences of alternative actions. Furthermore, any account of what it is to lead a good human life would seem to require an account of what kinds of experiences and activities are good in themselves. In order to understand the nature of a good life or the requirement to promote what is intrinsically good or better, we must understand what it is for something to be intrinsically good or intrinsically better than something else. We must also appreciate what kinds of things have this type of value and how the patterns and relationships between various goods and evils can affect the intrinsic value of a life or an outcome. Philosophical reflection on these issues may lead us to wonder whether there can be knowledge or warranted belief about what kinds of things have intrinsic value and, if so, what is the source of that warrant. In other words, we may ask what, if anything, makes some of our beliefs about intrinsic value more reasonable than others. Such philosophical reflection may also lead us to wonder about the objects of moral belief and knowledge, how such things as moral facts and properties are related to "natural" or nonethical facts and properties. In these ways, philosophical thought about intrinsic value and its nature raises questions of moral epistemology and moral ontology.

The past seven years have seen the publication of two very important books in the theory of intrinsic value. Roderick Chisholm's *Brentano and Intrinsic Value* appeared in 1986, and Panayot Butchvarov's *Skepticism in Ethics* appeared in 1989. Chisholm's book is a sympathetic treatment and development of the views of Franz Brentano, and Butchvarov's is devoted to a broad range of issues in addition to intrinsic value, issues that include the theory of right action. Though very different books, both are splendid and undoubtedly superior in many ways to this one. Both of these works, especially Chisholm's, have influenced the views presented here. Still, this work deals with some issues that they do not address. For example, Chisholm does not address issues of naturalism and moral epistemology, and Butchvarov does not deal with organic unities and the summation of values. Moreover, on certain topics of common interest, I defend substantially different positions. For example, I differ from Butchvarov on the bearers of value and from both Chisholm and Butchvarov on moral epistemology.

I have divided the book into two parts. The first six chapters, comprising Part I, deal with some basic issues in the theory of value. Among these are the explication of intrinsic value, the bearers of value, value and part–whole relations, pluralism, and hedonism. The final three chapters, comprising Part II, focus on matters traditionally belonging to metaethics, including those of moral epistemology and ontology. The view defended in these final three chapters may be considered a form of nonnaturalistic cognitivism. In this work, these issues are approached philosophically and conceptually rather than historically, though I discuss the views of certain important historical figures, such as Plato, Aristotle, Kant, and Brentano, where their views are relevant. I also discuss various relevant recent and contemporary views, such as those of Chisholm, Butchvarov, G. E. Moore, C. D. Broad, W. D. Ross, Gilbert Harman, Laurence BonJour, and David Brink.

In Chapter 1, I consider how we might explicate or explain the concept of intrinsic value, how we might explain what it is for something to be good in and for itself. I follow the approach of Brentano, Broad, A. C. Ewing, and Chisholm in defending the view that intrinsic value may be explicated in terms of the notions of ethically "fitting" or "required" emotional attitudes such as love, hate, and preference. With this approach we can explicate the concepts of intrinsic goodness, badness, preferability, and various forms of neutrality. If we explicate intrinsic value in this way, then we may think of something's being intrinsically good as being analogous to a proposition's being an axiom or self-evident. If one can understand what it is for something to be an axiom, and if one can understand the concept of ethical requirement, then one can understand the concept of intrinsic value.

In Chapter 2, I consider what are the bearers of intrinsic value. Among the main candidates are concrete particulars (e.g., people or cars) and abstract objects (e.g., properties or states of affairs). Following W. D. Ross, I argue that what has intrinsic value are *facts* or states of affairs that obtain. States of affairs that do not obtain can nonetheless be intrinsically worthy of love, hate, or preference. I argue that neither concrete individuals (e.g., John Smith), nor properties (e.g., being happy) have intrinsic value. What has intrinsic value is the fact that John Smith is happy.

Chapter 3 examines the principle of organic unities and the thesis of universality. The principle of organic unities tells us roughly that the intrinsic value of a whole should not be assumed to be equal in value to the sum of its parts. The thesis of universality tells us roughly that the intrinsic value of a part is essential to it and that its intrinsic value is not conditional on what other states of affairs obtain, that the intrinsic value of a thing is not dependent on the context in which it occurs. The principle of organic unities is accepted by Moore and Chisholm and, implicitly, by Brentano. Chisholm provides some of the most persuasive examples of the principle. The thesis of universality is implicitly rejected by Ross and, perhaps, by Immanuel Kant largely because of certain views on the value of pleasure. I argue that these views are mistaken.

Chapter 4 explores the belief that some intrinsic goods are "higher" than others, that a good of one kind can never be exceeded in value by any number of instances of goods of another kind. The existence of such goods is accepted by Brentano and Ross and, perhaps, by Aristotle, Plato, and John Stuart Mill. Some defenders of the existence of higher goods, such as Ross, have made what seem to be extravagant claims, for example, that no amount of pleasure can ever be intrinsically better than a single morally good act. Although such claims appear extreme and untrue, denying them raises certain problems for the existence of higher goods. These problems can be avoided, I argue, if we accept what I call the "principle of rank." This principle is analogous to the principle of organic unities. It tells us roughly that the axiological character of a whole as a higher good need not be the same as the character of its parts, that a whole can be a higher good even if none of its parts are higher goods. The existence of higher goods, along with the principle of organic unities, presents serious obstacles to the view that the value of a whole, even a whole world, can be construed as the sum of its intrinsically valuable parts.

Chapters 5 and 6 focus on some main traditional candidates for intrinsic value. These include pleasure, desire satisfaction, the experience of various morally good emotions, knowledge, understanding, consciousness, beauty, and the flourishing of at least some forms of nonsentient life. I defend the pluralistic view that attributes intrinsic value to each of these. Chapter 5 examines three views on the relations between sensory and nonsensory pleasure, the value of nonsensory pleasure, and the truth of hedonism. Chapter 6 explores the value of knowledge, understanding, and consciousness and the value of such things as nonsentient life and beauty, whose existence presupposes no form of consciousness whatever. I also discuss briefly some of the practical problems of value pluralism.

Chapter 7 includes a discussion of both traditional and "constitutional", naturalism. The former holds roughly that intrinsic value is identical with or analyzable by natural properties and facts. The latter maintains, among other things, that intrinsic value is constituted by natural properties or facts and that intrinsic value is a natural property or fact. I argue that we have no compelling reason to accept either view and some reason to think that both are false. In discussing traditional naturalism's identity claims, I make use of Chisholm's intentional criteria of identity for properties and states of affairs. In defending, the existence of distinctive ethical facts and properties, I consider Harman's views of explanation and evidence.

If there is knowledge or epistemically warranted belief about intrinsic value, and if intrinsic value is distinct from natural properties and facts, then how is such knowledge or justification possible? Either claims about intrinsic value can only be justified empirically or some of them can be justified a priori. Some traditional accounts of a priori knowledge and justification make this alternative highly doubtful. In Chapter 8, I argue that we need not accept these traditional accounts but that we should accept the notion of "modest" a priori knowledge and justification, which requires neither epistemic certainty nor indefeasibility. If we accept the possibility of modest a priori justification, then it is much more plausible to think that some claims about intrinsic value are known or warranted a priori. I defend the view that some propositions about intrinsic value are intrinsically acceptable, though not necessarily self-evident or axiomatic.

In Chapter 9, I examine critically two alternative accounts of how beliefs about intrinsic value derive their warrant: pure coherence theories and broadly empirical theories that take various emotional experiences as grounds or evidence for value beliefs. Some philosophers, such as BonJour and Brink, have sought to defend a coherence theory by attacking the possibility of basic or foundational beliefs. Both use versions of the doxastic ascent argument. I argue that the argument is unsuccessful and present some objections to coherence theories of justification. In contrast to coherence theories, other philosophers, including Brentano and Meinong, as well as some contemporary philosophers, have held that some of our beliefs about value are warranted in virtue of some form of emotional experience, either ordinary emotional experience or emotions that are experienced as fitting. I argue that this approach faces serious problems.

Finally, I have included two appendixes. In Appendix A, I examine Chisholm's definition of an organic unity. This definition has the advantage of defining the concept of an organic unity without making use of the problematic notion of a "sum" of values. I argue that it is not adequate to certain forms of organic unity that Chisholm himself distinguishes. In Appendix B, I examine and reject some naturalistic analyses of the concept of intrinsic preferability.

Acknowledgments

I am deeply indebted to Professors Fred Feldman and William Tolhurst. Their comments and criticisms lead me to abandon some rather bad arguments, and those that remain are not their responsibility. I am also grateful for the work of Professors Roderick Chisholm and Panayot Butchvarov. Their works on value theory are models of philosophical clarity and illumination. I have benefited over the years from discussions with various faculty members and graduate students. These include Steve Phillips, Robert Kane, Don Felipe, John Ellis, Jerry Pedersen, Mathias Steup, Marthe Chandler, Keith Nightenhelser, Roger Gustavsson, Dan Shannon, and Marcia McKelligan. I would especially like to thank my good friend Douglas Browning at the University of Texas for his encouragement, comments, and criticisms. Above all, I owe a special debt to my father, Ramon Lemos, Professor of Philosophy at the University of Miami. In addition to his encouragement and comments on every chapter, he introduced me to philosophy and has sought to teach his children to be lovers of wisdom. Finally, I would like to thank my wife, Lisa, whose love and support helped bring this work to completion.

I have included in this book revised portions of my articles "Coherence and Epistemic Priority," *Philosophical Studies* 41 (1982); "Warrant, Emotion, and Value," *Philosophical Studies* 57 (1989); and "Higher Goods and the Myth of Tithonus," *The Journal of Philosophy* 90 (1993). I would like to thank Kluwer Academic Publishers for permission to use material from the first two articles and *The Journal of Philosophy* for their permission to use revised portions of the third. I would like to thank DePauw University for providing me with a Summer Research Award during 1992.

Part I

Value, plurality, parts, and wholes

1

The concept of intrinsic value

My main concern in this chapter is to explicate the concept of intrinsic value. I discuss and defend the view that the concept of intrinsic value may be explicated in terms of the concept of "correct" or "required" emotion. I am not especially concerned with whether this explication amounts to a definition or philosophical analysis of the concept of intrinsic value, nor am I especially interested in "reducing" the concept of intrinsic value to certain other concepts. I am simply concerned with explaining what I take intrinsic value to be or, alternatively, what it is for something to be intrinsically valuable.

I wish to begin, however, by describing certain general views belonging to one traditional way of thinking about intrinsic value. These views are among the main theses of a tradition whose representatives include Franz Brentano, G. E. Moore, W. D. Ross, and A. C. Ewing. In stating these general views, I shall be describing, in part, the core of this tradition. I do this for two reasons. First, though I shall not undertake to defend them in this chapter, I think these theses pertaining to the nature and concept of intrinsic value are both plausible and true. Second, and more important, these remarks will provide some general background against which the explication of intrinsic value may proceed. It is hoped that these remarks will help illustrate in rough outline the concept with which I am concerned.

First, the traditional view holds that if something is intrinsically good, it is not intrinsically bad or intrinsically neutral or indifferent; and if something is intrinsically bad, it is not intrinsically good or indifferent. According to the traditional view, the claims that (1) X is intrinsically good and (2) X is intrinsically bad are contraries. Similarly, the traditional view assumes that if X is intrinsically better than Y, then it is false that Y is intrinsically better than X or that they are the same in intrinsic value.

The second feature is difficult to state precisely, but let us say that according to the traditional view, intrinsic value is a *nonrelational* concept.

3

When one says that something is intrinsically good, in the sense with which we are concerned, he means just that, that it is intrinsically good *period*. He does not mean that it is intrinsically good for me, for himself, for human beings, or for rational beings. In this respect, claims that something has intrinsic value are not like the claim "Boston is near," for in ordinary contexts the latter claim is meaningful only if one takes the speaker to be saying that Boston is near to something (e.g., to the speaker, to the person addressed, to Providence). If it is not clear what the speaker is saying Boston is near to, it is appropriate to ask, "Boston is near to what?" The tradition with which I am concerned does not take the concept of intrinsic value to be a relational concept, relative to persons, species, or anything else. If someone insists that he is concerned with such a relational concept or with what it is for something to be intrinsically good for someone, then he is talking about something other than the traditional concept of intrinsic value with which I am concerned.

Even if intrinsic value is not a relational concept, one can still talk meaningfully of something's being good for one person and not for another. One may say, for example, that insulin is good for a diabetic but not for an otherwise healthy person. But clearly, what this means is not that insulin is intrinsically good for one person and not for another. What is meant is roughly that insulin has an instrumental value when taken by someone with diabetes but not when taken by an otherwise healthy person. Furthermore, we may also say, for example, that a state of affairs is intrinsically better for one person than for another. We might say that the state of affairs consisting in Smith's being very happy and Brown's being very unhappy is intrinsically better for Smith than for Brown. But this may be taken to mean roughly that Smith and Brown have certain characteristics, F and G, such that Smith's having F is intrinsically better than Brown's having G. The fact that one person is better off than another when certain states of affairs obtain does not imply that intrinsic value is a relational concept.

Third, the philosophers in this tradition hold that we *know* that some things are intrinsically good, that some things are intrinsically bad, and that some things are intrinsically better than others. They are *cognitivists* about intrinsic value. There are significant differences among them concerning the nature of our knowledge of value and differences about how we have such knowledge, but they all agree that we know that some things are intrinsically valuable. They do not maintain, however, that we know or can know, upon reflection or investigation, the answer to every question of the form "Is X intrinsically good?" or "Is X intrinsically better

4

than Y?" Cognitivism about value does not imply or require omniscience about value. Withholding belief may be the epistemically reasonable stance to take with respect to certain claims about intrinsic value. Moreover, since knowledge implies true belief, this stance implies that it is true that some things are intrinsically good, others are intrinsically bad, and some are intrinsically better than others. There are truths about intrinsic value such that whoever denies them denies what is true.

The fourth feature of this tradition is also hard to state precisely, but we may say roughly that it takes intrinsic value to be *distinct* from any "natural" property, relation, or state of affairs. The philosophers in this tradition assume that we can distinguish ethical properties, relations, or states of affairs from natural entities. Intrinsic value is distinct from any natural entity in the sense that it is not identical with any such thing. Thus, if there is a property of being intrinsically good, that property is not identical with any natural property, such as being pleasant or being desired by most people. Similarly, if there is a state of affairs that is expressed by the sentence "John's being happy is intrinsically good," then the state of affairs expressed by that sentence is not identical with that expressed by the sentences "John's being happy would be approved by most people" or "John desires upon reflection that he be happy."

Although intrinsic value is not identical with any natural entity, many of the members of this tradition also hold that intrinsic value is dependent on nonethical features or facts, that whatever has intrinsic value has it in virtue of or because of the nonethical properties of that thing or in virtue of the obtaining of nonethical states of affairs. In this respect, they assume that intrinsic value is like certain other evaluative or normative concepts. Just as the beauty of a painting may be thought to depend on its colors and their arrangement or the goodness of an apple on its being sweet, juicy, ripe, and so on, intrinsic value may be thought to depend on certain nonethical facts or properties. The claim that intrinsic value is distinct from the natural must not, therefore, be taken to imply that intrinsic value does not supervene on or is not determined by the nonethical. It should not be taken to deny that intrinsic value is intimately related to the nonethical.

Finally, according to this tradition, the intrinsic value of a thing is not dependent on its being the object of any psychological attitude. If a thing has intrinsic value, it has it independently of its being the object of any psychological attitude or its being conducive to or productive of any such attitude. If a thing has intrinsic value, it does not have that value because, or in virtue of, its being the object of anyone's psychological attitude or

5

because it would be the object of such an attitude under some set of hypothetical conditions. We may also express this claim by saying that the intrinsic value that a thing possesses is not conferred on it by its being the object of such attitudes. Thus, if X is intrinsically good, then X is not intrinsically good because or in virtue of the fact that someone or some group likes or desires X or would like X if they were, say, "fully informed." This is an essentially negative view. It simply tells us what does not confer intrinsic value, what does not make things intrinsically valuable. It is important not to misunderstand this claim. Some writers in this tradition have held that if anything is intrinsically good, then that thing must have or contain consciousness as a part. Moore, for example, changed the position taken in *Principia Ethica* and writes in the later work, *Ethics,* that "it does seem as if nothing can be an intrinsic good, unless it contains both some feeling and also some other form of consciousness."[1] We must distinguish, then, between something's having consciousness as a part or implying that something is conscious from something's being the object of consciousness. It is possible that something have the first characteristic without having the second. For example, the state of affairs "there being at least 1,248 conscious beings" necessarily implies that something is conscious, but that state of affairs need not have been itself the object of anyone's psychological attitudes or consciousness. If we make this distinction, then we might consistently assert that every intrinsically good whole has consciousness as a part while denying that anything is intrinsically good because or in virtue of its being the object of consciousness.

CORRECT EMOTION AND INTRINSIC VALUE

What is it for something to be intrinsically valuable? What is it for something to be intrinsically good or bad or better than something else? One traditional way of answering these questions seeks to explicate the concept of intrinsic value in terms of the concept of correct, suitable, or fitting emotion. Among those favoring this approach are Franz Brentano, C. D. Broad, A. C. Ewing, and Roderick Chisholm. In spite of certain significant differences, these writers hold that something's being intrinsically good may be understood in terms of its being correct or fitting to love or like that thing in and for itself or for its own sake. Similarly, A's being intrinsically better than B may be understood in terms of the correctness or fittingness of preferring A in itself to B. Brentano, for example, says,

1. G. E. Moore, *Ethics* (Oxford: Oxford University Press, 1912), p. 107.

6

"We call a thing good when the love relating to it is correct. In the broadest sense of the term, the good is that which is worthy of love, that which can be loved with a love that is correct."[2] He adds, "One loves or hates correctly provided that one's feelings are adequate to their object – adequate in the sense of being appropriate, suitable, or fitting."[3] And again, "when we call certain objects good and others bad we are merely saying that whoever loves the former and hates the latter has taken the right stand."[4]

This approach to explicating the concept of intrinsic value has a certain intuitive appeal. It is plausible to think of the good as being worthy of, or meriting, love or favor and the bad as being worthy of, or meriting, dislike or disfavor. There thus seems to be at least this much truth in Brentano's remark – that whoever loves what is good and hates what is bad has taken the right stand. But what is it to take the right stand? We may say that it is a matter of loving, hating, or preferring fittingly. Whoever loves in itself what is intrinsically good loves that thing fittingly. It is plausible to think that there is some way in which the concept of value is related to our emotional attitudes, to "pro attitudes" and "anti attitudes." Although this approach does not tell us that such attitudes confer value on things or that value consists in our having such attitudes toward things, it does tell us that there is some sort of normative connection between the things that have value and our favoring and disfavoring.

The view that our emotional attitudes can be ethically appropriate or fitting to things has an ancient and venerable history reaching back at least as far as Aristotle's claim that there is a mean for emotion and feeling, as well as for action. For example, we find Aristotle claiming that there is a mean in anger, that anger toward certain forms of injustice is appropriate, whereas envy and spite consist in having inappropriate feelings of hatred or pleasure. He writes, "the man who is characterized by righteous indignation is pained at undeserved good fortune, the envious man, going beyond him, is pained at all good fortune, and the spiteful man falls so far short of being pained that he even rejoices [when someone suffers]."[5]

2. Franz Brentano, *The Origin of Our Knowledge of Right and Wrong,* English edition edited by Roderick Chisholm and translated by Roderick Chisholm and Elizabeth Schneewind (London: Routledge & Kegan Paul, 1969), p. 18.
3. Ibid., 74.
4. Franz Brentano, *The Foundation and Construction of Ethics,* English edition edited and translated by Elizabeth Hughes Schneewind (New York: Humanities Press, 1973), p. 131.
5. Aristotle, *Nicomachean Ethics,* translated by W. D. Ross in *The Basic Works of Aristotle,* edited by Richard McKeon (New York: Random House, 1941) Bk. II, Chapter 7,

According to Aristotle, it is ethically unfitting or inappropriate to take pleasure in the suffering of others and unfitting to be pained or displeased at the good fortune of those who merit good fortune. A similar view is expressed by Schopenhauer: "In a certain sense the opposite of envy is the habit of gloating over the misfortunes of others. At any rate, whereas the former is human, the latter is diabolical. There is no sign more infallible of an entirely bad heart, and of profound moral worthlessness than open and candid enjoyment of seeing other people suffer."[6] In addition to these examples, we may add that fear is fitting to certain sorts of dangers; gratitude toward certain sorts of favors; admiration toward excellences such as wisdom, courage, and aesthetic virtuosity; and remorse and guilt toward one's own wrongdoing. The list could, of course, go on, and one would be hard pressed to find a better study of the variety of fitting or appropriate attitudes and emotion than Aristotle's *Ethics*.

If the concept of intrinsic value can be explicated in terms of correct or fitting emotion, what form will the explication take? Some attempts seem pretty clearly unsatisfactory. Suppose, for example, we say, "X is intrinsically good just in case X is fittingly or correctly loved for its own sake." This view is unacceptable because it implies that the only things that are intrinsically good are those that are in fact loved. It is not at all clear that this is true, and it should not be a logical consequence of our explication of intrinsic value. Consider also the claim that "X is intrinsically good just in case if X is loved for its own sake, then X is correctly or fittingly loved." If the explanans is understood in terms of material implication, then one unhappy consequence is that anything that is not loved for its own sake is intrinsically good, and that is surely false.

Rather than consider all attempts to explicate the concept of intrinsic value in terms of correct emotion, a task that would be tediously long, I shall focus on one promising line of approach. C. D. Broad once suggested that "X is good" can "be defined as meaning that X is such that it would be a fitting object of desire to any mind which had an adequate idea of its non–ethical characteristics."[7] More recently, Roderick Chisholm has claimed that "p is intrinsically better than q" can be defined as follows:

1108b. Compare also Aristotle's remarks on pity and indignation in *Rhetoric*, translated by W. Rhys Roberts Bk. II, Chapter 9, 1386b.
6. Arthur Schopenhauer, *The Basis of Morality*, translated by A. Broderick Bullock (London: Swan Sonneschein, 1903), pp. 156–7.
7. C. D. Broad, *Five Types of Ethical Theory* (New York: Harcourt, Brace and Co., 1930), p. 283.

"p and q are necessarily such that, for any x, the contemplation of just p and q by x requires that x prefer p to q."[8]

Broad's definition involves one's having "an adequate idea" of something, and Chisholm's refers to the contemplation of just p and q. Why not say more simply "p and q are necessarily such that, for any x, p and q require that x prefer p to q"? One reason to favor the more complex formulation is that p and q might be very complicated states of affairs, too complex for some persons to conceive or contemplate, or p and q might involve concepts or properties that some persons cannot grasp. If there are states of affairs that some persons are incapable of conceiving, it is not clear that they can be required to have a pro-attitude toward them or that they can be required to prefer one such state of affairs to another.

In attempting to explicate the concept of intrinsic value in terms of correct or fitting emotion, one must say something about the sorts of emotional attitudes involved. Chisholm says:

One might qualify the definition by saying " . . . the contemplation of just p and q as such by x requires that x prefer p as such to q." One would thus be using the "as such" to stress the fact that the contemplation of a state of affairs as such is the contemplation of just that state of affairs as distinguished, for example, from the contemplation of some wider state of affairs which one may think that the given state of affairs brings along with it.[9]

Analogously, one could say that x is required to prefer p as such to q to emphasize that x is required to rank just those states of affairs, as distinguished from any wider states of affairs that might include them or any other states of affairs that might be among their causal consequences.

Chisholm's emphasis on preferring p as such to q reflects a distinction drawn by Brentano concerning our emotional attitudes. Within the sphere of emotional phenomena, Brentano distinguishes three basic types: love simpliciter, hate simpliciter, and preference simpliciter. To love something simpliciter is to love that thing *as such,* to feel favorably toward a thing *in and for itself.* Similarly, to hate something simpliciter is to hate that thing as such, to have an anti feeling toward it in and for itself. To prefer simpliciter p to q is to prefer p as such or in and for itself to q.

Love, hate, and preference simpliciter must be distinguished from loving, hating, or preferring something (1) as a means, (2) from choosing, and (3) having such attitudes *per accidens.* One may prefer taking aspirin

8. Roderick Chisholm, "Defining Intrinsic Value," *Analysis* 41, (March 1981), p. 100.
9. Ibid., p. 100.

to taking a sugar pill as a means of relieving a headache, but it does not follow that one prefers taking aspirin as such or in itself to taking a sugar pill. Preference simpliciter must also be distinguished from choice. If one chooses to bring about *A* rather than *B*, it does not follow that one prefers *A* in itself to *B*. Choosing to take an aspirin rather than a sugar pill does not imply that one prefers the former as such to the latter any more than choosing to spend a night at the movies rather than at the opera implies that one prefers the former in itself to the latter. Whether it is appropriate to choose *A* over *B* typically involves consideration of states of affairs that are wider than or different from *A* and *B* themselves, such as those states of affairs that are the consequences of bringing about *A* and those of bringing about *B*. Whether it is appropriate to choose a night at the movies over a night at the opera depends in part on the cost and consequences of doing the one or the other. Finally, loving, hating, and preferring simpliciter must be distinguished from having such attitudes *per accidens*. If one loves simpliciter a certain whole, then one may be said to love the parts of that whole *per accidens*. However, it does not follow that one loves every part of that whole simpliciter. Thus, one can love simpliciter Smith's overcoming temptation and one can love simpliciter Brown's remorse toward his wrongdoing, but it does not follow that one loves simpliciter Smith's being tempted or Brown's doing wrong. Similarly, one might hate simpliciter Smith's taking joy in his misdeeds, but it does not follow that one hates Smith's having joy as such.

It might be useful to compare the sort of approach we have been discussing with that adopted by Moore and Ross. Insofar as Chisholm stresses the notion that the contemplation of just *p* and *q* requires that one prefer *p* as such to *q,* there is some justification for saying that he adopts an "isolation approach" in explicating the concept of intrinsic value. We may say that his approach is *intentionally isolationist* because it stresses the intentional attitudes of contemplating and preferring states of affairs as such, in isolation from the contemplation and ranking of other, wider states of affairs. We may contrast this form of isolation approach with what we may call "ontological isolationism." Some writers, such as Moore and Ross, have suggested that "by calling a thing intrinsically good we mean that it would be good even if nothing else existed."[10] This sort of onto-logical isolationism is not very helpful since there are certain sorts of things that are intrinsically good but simply could not be the only things that

10. Moore, *Ethics,* p. 38; W. D. Ross, *The Right and the Good* (Oxford: Oxford University Press, 1930), p. 73.

exist. Consider the fact of Smith's being happy and let's suppose that it is intrinsically good. If there are certain abstract entities such as numbers or properties or states of affairs that necessarily exist, it would be impossible for Smith's being happy to be the only thing that exists. More important, though, is the fact that Smith's being happy could not exist without Smith's existing, as well as, I suppose, Smith's having certain pleasures and certain desires satisfied and his having certain beliefs to the effect that he had those pleasures and that his desires were satisfied. Since it is necessarily false that Smith's being happy could be the only existing thing, this sort of ontological isolationism is not very clear or very helpful.

We should note that, in spite of these different approaches, both Chisholm and Moore hold that if a thing has a certain intrinsic value, then it must have that value whenever it occurs. This thesis, sometimes referred to as the "thesis of universality," is implied by Chisholm's definition of intrinsic value. If p's being intrinsically better than q is a matter of p and q being necessarily such that the contemplation of both requires one to prefer p to q, then p will be intrinsically better than q whenever p and q occur. Similarly, Moore says with respect to intrinsic value:

it is impossible for what is strictly one and the same thing to possess that kind of value at one time, or in one set of circumstances, and not to possess it at another; and equally impossible for it to possess it in one degree at one time, or in one set of circumstances, and to possess it in a different degree at another, or in a different set.[11]

Thus, according to Moore and Chisholm, if Smith's being pleased is intrinsically better than Brown's suffering, then the former will always be intrinsically better than the latter whenever the two occur. Of course, both Moore and Chisholm allow that it is possible that things have different instrumental values in different contexts and under different conditions. Suffering might have instrumental value if it deters from wrongdoing, but it can, in some circumstances, harden the heart, stiffen resolve, and fail to deter. The instrumental value of suffering is not essential to it, but if Brown's suffering is intrinsically bad, it is intrinsically bad whenever it occurs. In Chapter 3, we consider some views on intrinsic value that reject the thesis of universality.

What is it for a fact or state of affairs to be intrinsically good or bad? I suggest that we can explicate intrinsic goodness and badness, and other

11. G. E. Moore, "The Conception of Intrinsic Value," *Philosophical Studies* (London: Routledge & Kegan Paul, 1922), pp. 260–1; see also G. E. Moore, *Principia Ethica* (Cambridge: Cambridge University Press, 1903), p. 30.

related value concepts, in terms of such concepts as "being intrinsically worthy of love" and "being intrinsically worthy of hate." But what is it for a state of affairs to be intrinsically worthy of love or hate? I propose to follow Chisholm in explicating such concepts in terms of the notion of "ethical requirement."[12] I shall also make use of the concepts of love and hate simpliciter, which Chisholm does not use, and that of preference simpliciter, which he does. Let us consider the following principles, where p and q stand for states of affairs and the attitudes of love, hate, and preference are taken to be attitudes simpliciter. Let us begin by accepting what Chisholm says about the concept of intrinsic preferability.

(P1) p is intrinsically worthy of preference to q if and only if p and q are necessarily such that, for any x, the contemplation of just p and q by x requires that x prefer p to q.

What is it for something to be intrinsically worthy of love or intrinsically worthy of hate? Let us say:

(P2) p is intrinsically worthy of love if and only if p is necessarily such that, for any x, the contemplation of just p by x requires that x love p and not hate p.

(P3) p is intrinsically worthy of hate if and only if p is necessarily such that, for any x, the contemplation of just p by x requires that x hate p and not love p.

There is, I think, a helpful analogy between a state of affairs being intrinsically worthy of love or hate and a proposition being an *axiom* or *self-evident*. What is it for something to be an axiom? Consider truths such as those expressed by "All men are men" and "If A is taller than B, then B is not taller than A." Robert Audi writes, "Such truths often called self-evident because they are obvious in themselves: if one comprehendingly considers them, one believes and knows them. One need not consult one's experience, nor even reflect on such propositions, to grasp – roughly to understand – them and thereby believe that they are true."[13] An axiom is a proposition that cannot be incorrectly believed and cannot be considered and accepted without its being evident to the person who accepts

12. For a discussion of the concept of requirement, see Roderick M. Chisholm, "Practical Reason and the Logic of Requirement," in Stephan Korner, ed., *Practical Reason* (Oxford: Basil Blackwell, 1974), pp. 2–13; also in *Practical Reasoning*, edited by Joseph Raz (Oxford: Oxford University Press, 1978), pp. 118–127.

13. Robert Audi, *Belief, Justification, and Knowledge* (Belmont, Calif.: Wadsworth Publishing Co., 1988), p. 51. See Chisholm: "*h* is an axiom = Df.*h* is necessarily such that (i) it is true and (ii) for every *S*, if *S* accepts *h*, then *h* is certain for *S*." *Theory of Knowledge*, 2nd edition (Englewood Cliffs, N.J.: Prentice-Hall, 1978), p. 42.

it. Thus, we may say that whoever accepts an axiom accepts correctly, "has taken the right stand," both from the standpoint of accepting what is true and from the standpoint of accepting what he is epistemically justified in believing. The analogy between an axiom and that which is intrinsically worthy of love consists in this: Whoever considers and accepts an axiom believes in a way that is *epistemically* required, and whoever considers and loves as such what is intrinsically worthy of love loves in a way that is *ethically* required. If one understands what it is for a proposition to be an axiom, and understands the concepts of ethical requirement and love simpliciter, one can understand what it is for something to be intrinsically good. I say more about the concept of an axiom and the analogy to what is intrinsically valuable in Chapter 8.

What is it for a state of affairs to be neutral? Roughly, a state of affairs is neutral just in case it is not intrinsically worthy of love and not intrinsically worthy of hate. I suggest, however, that we should distinguish between several different types of neutral states of affairs. Such distinctions are called for because the sorts of attitudes that are appropriate to various neutral states of affairs are not the same. We will use the following distinctions in discussing the value of things like pleasure, knowledge, and beauty. Let us consider the following two propositions:

(P4) p is *strictly* neutral if and only if p is necessarily such that, for any x, the contemplation of just p by x requires both that x not love p and that x not hate p.

(P5) p is *merely* neutral if and only if p is necessarily such that, for any x, the contemplation of just p by x does not require that x love p and does not require that x hate p.

(P5) is clearly a more latitudinarian notion than (P4). The difference between them is important. If a state of affairs is merely neutral, then it is possible for someone who has contemplated it to love it or hate it without violating any requirement. Similarly, to the extent that taking pleasure in a thing in and for itself appears to involve loving that thing simpliciter, it is possible for someone contemplating a merely neutral state of affairs to take intrinsic pleasure in it without violating any requirement. In contrast, anyone who takes pleasure in or loves simpliciter a strictly neutral state of affairs violates an ethical requirement in doing so. Consider the state of affairs *there being stones*. Suppose that someone contemplates just this state of affairs and loves or takes intrinsic pleasure in it. If *there being stones* is strictly neutral, then his loving or taking pleasure in it violates an ethical requirement. If, on the other hand, it is merely neutral, then his loving

13

or taking pleasure in it does not. It seems that however odd or unusual it would be, one does not violate any ethical requirement simply by taking intrinsic pleasure in or loving simpliciter the existence of stones. Consequently, I believe that the state of affairs *there being stones* is merely rather than strictly neutral.

Are there any states of affairs that are strictly neutral? A likely candidate would be a state of affairs in which intrinsic goods and evils are "balanced off," for example, Smith's having five units of pleasure and Brown's having five units of pain. Given that this state of affairs involves as much good as evil and vice versa, it is appropriate that one not love or hate it simpliciter. Of course, it has "parts" that it is appropriate to love and to hate simpliciter.

In addition to the strictly and merely neutral, we may also distinguish between the *positively* and *negatively* neutral. Let us say:

(P6) p is *positively* neutral if and only if p is necessarily such that, for any x, the contemplation of just p by x requires that x not hate p and the contemplation of just p by x does not require that x love p.

(P7) p is *negatively* neutral if and only if p is necessarily such that, for any x, the contemplation of just p by x requires that x not love p and the contemplation of just p by x does not require that x hate p.

The importance of distinguishing the positively and negatively neutral can be brought out by reflecting on the absence of a good or evil. Consider the state of affairs *there being no one who is happy*. This state of affairs can be thought of as the absence of a good. Is this state of affairs intrinsically bad? Many writers have said that it is not. Oskar Kraus writes, "The nonexistence of a good is not an evil and the nonexistence of an evil is not a good; one can say only that the existence of a good is *preferable* to its nonexistence, and conversely for evil."[14] The same view is taken by Chisholm and Ernest Sosa.[15] Suppose that these writers are correct and *there being no one who is happy* is *not* an intrinsically bad state of affairs. I suggest that the contemplation of this state of affairs requires that one not love it in and for itself. It is inappropriate to love in and for itself or to take intrinsic pleasure in the absence of a good. If this is right, then *there being no one who is happy* is not merely neutral. It also seems, however, that there is no requirement that one not hate the absence of a good. If

14. Roderick Chisholm, *Brentano and Intrinsic Value* (Cambridge: Cambridge University Press, 1986), p. 61.
15. Roderick Chisholm and Ernest Sosa, "On the Logic of 'Intrinsically Better'," *American Philosophical Quarterly* 3 (July 1966), pp. 244–9.

14

this is so, then *there being no one who is happy* is not strictly neutral. I suggest that this state of affairs is negatively neutral. Similarly, consider the absence of an evil such as *there being no one in pain*. We may say that the contemplation of this state of affairs requires that no one hate it simpliciter, but the contemplation of it does not require that anyone love it simpliciter. It is an example of the positively neutral. We may say that the absence of an evil is a positive neutral and the absence of a good is a negative neutral.

We have distinguished four forms of neutral states of affairs. Shall we say that some forms of neutrality are intrinsically worthy of preference to other forms of neutrality, that, for example, anything that is positively neutral is intrinsically worthy of preference to anything that is negatively neutral? I see no reason to think so. I see no reason to hold that there being no one in pain is intrinsically preferable to there being no happy people. Holding that neither of these states of affairs is preferable to the other is quite compatible with there being a requirement not to hate the former and a requirement not to love the latter.

What is it for a fact to be intrinsically good or bad? Again, taking p and q to stand for states of affairs, let us say:

(P8) p is intrinsically good if and only if p obtains and p is intrinsically worthy of love.

(P9) p is intrinsically bad if and only if p obtains and p is intrinsically worthy of hate.

(P10) p is intrinsically neutral if and only if p obtains and p is not intrinsically worthy of love and not intrinsically worthy of hate.

(P11) p is intrinsically better than q if and only if p and q obtain and p is intrinsically worthy of preference to q.

If a fact is intrinsically good, then the contemplation of just that obtaining state of affairs requires that one not hate it in and for itself. Thus, if Smith's being pleased is intrinsically good and one contemplates that state of affairs, there is a requirement that one not hate it simpliciter. As Aristotle suggests, such a hatred would be ethically unfitting and a mark of the envious man. To be indifferent or not to love as such someone's being pleased is not precisely to be envious, but it is a mark of, at best, a small-minded niggardliness and, at worst, an ungenerous lack of goodwill to others. Similarly, the contemplation of something intrinsically bad requires that one not love it simpliciter. Thus, if someone's being in pain is intrinsically bad, then anyone who considers that state of affairs is required not to love it in itself. To love as such someone's being in pain is, according to Aristotle, spiteful and, according to Schopenhauer, diabolical. It is an ethi-

15

cally incorrect attitude. In contrast, it is a mark of the ethically good man to love as such what is intrinsically good and to hate as such what is intrinsically bad.

SOME OBJECTIONS TO THIS APPROACH

Let us consider four objections to the view that intrinsic value can be explicated in terms of required love, hate, and preference. The first objection is that in explicating the notion of intrinsic value in terms of an ethical requirement, we are confusing intrinsic value with *moral* value, that is, we are confusing intrinsic goodness with moral goodness and intrinsic badness with moral badness. But clearly, we are *not* confusing intrinsic goodness with moral goodness where the latter is construed as a certain kind of character or property of the person, the will, or certain actions. Of course, we are saying that the ethically or morally correct attitude toward what is intrinsically good is one of love rather than hate or indifference. Thus, if the suffering of an animal is intrinsically bad or the existence of a beautiful painting is intrinsically good, then for anyone who considers such things, the ethically correct attitude toward the former is one of hate and that toward the latter is one of love or favor. Presumably, a morally good person would not hate or be indifferent to what is worthy of love, or love or be indifferent to what is worthy of hate.

A second objection to this approach is the following: "Consider the following states of affairs: something's happening that is very likely to make 100 people happy (p) and something's happening that is very likely to make 100 people unhappy (q). It is false that p is intrinsically preferable to q, but the view previously described incorrectly implies that it is, for if one considers just p and q, then the contemplation of just p and q requires that one prefer p as such to q." The response to this objection is that the contemplation of just p and q does *not* require that one prefer p *as such* to q. p involves a state of affairs that is intrinsically worthy of love, namely, there being 100 happy people, and q involves a state of affairs that is intrinsically worthy of hate, namely, there being 100 unhappy people. But from the fact that there is a requirement to prefer as such there being 100 happy people to there being 100 unhappy people, it does not follow that there is a requirement to prefer p in itself to q in itself. We may also add that the contemplation of just p (unlike the contemplation of the different state of affairs, there being 100 happy people) does not require that one love p in and for itself.

A third objection urges that two things might be the same in intrinsic value, whereas the attitudes and feelings that are appropriate to one might be inappropriate to the other. Consider the suffering of one's own child and the equal suffering of a child starving in Ethiopia. We may reasonably believe that the suffering of some child unknown and distant is every bit as bad as the suffering of our own child, but is it plausible to believe that the attitudes and feelings that are appropriate to the one state of affairs are also appropriate to the other? Brand Blanshard writes, "There are many feelings, felt with great intensity, that are obviously suitable in the case of our own child, which we could hardly be expected to show about one that was remote and all but unknown."[16] Toward the suffering of our own child we feel acute grief and distress, but only a certain melancholy and sadness about the suffering of faraway strangers, and we do so without any sense that the difference in our attitudes is inappropriate. But if the difference in our attitudes is appropriate, if it is fitting for us to have different attitudes toward these states of affairs, then how can we say that they have the same intrinsic value?

In response to this objection, one might urge that it is *not* fitting or appropriate for us to have different feelings toward our own child's misfortune and that of a total stranger. One might urge that the same acute grief or the same cool sadness, or perhaps something in between, is the fitting attitude to take toward both. Consider the advice of the Stoic Epictetus:

when some other person's slave-boy breaks his drinking cup, you are instantly ready to say, "That's one of the things which happen." Rest assured, then, that when your own drinking-cup gets broken, you ought to behave in the same way that you do when the other man's cup is broken. Apply now the same principle to the matters of greater importance. Some other person's child or wife has died; no one but would say, "Such is the fate of man." Yet when a man's own child dies, immediately the cry is, "Alas! Woe is me!" But we ought to remember how we feel when we hear of the same misfortune befalling others.[17]

I cannot believe that this response is right. We often have at different times different emotional attitudes and feelings toward a single event and take these different attitudes and feelings to be appropriate. Different emotions and feelings toward the death of one's child or one's parents seem more appropriate to these events when they are recent than when they have receded into the past. It seems inappropriate to have precisely the

16. Brand Blanshard, *Reason and Goodness* (New York: Humanities Press, 1978), p. 287.
17. Epictetus, *The Encheiridion,* in Oliver Johnson, *Ethics,* 6th edition (Fort Worth, Tex.: Holt, Rinehart, and Winston, 1989), p. 96.

same emotions and feelings about their death at different times, for there comes a point when it is appropriate not to feel acute grief and sadness, to let these feelings pass, and to feel in their place a sadness that is less intense. If different emotions and feelings can be appropriate to the same event when the intrinsic value of that event has not changed, there is no obvious reason why different emotions and feelings cannot be appropriate to different events of the same value.

Now even if we concede that it is more appropriate to have a more intense feeling of grief of sadness toward the suffering of one's own child than toward the suffering of a total stranger, this concession does not imply that we cannot explicate intrinsic value in terms of required love, hate, and preference. This is so simply because grief, sadness, and melancholy are not the same attitudes as love, hate, and preference simpliciter. It is not at all obvious that one's contemplation of just the states of affairs *my child's suffering* and *an unknown child's suffering* requires that one prefer the latter as such to the former.

It should be emphasized that claiming that there is no requirement that one prefer in itself the latter to the former *is* compatible with holding that there is a requirement to alleviate the one rather than the other. It has already been noted that preference simpliciter is not the same thing as choosing, and which case of suffering one is required to alleviate depends on considerations other than the contemplation of just those states of affairs. These other considerations might include the nearness of the children, the probability of success in alleviating their pain, the costs of doing so, and even considerations of loyalty to one's children. But even if, in light of these other factors, there is a requirement to choose to alleviate the suffering of one's own child, it does not follow that one is required to prefer simpliciter the suffering of the unknown child.

Let us consider a fourth objection to the view that intrinsic value can be explicated in terms of required love, hate, and preference. According to this objection, if something merits favor, it can only be because or in virtue of the fact that it is good, and if it is correct or fitting to prefer one thing as such to another, it can only be because the former is better in it self than the other. Blanshard says, "If saintliness and generosity are such as to merit favoring, it must be because there is something in them that goes beyond their 'factual characteristics' and equally goes beyond a mere blank cheque on our favor. What is this? I think we must answer, a goodness that they have already."[18] According to this objection, if it is

18. Blanshard, *Reason and Goodness*, p. 287.

fitting to favor something only because it is good already, if something's being good is the ground or reason why it is fitting to favor that thing, then the goodness of that thing cannot be identical with its being fitting to favor it and its being good cannot be defined in terms of its being fitting to favor it.

Strictly speaking, this is not an objection to the view presented earlier. Rather, it is an objection to the view that we can *eliminate* the concept of goodness in favor of the concepts of correct or required emotion. The objection insists that we cannot eliminate intrinsic goodness in this way because it is the goodness of a thing that explains why it is a required object of love. Of course, this is not an objection to the view I have offered, since I have only tried to explicate intrinsic goodness, not eliminate it. Still, this objection is not fatal even to those who do propose to eliminate goodness in favor of required attitudes. The mistake that underlies this objection is the assumption that it can only be the value of a thing that makes it required or appropriate to favor it. Why must there be something else in addition to the "factual characteristics" of saintliness, generosity, wisdom, or pleasure that makes them worthy of favor, that makes it appropriate to look favorably on their instances? Surely it is plausible to think that there are other sorts of evaluative and normative features of things that they have in virtue of their factual or nonevaluative characteristics. The goodness of an apple would seem to depend on its being sweet, juicy, and so on. The beauty of a painting would seem to depend on such factual characteristics as its colors and their arrangement. The rightness of an action may depend on its factual characteristics, such as whether it produces a greater balance of pleasure over pain than any alternative, whether it is the keeping of a promise or an instance of gratitude or loyalty. There is, therefore, no obvious reason why the fittingness of an emotional attitude should be thought to depend on something other than the nonevaluative nature of its object. If so, there is no obvious reason to think that the fittingness of an attitude must depend on an additional distinct feature or characteristic of value. Moreover, it would seem hard to deny that what has value has it because or in virtue of its having some factual, nonevaluative characteristic or because of the obtaining of some nonevaluative state of affairs. But if value is itself dependent on the factual and the nonevaluative, then it is strange to argue that meriting favor or disfavor cannot be similarly dependent. Why should there be any difference between the two? As far as I can see, there simply isn't any.

2

The bearers of intrinsic value

In this chapter, I consider what are the bearers of intrinsic value or what are the kinds of things that are intrinsically valuable. Are they abstract objects or concrete, particular things or both? If they are abstract objects, then are they properties, facts, or states of affairs? If they are particulars, are such things as persons, apples, and cars bearers of intrinsic value?

THE BEARERS OF VALUE: ABSTRACT OBJECTS

What are the bearers of intrinsic value? What are the kinds of things that have intrinsic value? Among the traditional candidates, we may distinguish between those that are abstract objects and those that are concrete, individual things such as persons, dogs, and cars. Let us begin by considering the former.

Concerning abstract objects, there are at least three main candidates: properties, states of affairs, and facts or states of affairs that obtain. Ordinary discourse sometimes suggests that properties are intrinsically good or bad. People sometimes say such things as "Pleasure and wisdom are intrinsically good" and "Pain is intrinsically bad." The view that some properties are intrinsically good has been defended by Panayot Butchvarov. Some philosophers, including Chisholm, have held that states of affairs are the bearers of value. Others have held that facts are bearers of value. This view has been defended by W. D. Ross, who writes, "what is good or bad is always something properly expressed by a that-clause, i.e. an objective, or as I shall prefer to call it, a fact."[1] In this section, I defend the view that facts or states of affairs that obtain have intrinsic value, whereas properties and states of affairs that do not obtain do not have intrinsic value.

In discussing the bearers of value, I make certain metaphysical assumptions about properties and states of affairs. I make further use of these

1. W. D. Ross, *The Right and the Good* (Oxford: Oxford University Press, 1930), p. 137.

concepts in Chapter 7 in connection with the "distinctiveness" of intrinsic value. Let us define "x is a property" as "It is possible that there is something that exemplifies x."[2] According to this definition, we must say that there are no properties that cannot be exemplified. Thus, although there is a property of being round and a property of being square, there is no property of being a round square. I make the following metaphysical assumptions about properties. I assume that there are properties that exist and are exemplified, and that there are properties that exist but are not exemplified. For example, I assume that the property of being female exists and is exemplified but that the property of being a mermaid exists but is not exemplified. The view that there are properties that are not exemplified is sometimes taken to be a mark of *extreme realism*. I also assume that properties can be the objects of certain intentional attitudes, that they can be conceived, considered, and attributed. I assume that one can, for example, consider and attribute the property of being a mermaid, even if nothing has that property. For example, a drunken sailor with poor vision at dusk might attribute to a sea-weed-draped manatee the property of being a mermaid.

The following passage from Chisholm's *Person and Object* will help clarify the concept of a state of affairs that I employ:

> States of affairs, as they are being considered here, are in no way dependent for their being upon the being of concrete, individual things. Even if there were no concrete, individual things, there would be indefinitely many states of affairs. States of affairs, so conceived, resemble what have traditionally been called *propositions* in the following respect. Even though the author of *Waverly* was the author of *Marmion,* "the author of *Waverly* being knighted" expresses a different state of affairs than "the author of *Marmion* being knighted" (the former state of affairs but not the latter could obtain in worlds in which there is no *Marmion,* and the latter but not the former could obtain in worlds in which there is no *Waverly*.[3]

I make the following assumptions concerning states of affairs. First, I assume that there are states of affairs that exist but do not obtain, and that there are states of affairs that exist and do obtain. The state of affairs *everyone's being wise and virtuous* exists but does not obtain, and the state of affairs, *someone's being happy* exists and obtains. Second, there are states of affairs that necessarily obtain and states of affairs that necessarily do not

2. See Roderick Chisholm's definition of an "attribute" in *On Metaphysics* (Minneapolis: University of Minnesota Press, 1989), p. 100. Chisholm says, "*P* is an attribute = *Df.P* is possibily such that there is something that exemplifies it."
3. Roderick Chisholm, *Person and Object* (LaSalle, Ill.: Open Court Publishing Co., 1976), p. 114.

obtain. The latter may be said to be "impossible" states of affairs. An example of the latter is the state of affairs *there being something that is round and square*. (Of course, if what I've said concerning properties is correct, this state of affairs does not involve a property of being round and square. We may say instead that it involves the property of being round and the property of being square.) Third, I say that a fact is a state of affairs that obtains. Thus, we may say that someone's being happy is a fact, but everyone's being wise and virtuous is not a fact. Finally, I assume that states of affairs can be the objects of intentional attitudes. They may be considered and contemplated, accepted or rejected, loved or hated, desired or preferred, and so on. The state of affairs *there being a snake in the grass* is such that one can consider it, accept it, and fear it.

Let us begin by considering the view that properties are bearers of value. In considering this claim, we may note that in ordinary discourse people say such things as "Pleasure is good for its own sake" and "Perfect justice is good in itself." But such talk is not a very good reason, if it is any reason at all, for accepting the view that properties as such are intrinsically good or bad. It may be that what people really mean is more accurately expressed by the more complicated locution "Someone's being pleased is good for its own sake" and "There being perfect justice is good in itself." Butchvarov's defense of the thesis that properties are bearers of value does not rest on dubious considerations about ordinary language. Instead he writes:

We may say that a certain person's life is good, but we may also say that happiness as such, that is the property a life may have of being happy, is good. Now, I suggest, a person's life can be said to be good on the grounds that it is happy only if happiness itself can be said to be good, and in general a concrete entity can be said to be good only on the grounds that it has some other property or properties that themselves have the property of being good.[4]

We may surely agree with Butchvarov that (1) a life may have the property of being happy and (2) a person's life can be said to be good on the ground that it is happy. But does it follow from these assumptions that the property of being happy, as distinguished from the particular happy life, is itself good, that the property of being happy has the property of being good? I don't think so. In response, we should consider the following two points. First, we may recognize (a) that something can have the property of being colored and (b) that a thing can be said to be extended on the grounds

4. Panayot Butchvarov, *Skepticism in Ethics* (Indianapolis: Indiana University Press, 1989), p. 14.

that it is colored, but it does not follow from these assumptions that the property of being colored has the property of being extended. I assume that the property of being colored, unlike particular colored things, is not extended. In general, from the fact that *X* has *G* because *X* has *F*, it does not follow that the property of being *F* has the property of being *G*. Second, let us consider the parallel case of rightness. We may assume that right actions are right in virtue of their having certain properties. For the sake of argument, suppose that some actions are right because they have the property of maximizing intrinsic value. Must we say that an action is right only because it has some property that itself has the property of being right? I am not sure that this makes any sense, for right and wrong seem to be properties of actions and not of properties. If we say "Maximizing value is right," surely what this means is not that the property of maximizing value is right, but rather something to the effect that any action that has that property is right. If this is so, then Butchvarov's remarks provide no compelling reason for us to think of goodness as a property of properties.

I suggest that, strictly speaking, it is not pleasure or perfect justice considered as abstract properties that have intrinsic value. What has intrinsic value is surely more accurately thought to be the exemplification or possession of these properties, or, we may say, the *fact* that someone is pleased or that a community is perfectly just. A world containing nothing that exemplifies properties such as wisdom, beauty, or pleasure, or that has no concrete particulars at all, would be a world without anything intrinsically good, even if it contained the abstract, unexemplified properties of wisdom, beauty, or pleasure. But even if such properties are not themselves intrinsically good, we may say that properties such as pleasure, wisdom, and beauty, are "good-making" properties in the sense that the fact that something has them is intrinsically good.

Are facts bearers of value? I assume that the answer is "yes." If it is a fact that someone is suffering, then that fact is intrinsically bad; and if it is a fact that someone is happy, then that fact is intrinsically good. If facts are states of affairs that obtain and if facts are bearers of value, then there is an understandable temptation to say that some states of affairs are bearers of value. This is simply because facts are states of affairs that obtain. But for the sake of precision and clarity, it is useful to distinguish facts and states of affairs and to speak of facts as bearers of value.

What of those states of affairs that do not obtain, that are not facts; are they intrinsically good or bad? Do they have intrinsic value? There are considerations both for and against an affirmative answer, but I think the

23

correct answer is "no." Let us consider the case for an affirmative answer. The weightiest reason for an affirmative answer arises from thinking of intrinsic value in terms of correct or fitting emotional attitudes. Suppose "A is intrinsically good" means "A is worthy of love" or "A is necessarily such that, for any x, the contemplation of just A by x requires that x love A as such." Whether a state of affairs is worthy of love or a pro-attitude does not depend on whether it obtains or is a fact. We can say, correctly I think, that someone's being perfectly honest is worthy of love even if no one is perfectly honest. Similarly, we may say that it is fitting to prefer everyone's being very happy to everyone's being slightly happy even if no one is happy. Therefore, if A is intrinsically good just in case A is worthy of love, then A can be intrinsically good even if it is not a fact.

Against this view, however, is the main consideration raised against the view that properties are bearers of value, namely, that what seems to be intrinsically good is the actual exemplification of certain good-making properties such as wisdom or pleasure. What seems to be intrinsically valuable is that something *has* these properties, that a certain state of affairs involving these properties obtains. Again, I would urge that a world in which nothing exemplified such good-making properties as beauty, wisdom, or pleasure would be a world that contained nothing that is intrinsically good, even if it contained the nonobtaining state of affairs *someone's being wise and happy*. That intrinsic value requires the exemplification of certain sorts of properties is strongly suggested in the following passage from Ross:

However much one were convinced that conscientiousness, for example, is good, . . . no one would say "A's conscientiousness is good" if he were convinced that A is not in fact conscientious. . . . We might say "perfectly conscientious action is good" even if (as Kant suggests) we are not convinced that there ever has been such an action. But this is only a shorthand way of saying that without being sure that such an action has ever existed, we can be sure that if any existed it would be good. Hypothetical goodness presupposes hypothetical existence just as actual goodness presupposes actual existence.[5]

If it is true that states of affairs that do not obtain are not intrinsically good or bad, then we might say, speaking very loosely, of the states of affairs *everyone's being wise and happy* and *everyone's being perfectly just* not that these states of affairs *are* good, but that they *would be* good if they were to obtain. But even this is not quite right, for it would not be, strictly speaking, the state of affairs *everyone's being wise and happy* that would be intrinsically

5. Ross, *The Right and the Good*, pp. 96–7.

24

good, but the *fact* that everyone was so. Perhaps we could say that it would be good if the state of affairs were to obtain. Furthermore, if some non-obtaining states of affairs are worthy of love, then we should say that being intrinsically good implies being worthy of love, but being worthy of love does not imply being intrinsically good.

There is an objection to the view that facts are the bearers of value that is worth considering. As we have seen in the last chapter, both Chisholm and Moore accept the thesis of universality. We may take this thesis to imply that if A is intrinsically good, then it is not possible for A to exist and not be intrinsically good. Now consider the following argument. (1) If p is a contingent state of affairs, then p is a fact in some possible worlds but not in others. (2) Suppose the state of affairs p is intrinsically good in those worlds in which it obtains. (3) There are possible worlds in which the state of affairs p exists but does not obtain. (4) In those worlds p is not intrinsically good. (5) Therefore, p is intrinsically good in some worlds, but not in others in which it exists and does not obtain. The conclusion of this argument conflicts with the thesis of universality, since it implies that the intrinsic value of a thing is not essential to it. Should we abandon the thesis of universality on the basis of this argument? I do not think so. The argument assumes in the second premise that states of affairs rather than facts are the bearers of value. I have argued that it is the *fact* that p that is intrinsically good. If we are careful to distinguish between facts and states affairs, we may say that although the state of affairs that p can exist in possible worlds where it does not obtain, the fact that p does not exist in those worlds. There is no fact that p in those worlds where p does not obtain. Thus, in a world where p does not obtain, we cannot say that the fact that p exists in that world and is not intrinsically good. If we are careful to distinguish between states of affairs and facts, then we can say: If the fact that p is intrinsically good, then it is not possible for the fact that p to exist and not be intrinsically good. In other words, we can still hold that it is impossible for the fact that p to exist without being intrinsically good.

If the preceding remarks are correct, then, strictly speaking, we should not say that those states of affairs that do not obtain, that are not facts, *are* intrinsically good or bad. We may say of certain states of affairs that do not obtain that they are such that it would be good for them to obtain or bad for them to obtain. Similarly, we should not say that one state of affairs is better than another unless they both obtain. Admittedly, in ordinary discourse, we often say with respect to states of affairs that do not obtain, and in some cases where both cannot obtain, that one is better than the other. Ordinarily we might say, for example, that Socrates's having exactly ten units of pleasure is better than Socrates's having exactly five units of pleasure. But if neither state of affairs obtains, then, strictly speaking, we cannot say that one *is* better than the other. Could we say that Socrates's having exactly ten units of pleasure and Socrates's having exactly five units of pleasure are such that if they were to obtain, the former would be better than the latter? This is problematic, since these states of affairs cannot both obtain at the same time. Instead let us say, somewhat more awkwardly, that there is some state of affairs, q, such that if q and Socrates's having exactly ten units of pleasure were to obtain, then Socrates's having exactly ten units of pleasure would be better than q, and if q and Socrates's having exactly five units of pleasure were to obtain, then q would be the same in value or better than Socrates's having exactly five units of pleasure.

THE BEARERS OF VALUE:
CONCRETE PARTICULARS

At this point, I wish to turn from consideration of abstract objects such as properties, facts, and states of affairs and discuss whether certain concrete, particular things are also bearers of value. The concrete particulars I wish to consider are individual things such as human beings, dogs, apples, and cars. These things are not abstract objects; they are not properties, facts, or states of affairs. I argue that such concrete particulars are not bearers of intrinsic value.

We often judge that such things as apples, people, and dogs are good or bad. We judge that a particular apple or car is good or bad. But clearly, some judgments of value are not judgments of intrinsic value, and it hardly follows from the fact that a person or an apple is good in *some* sense that it is *intrinsically* good. Such things as apples, cars, and human beings might have instrumental value, but if they are good in this sense, it does not follow that they have intrinsic value. Particular apples, cars, and people may also be good in the sense of being *good members of their kind*. But the fact that something is a good member of its kind does not imply that it has intrinsic value. If we agree that a particular knife can be a good knife or that a particular toothpick can be a good toothpick, without either one having intrinsic value, then clearly, being a good member of a kind does not imply being intrinsically valuable.

I must note that I shall not consider here whether individual actions, events, or lives are intrinsically good. My reason for not considering these latter sorts of things is that there is some question of whether they are concrete particulars or whether they are more properly construed as abstract objects, as either species of properties, states of affairs, or facts, or akin to such things. We might, for example, think of an event or an action that occurs as a state of affairs that obtains. Thus, the occurrence of an event such as something's falling, and the occurrence of an action such as someone's walking, might both be understood in terms of the obtaining of certain states of affairs. Trying to decide whether events are abstract objects or concrete particulars would take us too far afield. Instead, let me say simply that I have no doubt that some actions, events, and lives are intrinsically good, and if it is reasonable for us to believe that such things are concrete, particular things, then it is reasonable for us to believe that some concrete particulars are intrinsically good and that others are intrinsically bad.

Let us consider, then, whether such things as human beings, apples, dogs, and cars can be bearers of intrinsic value. It is not at all clear that such concrete, individual things are bearers of intrinsic value. In considering whether properties and states of affairs are bearers of value, it was urged that it is not they that have intrinsic value, but rather the exemplification or possession of certain properties or the obtaining of certain states of affairs. If this is right, then it seems at least prima facie plausible that it is not a dog, an apple, or a person as such that has intrinsic value but rather such things as a dog's being pleased, a person's being wise, or even, perhaps, the fact that there are persons and dogs.

Among those concrete individuals that may seem most plausibly to be bearers of value are persons and human beings. If persons and human beings do not have intrinsic value, then it is doubtful that such value is had by any concrete particulars. Now as with cars and apples, the mere fact that persons and human beings are good in some sense does not imply that they are intrinsically good. The fact that John is a good painter or a good thief does not imply that John is intrinsically good any more than the fact that X is a good pencil implies that X is intrinsically good. Even the fact that John is morally good does not imply that *he* is intrinsically good. We may note that even if the fact that John is morally good is itself intrinsically good, it does not follow that *John* is intrinsically good. In general, if someone's having property F is intrinsically good, it does not follow that either (1) the person who has F or (2) the property of F itself is intrinsically good. On the other hand, it does seem reasonable to hold that *if* some concrete, individual, A, *were* intrinsically good, then the fact that A exists *would be* intrinsically good.

27

The existence of persons does seem to be necessary for the existence of some important intrinsic goods. If, for example, the properties of being wise and having morally good emotions can only be had by persons, and if the having of these properties is intrinsically good, then the existence of persons is necessary for their existence. But the fact that persons are necessary for the existence of such goods does not imply that persons are themselves intrinsically good. The existence of such goods depends just as much on the existence of the properties of being wise and having morally good emotions. Since we have already seen that properties are not bearers of value, the fact that persons are necessary for the existence of such goods does not imply that they are bearers of intrinsic value.

I am skeptical that persons are bearers of intrinsic value. Imagine a world in which nothing is beautiful or wise or morally good, a world that contains no pleasure or pain, but contains persons in a deep, dreamless sleep, their bodies tended by machines, a world in which the only living things are these sleepers. Now, such a world might perhaps be thought to have a greater potential for the exemplification of intrinsic value than an otherwise similar world that lacked any persons at all. One might make such a claim thinking that there was a greater potential in the former for the realization of such things as moral goodness, wisdom, and pleasure. (Of course, the potential for moral wickedness, stupidity, and pain might be just as great.) But even if that were true, such a potential would be irrelevant to the assessment of the world's intrinsic value, since the fact that one state of affairs or fact is more likely to lead to the exemplification of intrinsic value than another implies nothing about the intrinsic value of either state of affairs or fact. When we consider the question of intrinsic value, such a world seems to be without any intrinsic value; it does not seem to be a world that anyone should desire or favor in and for itself. The mere fact that there are persons in that world contributes no intrinsic goodness to it. And the mere fact that there are persons does not seem to be desirable in and for itself or intrinsically good. But if the fact that there are persons is not intrinsically good, then it seems reasonable to believe that persons are not intrinsically good, since if individual persons had intrinsic value, the fact that they exist would be intrinsically good.

On reflection, I suggest that what we find intrinsically good are not concrete, individual persons or the mere fact that they exist, but such things as their being wise or happy or morally good, states of affairs that do not obtain in our imagined world. If persons and human beings as such are not intrinsically good and if they are the most plausible candidates among concrete, individuals for bearers of value, then we have reason to doubt that any concrete, individual things are bearers of value.

Finally, let me advance one last set of considerations against concrete, individual things as bearers of value. In asking whether such things are bearers of intrinsic value, we should consider what is involved in the attitudes of love, hate, and preference and the related attitudes of desiring and wanting. There is reason to believe that the objects of such attitudes are not simply concrete, individual things, such as a dog, an apple, or a person, but more complex sorts of things, such as states of affairs, facts, and perhaps events. In ordinary contexts, when someone says, "I want a yacht," what he wants, the object of his want, is not simply a yacht, but more precisely his owning or having a yacht. Similarly, if someone says, pointing to a piece of apple pie, "I want that," typically what he wants is to eat it or taste it. In this case, the object of his want or desire, what he wants or desires, is not merely the piece of pie. When people say such things as "I desire X" or "I want X," where X is some concrete, individual thing, we must often gather from the context the object of their want or desire. If Mary says, "I want a little lamb," she may mean that she wants to own a lamb, or to play with a lamb, or to have a little more lamb on her plate. We can usually tell in a given context what is wanted or desired. But what I chiefly wish to emphasize is that the object of the want or desire always seems to be an object of a more complex and different sort than the mere concrete, individual thing.[6]

This feature of our wants and desires appears to belong to our preferences as well. If someone says, "I prefer X to Y," where X and Y are concrete, individual things, what is more accurately said to be the object of his preference is not merely X and Y, but some other, more complex sort of thing. Thus, if someone says he prefers a piece of chocolate cake to a piece of apple pie, the object of his preference might be more precisely said to be his eating or tasting chocolate cake to his eating or tasting apple pie. Similarly, if someone says he prefers Mary to Jill, his attitude might be more accurately said to be his preferring to be in Mary's company to Jill's or to have Mary as a boss to having Jill as a boss or to read Mary's books to reading Jill's.

The view that the objects of desires, wants, and preferences are not merely concrete individuals may be further supported by reflecting on the

6. Ibid., p. 96: "But obviously it is only a rough and ready description of my desire to say that I desire a primrose. What I desire is to be seeing it or smelling it or possessing it."

peculiarity of supposing that someone should want or desire a concrete individual without wanting or desiring some more complex object that somehow involved that thing. Think how strange it would be were someone to insist that he wants a yacht while denying that he wanted to own a yacht or that he wanted a yacht to sail, steer, see, touch, care for, admire, run aground, and so on. It does not seem possible that anyone can merely or simply want or desire a concrete, individual thing.

These remarks about the objects of emotional attitudes such as desiring and preferring are relevant to the question of whether concrete, individual things are bearers of intrinsic value. For if what we have said about the objects of preference is correct, if they are not mere concrete individual things but more complex objects, then the sorts of things that it can be fitting or appropriate to prefer must be objects of a complex kind, different from such things as a dog or a human being. Consequently, if we assume that whatever is intrinsically good is preferable to whatever is intrinsically bad, then both what is intrinsically good and what is intrinsically bad must be possible objects of preference. But if what is a possible object of preference is not merely a concrete individual such as a dog or a human being, then such things are not, strictly speaking, intrinsically good or intrinsically bad; they are not bearers of intrinsic value. If we assume, therefore, that whatever is intrinsically good is preferable to whatever is intrinsically bad, then the sorts of things that are intrinsically good or bad must be complex objects like states of affairs or facts.

The preceding remarks offer some support for the view that concrete, individual things are not bearers of intrinsic value. Some philosophers have argued that what has been said about the objects of desiring, wanting, and preferring also pertains to the objects of love and hate. According to this view, the objects of love and hate are not mere concrete, individual things but more complex objects. There are several forms that this view might take. For example, one might hold that loving and hating concrete, individual things can be reduced to the phenomena of preference. In its simplest form, this view would claim that loving X, where X is a concrete, individual thing, is a matter of preferring the state of affairs X's *existing* to any state of affairs to which one is indifferent. (One is indifferent to a state of affairs when one does not prefer it to its negation and vice versa.) Thus, to say that I love my old rocking chair is to say that I prefer my old rocking chair's existing to any state of affairs to which I am indifferent. If the phenomena of love and hate can be reduced to that of preference, then the objects of love and hate, like that of preference, would seem to be complex objects like states of affairs and facts.

An alternative view might claim that the objects of love and hate are not mere concrete, individuals, without reducing love or hate to preference. To love someone, according to this view, is typically, though not always, a matter of loving such things as his being or existing, his being healthy, his being happy, to see him and to spend time in his company. It is to love a constellation, and possibly a shifting variety, of complex objects. This view about the objects of love is expressed in the following passage by Everett Hall:

"John loves Mary" would then need to be interpreted as elliptical. What John loves is Mary's having a pair of blue eyes, a dimple in her right cheek, a way of turning suddenly pensive in the midst of a playful mood, a. . . , a. . . , etc. No one of the characterizations is a sufficient (unless John is a very, very simple boy); it is only the ensemble that is the object of his passion. It would follow that when John tells Mary, "I love you", he is saying something very complex, indeed. . . . I am suggesting . . . that a complete description of an emotion must, besides the emotive verb, contain a secondary one subordinate to it, either in an oblique participial phrase or in a substantive clause in the accusative.[7]

According to this view, the object of love is not merely the concrete, individual thing, nor is it a mere bundle of properties or characteristics. John's loving Mary is not merely a matter of his loving the property of having blue eyes, a dimple, and so on. The object of John's love is also not merely some existential generalization such as someone's having blue eyes or someone's existing. The object of John's love is not simply Mary but some more complex objects that, to speak very loosely and roughly, involve Mary.

I am not entirely sure that either of these views about the objects of love is correct. Yet if either is correct, we have one more reason to think that the bearers of intrinsic value are not concrete, individual things. For if p is intrinsically good implies that p is worthy of love, then p must be the sort of thing that can be loved, p must be a possible object of love. But if the preceding remarks are correct, and the objects of love and hate are not concrete, individual things, then such things are not bearers of value. If mere concrete, individual things are not the objects of love or hate or preference, then such things are not bearers of intrinsic value.

7. Everett Hall, *Our Knowledge of Fact and Value* (Chapel Hill: University of North Carolina Press, 1961), p. 147.

3

Organic unities and the principle of universality

In Book X of the *Nicomachean Ethics,* Aristotle refers to a kind of argument intended to show that pleasure is not the only intrinsic good:

Plato uses a similar argument in his refutation that pleasure is the good; a pleasant life, he says, is the more desirable when combined with practical wisdom than without it; but if pleasure is better in combination with something else, it is not the good, since the good cannot become more desirable by the addition of something to it.[1]

The argument presupposes the general principle that if a whole consisting in *A* and *B* is intrinsically better than its part *A,* then *B* must also be intrinsically good. Given this assumption, one may argue that since the whole consisting in pleasure and practical wisdom is better than pleasure alone, it follows that practical wisdom must also be intrinsically good and that pleasure is not the sole intrinsic good. The principle presupposed in this argument seems initially plausible, for it seems plausible to think that if a whole is better than one of its parts, then its greater value must be due to the presence of another good part. The assumption on which this argument rests implicitly denies what Moore called the "principle of organic unities."

In *Principia Ethica,* Moore states and accepts two principles concerning intrinsic value. These are the *principle of organic unities* and the *thesis of universality.* According to the principle of organic unities, "the value of a whole must not be assumed to be the same as the sum of the values of its parts."[2] We may understand the principle of organic unities to tell us that the value of some wholes is not the same as the sum of the values of their parts. According to the thesis of universality, "The part of a valuable whole retains exactly the same value when it is, as when it is not, a part of that

---

1. Aristotle, *Nicomachean Ethics,* translated by Martin Ostwald (Indianapolis: Bobbs-Merrill Co., 1962), Book X, Chapter 2, 1172b, 27–33.
2. G. E. Moore, *Principia Ethica* (Cambridge: Cambridge University Press, 1903), p. 28.

32

whole. If it had value under other circumstances, its value is not any greater, when it is part of a far more valuable whole; and if it had no value by itself, it has none still, however great be that of the whole of which it now forms a part."[3] The principle of organic unities may be contrasted with the *principle of summation,* which tells us that the value of every whole is merely a sum of the values of its parts. If the principle of organic unities is true, then the principle of summation is false, and vice versa. The principle of universality may be contrasted with what we may call the *principle of conditionality.* The principle of conditionality tells us that the intrinsic value of a fact is conditional on what other states of affairs obtain, that is, that the value of a part of one whole can be different when it is part of a different whole. If the principle of universality is true, then the principle of conditionality is false, and vice versa.

In this chapter, I wish to explicate and defend the principle of organic unities and the principle of universality. To this end, I illustrate the principle of organic unities by means of certain examples, most of which involve an appeal to certain judgments about the value of pleasure and pain, including such things as "pleasure in the bad" and "displeasure in the bad." These examples are among the most promising and common illustrations of organic unities. In the following section, I explain how these examples presuppose the thesis of universality. The main concern of that section, however, is to defend the thesis of universality against a certain view of pleasure and pain represented by W. D. Ross and, perhaps, Immanuel Kant. I shall try to show that Ross's and Kant's view that pleasure and pain are only prima facie or conditionally good or bad is less reasonable than the view presupposed in our examples of organic unities.

Both the principle of organic unities and the thesis of universality are stated in terms of the concept of a "part." How shall we understand the concept of a part in relation to these theses about value? It was urged in the last chapter that the clearest candidates for bearers of value are facts or states of affairs that obtain. In light of this, I suggest that the relevant notion of a part is one that pertains to states of affairs. But what is it for one state of affairs to be part of another? Let us say,

(D1) p is a part of q = Df. q is necessarily such that (1) if q obtains, then p obtains, and that (2) whoever entertains q entertains p.[4]

3. Ibid., p. 30.
4. This is Chisholm's definition of "part" in *Brentano and Intrinsic Value,* p. 73. But in discussing the concept of "organic unities," we need to use the more specific notion of a proper part. Roderick Chisholm, *Brentano and Intrinsic Value* (Cambridge: Cambridge University Press, 1986).

Entertaining a state of affairs is an intentional attitude akin to believing and wanting. Just as one can believe, accept, or want states of affairs that do not obtain, one can entertain states of affairs that do not obtain. For example, one can entertain the state of affairs *there being unicorns*. One can also entertain a state of affairs without wanting or accepting or believing it. Someone can entertain there being unicorns without accepting it or wanting it to obtain. Since (D1) makes use of the intentional concept of entertaining, we may say that it is an intentional definition of the concept of a part. According to (D1), *something's being red* is a part of *something's being red and round*. The latter state of affairs implies the former, and whoever considers the latter considers the former. *Something's being red* is not part of *something's being red or round,* for the latter does not imply the former. *There are unicorns* is not part of *Smith's believing that there are unicorns.* Smith's believing that there are unicorns does not imply that that there are any. One feature of (D1), however, is that every state of affairs is a part of itself. So let us say:

(D2)   *p* is a proper part of *q* = Df. *p* is a part of *q* and *q* is not a part of *p*.

Henceforth, when I refer to "parts," I shall be referring to proper parts unless otherwise indicated.

EXAMPLES OF ORGANIC UNITIES

In the preface to *Principia Ethica,* Moore points out the similarity between his view of value and that of Brentano, but he claims that one difference between his view and Brentano's is that the latter "does not recognise, but even denies by implication, the principle which I have called *the principle of organic unities.*"[5] Yet in *Brentano and Intrinsic Value,* Chisholm notes that Brentano's treatment of certain cases of pleasure and displeasure presupposes the principle. Chisholm suggests that we can understand the principle better if we consider what Brentano says about these examples of pleasure and displeasure.

To appreciate properly these examples, we must bear in mind certain points about pleasure and displeasure. First, pleasure or displeasure *can* be construed as intentional attitudes akin to such as things as believing, en-

---

5. Moore, *Principia Ethica,* p. xi. There is no question that Moore thought very highly of Brentano's work on the theory of value. In a review of Brentano's *On the Origin of Our Knowledge of Right and Wrong,* Moore wrote, it is "a far better discussion of the most fundamental principles of ethics than any other works with which I am acquainted." See Moore's review in the *International Journal of Ethics* (October 14 1903), pp. 115–23.

tertaining, fearing, hoping, desiring, and so on. One can be pleased or displeased *that* certain states of affairs obtain. In other words, pleasure and displeasure can be construed as intentional attitudes that take states of affairs as their objects. Second, just as one can accept, entertain, or want states of affairs that do not obtain, one can also be pleased or displeased about states of affairs that do not obtain. For example, if you tell me that my wife has won the lottery and I believe you, I shall be pleased that my wife has won. But even if, unknown to me, what you have told me is false, the fact remains that I am pleased that she has won. I am pleased even though the state of affairs that is the object of my pleasure does not obtain. One can also be displeased or pained about something that he mistakingly believes to be true. Thus, my being displeased or pained that someone has stolen my wallet is quite compatible with the fact that no one has done so. Finally, pleasure and displeasure can be taken in states of affairs that are themselves intrinsically good or bad or intrinsically worthy of love or hate. "Pleasure in the good" consists in one's taking pleasure in a state of affairs which is intrinsically good or worthy of love. If, for example, Smith's being wise is intrinsically good or worthy of love, then Jones's being pleased that Smith is wise is an instance of pleasure in the good. Similarly, pleasure in the bad might consist in Jones's taking pleasure in a state of affairs that is intrinsically bad or worthy of hate, such as Smith's suffering.

In presenting examples of organic unities, we may compare (1) pleasure in the bad, (2) displeasure in the bad, (3) pleasure in the good, and (4) displeasure in the good. We may also consider (5) indifference to the good and (6) indifference to the bad. These last two consist in one's being aware of certain good or bad states of affairs and one's being indifferent to them.

In "Two Unique Cases of Preferability," Brentano considers the values of pleasure in the bad and displeasure in the bad. He writes:

> What of pleasure in the bad? Is it itself something that is good? Aristotle says that it is not, and in a certain sense he is undoubtedly right. He writes in the *Nicomachean Ethics* . . . "No one would wish to feel joy in what is base, even if he were assured that no harm would come from it."[6]

He adds, "Pleasure in the bad is, as pleasure, something that is good, but at the same time, as an incorrect emotion, it is something that is bad. Even if it

---

6. Brentano, "Two Unique Cases of Preferability," *The Origin of Our Knowledge of Right and Wrong,* translated by Roderick Chisholm and Elizabeth Schneewind (London: Routledge & Kegan Paul, 1969), p. 90. Aristotle's remark is from the *Nicomachean Ethics,* Book X, Chapter 3, 1174a, 1–4.

is predominantly bad, because of this incorrectness, it cannot be said to be purely bad."[7] With respect to displeasure in the bad, Brentano says:

> Consider what occurs when a magnanimous person is pained at the sight of innocent victims of injustice, or when a man feels remorse about some misdeed committed in the past. Now we have the reverse of the situation previously considered. Here we have a feeling that strikes us as being predominantly but not purely good.[8]

Brentano's comments about the magnanimous attitude toward the suffering of the innocent is in keeping with Aristotle's remarks in the *Nicomachean Ethics* about righteous indignation[9] and the following observation by W. D. Ross: "We think that the pleasure taken either by the agent or by a spectator in, for instance, a lustful or cruel action is bad; and we think it a good thing that people should be pained rather than pleased by contemplating vice or misery."[10]

Bearing in mind the intentional aspect of pleasure and displeasure, let us consider pleasure in the bad. Consider the state of affairs *Jones's being pleased that Smith is suffering, q*. Let us assume that this state of affairs is intrinsically bad. Brentano would say that q is predominantly bad but not purely bad. It is not purely bad because it has a part that is good, namely, *Jones's being pleased*. Does q have any part that is intrinsically bad? No, for *Smith is suffering* is *not* a part of q. Jones's being pleased that Smith is suffering does not imply that Smith is suffering. Jones might be mistaken in believing that Smith is suffering. Q is thus an intrinsically bad whole with a good part and no bad parts.[11] In this respect, it illustrates the principle of organic unities, for its intrinsic value is not a mere sum of the values of its parts.

Displeasure in the bad also illustrates the principle. Let's assume that *Jones's being displeased that Smith is suffering, p*, is intrinsically good. Brentano would say that p is predominantly but not purely good. It is not purely good because it has a part that is bad, namely, *Jones's being displeased*.

---

7. Brentano, *The Origin of Our Knowledge of Right and Wrong*, p. 90.
8. Ibid., p. 91.
9. Aristotle, *Nicomachean Ethics*, Book II, Chapter 7, 1108b, 1–6.
10. W. D. Ross, *The Right and the Good* (Oxford: Oxford University Press, 1930), p. 137.
11. Could one say that a bad part of q is someone's having an incorrect emotion? No, since one can entertain q without entertaining the latter. Furthermore, even if we assume that *Jones's being pleased* is not a *good* part of q, but, say, merely neutral, we still have an example of an organic unity, for then q would be a bad whole with no good parts and no bad parts. It would still be a whole whose value was not equal to the sum of the value of its parts.

P is an intrinsically good whole with a bad part and no good parts.[12] Here again we find a state of affairs whose value is not a mere sum of the values of its parts.

The states of affairs *Jones's being pleased that Smith is suffering, q,* and *Jones's being displeased that Smith is suffering, p,* illustrate the principle even if we do not assume that p is intrinsically good. If we assume merely that p is intrinsically better than q, then we may say that p is better than q even though p has bad parts and no good parts and q has good parts and no bad parts.

The principle of organic unities may also be illustrated by comparing pleasure in the good and pleasure in the bad. Compare *Jones's being pleased that Smith is suffering, q,* and *Jones's being pleased that Smith is happy, r.* The former is an instance of *Schadenfreude,* taking pleasure in the suffering of another. Brentano would tell us that it is predominantly but not purely bad. The latter is an instance of *Mitfreude,* taking pleasure in the joy or happiness of another. It is purely good with no bad part. R and q illustrate the principle insofar as r is better than q, even though the only good part of each is *Jones's being pleased.* The difference in their value is not a result of q's having a bad part that r lacks or r's having a good part that q lacks.

Along with the examples just presented, we may include indifference to the bad and indifference to the good. Let's assume that the state of affairs *Jones's believing that Smith is suffering and being indifferent to it* is intrinsically bad. This state of affairs has no bad part. Like pleasure in the bad, it is a bad whole that contains no bad parts. Similarly, the state of affairs *Jones's believing that Smith is happy and being indifferent to it* seems intrinsically bad. If it is bad, it is also a bad whole with no bad parts.

In addition to the preceding examples, some philosophers have claimed that the principle of organic unities can be discerned in the importance of order and arrangement. Brentano offers three sorts of cases that illustrate this importance. These are (1) the value in retribution and requital, (2) the *bonum variationis,* and (3) the *bonum progressionis.*

How does the value of retribution and requital bear on the principle of organic unities? According to Chisholm, Brentano writes in an unpublished fragment that wickedness accompanied by sorrow is better than

---

12. Again, even if we assume that *Jones's being displeased* is not a *bad* part of p, we still seem to have an example of an organic unity, for p would then be a good whole with no good parts and no bad parts. Its value would not be equal to the sum of the value of its parts.

the same wickedness accompanied by pleasure.[13] Just as displeasure in the suffering of another is intrinsically better than pleasure in the suffering of another, so Brentano suggests that feeling remorse or sorrow at one's wickedness is intrinsically better than taking pleasure in one's wickedness. Brentano would tell us that *someone's feeling sorrow toward his wicked actions,* is predominantly but not purely good. It has a part that is intrinsically bad, namely, *someone's feeling sorrow.* In contrast, *someone's being pleased about his wicked actions* is predominantly but not purely bad. It has a good part, namely, *someone's being pleased.* If someone's feeling sorrow toward his wicked actions is intrinsically better than someone's being pleased about his wicked actions, then these states of affairs illustrate the principle of organic unities insofar as the former is better, even though it has bad parts and no good parts and the latter has good parts and no bad parts.

In connection with the value of retribution, Brentano writes, "if at the Last Judgment a greater amount of bliss were given to a person who actually deserved it less, then he would have a greater amount of good than he otherwise would have, but the good in the universe considered as a whole would be less."[14] A similar point is made by Ross: "If we compare two imaginary states of the universe, alike in the total amounts of virtue and vice and of pleasure and pain present in the two, but in one of which the virtuous were all happy and the vicious miserable, while in the other the virtuous were all miserable and the vicious happy, very few people would hesitate to say that the first was a much better state of the universe than the second."[15] The following will serve to illustrate Brentano's point. Let us assume that *A's being happy, p,* has the same intrinsic value as *B's being happy, q.* Now consider the state of affairs *A's being wicked and B's being virtuous, r.* According to Brentano, the whole that consists of *p* and *r* has less intrinsic value than the whole that consists of *q* and *r.* Such a case appears to be one in which the value of the whole is not a mere sum of the values of its parts.

Chisholm says, "The principle of the *bonum variationis* might be formulated this way: other things being, equal it is better to combine two dissimilar goods than to combine two similar goods."[16] Chisholm suggests the following as an example of the principle: Suppose that *A* is a beautiful painting, that *B* is a painting exactly like *A,* and that *C* is a beautiful piece

13. Chisholm, *Brentano and Intrinsic Value,* p. 72. Brentano's unpublished fragment is entitled "On the good that there is in order or arrangement."
14. Brentano, *The Origin of Our Knowledge of Right and Wrong,* p. 149.
15. Ross, *The Right and the Good,* p. 138.
16. Chisholm, *Brentano and Intrinsic Value,* pp. 70–1.

of music. Let us assume that the aesthetic contemplation of *A* has the same value as that of *B* and the same as that of *C*. The whole that is the aesthetic contemplation of *A* followed by the aesthetic contemplation of *C* is in-trinsically better than that whole that is the aesthetic contemplation of *A* followed by the aesthetic contemplation of *B*. Other writers have suggested that other things being equal, a variety of goods is preferable to a lack of variety.[17]

Finally, with respect to the *bonum progressionis*, Chisholm cites the following remark by Brentano:

> Let us think of a process which goes from good to bad or from a greater good to a lesser good; then compare it with one which goes in the opposite direction. The latter shows itself as the one to be preferred. This holds even if the sum of the goods in the one process is equal to that in the other.[18]

Chisholm suggests that the principle of the *bonum progressionis* may be put by saying, "If *A* is a situation in which a certain amount of value *x* is increased to a larger amount *y*, and if *B* is like *A* except that in *B* there is a decrease from the larger amount of value *y* to the smaller amount *x*, then *A* is preferable to *B*."[19] Chisholm emphasizes that in comparing the two processes, *A* and *B*, we should think of them as mirror images of one another and that one does not include, for example, a pleasure of anticipation unless the other includes a corresponding equal pleasure of recollection.

The principle of the *bonum progressionis* is also implicit in the following example suggested by A. C. Ewing: "A life the earlier part of which was morally inferior and the later part morally superior would be intrinsically more valuable than a life the earlier part of which was superior in the

---

17. In his discussion of the problem of evil, A. C. Ewing writes, "The more different kinds of goods realized the better, but they need not all be realized at once." A. C. Ewing, *Value and Reality* (London: George Allen & Unwin, 1973), p. 221. Consider also the following passage from William Frankena's *Ethics*: "the good life will be a 'mixed life,' as Plato said, consisting of activities and experiences of the kinds listed earlier, that is, of activities and experiences that are enjoyable or both excellent in some degree and enjoyable. . . . D. H. Parker, staying close to Plato, thought that one's life should have such features as unity in variety, balance, rythymn, and hierarchy. A. N. Whitehead, closer to romanticism and evolutionism, thought it should include novelty and adventure, as well as continuity and tradition, and that it should include them in some kind of rythymn of alternation." William Frankena, *Ethics*, 2nd edition (Englewood Cliffs, N. J.: Prentice-Hall, 1973), p. 92.
18. Chisholm, *Brentano and Intrinsic Value*, p. 71. The passage is from Brentano, *The Foundation and Construction of Ethics*, translated by Elizabeth Schneewind (New York: Humanities Press, 1973), pp. 196–7.
19. Chisholm, *Brentano and Intrinsic Value*, p. 71.

same degree and the later part equally inferior."[20] Ewing stresses that the ascent from the inferior to the superior is better than the descending process, quite apart from any possible delight or pleasure one feels toward one's improvement or any possible pain one takes in one's moral deterioration. He holds that the ascending life is better than the descending life even if, in the former, one is too modest to take pleasure in the improvement and, in the latter, too callous to be pained by the moral disintegration. A similar point about temporal order was made by C. I. Lewis: "It may be that a life which begins badly but ends well is better than one which begins well but ends badly, even though the ingredient experiences which make it up should be as nearly comparable as could well be imagined and should differ only by what is involved in the different temporal order of them."[21]

THE PRINCIPLE OF UNIVERSALITY

Let us turn to the thesis of universality. Moore takes this to be the thesis that "the part of a valuable whole retains exactly the same value when it is, as when it is not a part of that whole." Let us consider the following state of affairs:

(1) A is pleased that someone is happy.
(2) A is pleased that someone is suffering.
(3) A is pleased and A is wicked.
(4) A is pleased and A is virtuous.
(5) A is pleased.

Given the notion of a "part" presented in (D2), we may say that (5) is a part of (1)–(4). If the considerations in the last section are correct, (1)–(5) are not of equal intrinsic value. It is reasonable to believe, for example, that (1) is intrinsically better than either (2) or (3). The thesis of universality tells us that (5) has the same value as (1)–(4). It tells us, for example, that the intrinsic value of A's being pleased is the same whether A is wicked or virtuous. It does *not* tell us that larger wholes of which (5) is a part, such as (3) and (4), are of equal intrinsic value.

What we have said in the last section concerning pleasure in the good and pleasure in the bad implies that (5) is an intrinsically good part of each of the other states of affairs. We have said, for instance, that (2) is an

20. Ewing, *Value and Reality*, p. 219.
21. C. I. Lewis, *An Analysis of Knowledge and Valuation* (LaSalle, Ill.: Open Court Publishing Co., 1946), p. 488.

example of an organic unity since it is an intrinsically bad whole with a good part, namely, (5), and no bad parts. In this respect, then, the claim that (2) is an organic unity presupposes the claim that (5) has the same intrinsic value, that it is intrinsically good, even when it is part of a whole that is bad.

Anyone who denies that (5) has the same intrinsic value in (1)–(5) rejects the thesis of universality. While the thesis of universality has been accepted by philosophers such as Moore, Brentano, and Chisholm, it has been implicitly rejected by W. D. Ross and, perhaps, Immanuel Kant. Since probably the clearest and most familiar objections to the thesis of universality arise in connection with the value of pleasure, the rest of this section will focus on the value of pleasure.

In *The Right and the Good*, Ross tell us that

reflection on the conception of merit does not support the view that pleasure is always good in itself and pain is always bad in itself. For while this conception implies the conviction that pleasure when deserved is good, and pain when undeserved is bad, it also suggests strongly that pleasure when undeserved is bad and pain when deserved is good.[22]

Reflection on merit, pleasure, and pain leads Ross to hold that pleasure is conditionally or prima facie good and that pain is conditionally or prima facie bad. He claims, "a state of pleasure has the property, not necessarily of being good, but of being something which is good if the state has no other characteristic which prevents it from being good."[23] In this respect, the goodness of states of pleasure is akin to the prima facie rightness of certain kinds of actions. Ross suggests that there are two sorts of features that override the prima facie goodness of a state of pleasure: (1) its being contrary to the desert of the person pleased and (2) its being a state that is the realization of a bad disposition. He goes on to say that there are two sorts of pleasures that we can say without doubt are good, namely, the pleasures of nonmoral beings (animals) and the pleasures of moral beings that are deserved and are either the realizations of good moral dispositions or the realizations of natural capacities.

We may express Ross's view toward the pleasures of the wicked in the following way. We must distinguish between (3) and (5), between the fact that A is wicked and A is pleased and the fact that A is pleased. Ross calls the former the "total" fact, and this total fact includes the simpler fact that A is pleased. Ross's view is that the total fact is not good in itself.

22. Ross, *The Right and the Good*, p. 136.
23. Ibid., p. 138.

So far, this seems very plausible. But now Ross holds that the total fact overrides the prima facie goodness of the simpler fact that A is pleased. In other words, the prima facie goodness of (5) is overridden by the fact that (3) obtains. Ross's view is that (5) is not good when (3) obtains and that (5) is not a good part of (3). Just as an act is not right when its prima facie rightness has been overridden, so (5) is not good when its prima facie goodness is overridden by (3)'s obtaining. The goodness of (5) is thus mere *conditional* goodness insofar as (5) is good provided that certain other conditions do not obtain. Given what Ross says about pleasures that are the realizations of bad dispositions, we might also say that the goodness of (5) would be overridden by the obtaining of (2), by its being a fact that A is pleased that someone is suffering. This view of the intrinsic value of (5) is incompatible with the thesis of universality.

Ross's rejection of the thesis of universality and his views on the conditional value of pleasure resemble remarks by other philosophers. Certain remarks by Brentano and St. Thomas *appear* to suggest a rejection of the thesis. "Evil," says Brentano, "appears as something in the world only when it is considered together with the whole. And isolation is a fiction."[24] St. Thomas says, "Initially and without qualification something may be judged to be good or evil, yet this decision may have to be reversed when additional circumstances are taken into account" and "something may be good according to a particular judgment which is not good according to a wider judgment, and conversely. . . ".[25]

Ross's views on the value of pleasure are influenced by and resemble Kant's. Kant writes, "a rational and impartial spectator can never feel approval in contemplating the uninterrupted prosperity of a being graced by no touch of a pure and good will, and that consequently a good will seems to constitute the indispensable condition of our very worthiness to be happy."[26] Although Kant's views on value are more difficult to interpret than Ross's, it is commonly held that Kant denies that pleasure or happiness is good when it is the pleasure or happiness or a being that lacks a good will.[27] In order for someone's being pleased or happy to be good,

---

24. Chisholm, *Brentano and Intrinsic Value*, p. 96.
25. Ibid., p. 97. Chisholm holds that neither Brentano's remark, cited earlier, nor these remarks by St. Thomas reflect these thinkers' considered views.
26. Immanuel Kant, *Groundwork of the Metaphysics of Morals,* translated and analyzed by H. J. Paton (New York: Harper & Row, 1964), p. 61.
27. This view has been attributed to Kant by H. J. Paton, Christine Korsgaard, and Ross himself. See Paton's "Analysis of the Argument" in his translation of Kant's *Groundwork of the Metaphysic of Morals,* p. 17; see also Christine Korsgaard, "Two Distinctions in Goodness," *The Philosophical Review* 14 (April 1983), p. 179.

certain conditions must be met, specifically, that the person being pleased or happy is *worthy* of pleasure or happiness, and this, in turn, requires that he have a good will. Thus, it seems to be Kant's view, like Ross's, that (3) earlier is not intrinsically good and, more important, that (5) is not good when (3) obtains. It seems that Kant, like Ross, accepts the principle of conditionality.

Shall we say, with Ross and Kant, that (5) is not good when certain other states of affairs obtain? That it is not good when it is a part of (3)? Or shall we say, with Moore and other proponents of the thesis of universality, that the intrinsic value of (5) is unaffected by what else is the case? That (5) retains the same value in whatever whole it is found?

One might attempt to illustrate and support Ross's rejection of the thesis of universality by appealing to an aesthetic analogy involving parts and wholes. Imagine that we have two patches of color that are exactly alike, A and A'. Suppose that we lay A beside a patch of color B that harmonizes with it and put A' beside patch C, which clashes with it. One might say that in this context A is beautiful and A' is ugly, and that the aesthetic values of A and A' thus appear to change, depending on the whole to which they belong. But if the aesthetic values of A and A' depend on the wholes to which they belong, then why should we deny that the value of a pleasure might also change when it belongs to different wholes? Yet whatever the merits of this analogy, it is not endorsed by Ross. He considers this very illustration in *The Right and the Good* and rejects the claim that the beauty or ugliness of A and A' change. He says, "it is not the two patches A, A' that would be respectively beautiful and ugly, but the wholes A B, A' C. On reflection we should admit that though A B is beautiful and A' C ugly, still if A is beautiful, A' if exactly like it must be beautiful too; though to apprehend its beauty we should have to do what may be difficult to do, viz. contemplate it in abstraction from C."[28] Given his straightforward rejection of this aesthetic analogy, Ross's treatment of the value of pleasure seems puzzling. Though his treatment of pleasure as conditionally or prima facie good is logically consistent with his rejection of the aesthetic analogy, one wonders whether there is any good reason for treating the aesthetic and value cases differently.

I am inclined to agree with Moore and the defenders of universality. The chief difficulty with Ross's view is that it misses what apparently makes so offensive the prosperity of the wicked and states of affairs such as (3). What is it that makes the wicked man's being happy, "the unin-

28. Ibid., p. 123.

terrupted prosperity" of the wicked, so offensive? I suggest that it is offensive precisely because we think that the wicked man has a *good* that he deserves not to have. Contrary to Ross, the judgment that the prosperity of the wicked is not good, that no rational and impartial spectator could approve of it, presupposes the judgment that his being pleased *is* good; it is a good that is contrary to what he deserves. Compare our attitude toward the prosperity and pleasure of the wicked with our attitude toward the hair color of the wicked. The attitudes are very different. No one finds it particularly offensive that a wicked man might be a blond or a brunette. The fact that *A* is wicked and blond is not as offensive as his being wicked and happy. This is because we don't think of being blond or brunette as intrinsically good. We don't think that the blond wicked man is ipso facto in possession of a *good* that he deserves not to have.

Now one might object that what makes the prosperity of the wicked not good is simply the fact that the wicked desire to be pleased and prosperous, and it is not good that the wicked have their desires satisfied. But this suggestion is not very plausible, for even the wicked might have *some* desires which are such that their satisfaction is good. Even a wicked person might desire that some deserving person be happy or pleased or that some innocent animal be pleased, but there is no reason to suppose that the satisfaction of such desires is not good.

Perhaps one might more plausibly object that what makes the prosperity of the wicked man not good is simply that he has something that he deserves not to have. One might suggest that the judgment that the prosperity of the wicked is not good presupposes not the belief that the wicked man has something *good*, but just that he has *something* he deserves not to have. But I suggest that this view does not adequately capture what underlies our attitude toward the pleasure and prosperity of the wicked. Consider the following observation from Aristotle's *Rhetoric*:

Most directly opposed to pity is a feeling called Indignation. Pain at unmerited good fortune is, in one sense, opposite to pain at unmerited bad fortune, and is due to the same moral qualities. Both feelings are associated with good moral character; it is our duty both to feel sympathy and pity for unmerited distress, and to feel indignation at unmerited prosperity; for whatever is undeserved is unjust, and that is why we ascribe indignation even to the gods.[29]

Both unmerited bad fortune and unmerited good fortune imply someone's having something that he deserves not to have, but, as Aristotle

29. Aristotle, *Rhetoric*, translated by W. Rhys Roberts in *The Basic Works of Aristotle* edited by Richard McKeon (New York: Random House, 1941) Bk. II, Chapter 9, 1386b.

points out, the former is a fitting object of pity and the latter a fitting object of indignation. What underlies our attitude, our indignation, toward the prosperity of the wicked is not, therefore, merely that he has *something* that he deserves not to have, but that he deserves not to have some particular *good*.

I conclude that reflection on the unmerited pleasures of the wicked does not support the view that the thesis of universality is false, that the goodness of A's being pleased is overridden by the fact that A is also wicked. On the contrary, reflection supports the view that A's being pleased retains its goodness, and for this reason, indignation is appropriate toward A's being wicked and pleased or happy, that is, toward A's unmerited good fortune.

Let us turn to those pleasures Ross refers to as the "realizations" of a bad disposition. Ross claims that any state of pleasure that is the realization of a bad disposition is not good, that its goodness has been overridden by the fact that it is the product of such a disposition. We may take Ross to hold that (4), A's being pleased, is not good when certain other state of affairs obtain, such as the fact that A's being pleased is the realization of a bad disposition, such as malice, envy, or spite.[30] According to this view, if A is pleased that someone is suffering, (2), and this is the realization of a bad disposition, then (5) is not good. Thus, this view contrasts sharply with Brentano's view that, although (2) is predominantly bad, it has a part, (5), that is good.

There are at least two problems with Ross's view. First, suppose that A is a wicked man whose exercise of bad dispositions brings him pleasure. The mere fact that A is pleased seems clearly contrary to his desert, and suppose that we agree with Ross that the fact that A is wicked and pleased is not good. But as I have argued, if we are indignant that A is wicked and pleased, then our indignation presupposes the fact that A's being pleased is good, that it is a good that A deserves not to have. But if this is so, then the fact that A is pleased, (5), is good even though it results from the exercise of his bad dispositions.

Second, suppose that we assume that a pleasure is the realization of a bad disposition just in case it is a pleasure that is brought about by the exercise of that bad disposition. Given this assumption, it is not clear that all such pleasures are bad. Suppose, for example, that B is a nepotist and

---

30. See Aristotle's remark that "The pleasure proper to a morally good activity is good, the pleasure proper to a bad activity evil." *Nicomachean Ethics,* Bk. X, Chapter 5, 1175b, p. 284.

that nepotism is understood as a disposition to give unfair or undue preference to the welfare of one's relatives. Imagine that B's nepotism leads B to promote the pleasure of his nephew, C. It is far from clear that we should think that C's being pleased is not good simply because it results from the realization of B's bad disposition. Suppose that C is himself a good man and deserving of pleasure, but that his uncle is unaware of and unmotivated by any consideration of C's merit. C's pleasure could be both deserved *and* the product of his uncle's nepotism. C's pleasure could be both deserved and the realization of a bad disposition. This would be an unhappy consequence for Ross, since he holds that deserved pleasures are good and that pleasures that are the realization of bad dispositions are bad. Given his assumptions, this would entail that C's being pleased is both intrinsically good and intrinsically bad.

Perhaps neither of the problems mentioned earlier is fatal to Ross's view, but they should at least make us wary of embracing it. More important, reflection on pleasures that are the realization of bad dispositions does not really support a rejection of the thesis of universality or require us to say either that (1) the state of affairs *someone's being pleased* is only prima facie good or that (2) the property of *being pleased* is not an intrinsically good-making property. At best, such reflection supports a view that says roughly that some kinds of pleasure are not intrinsically good. To claim that some kinds of pleasure are not intrinsically good is only to say roughly that some states of affairs that imply pleasure and no pain are not intrinsically good. But on this point, we may take Brentano and Ross to be in complete agreement. Both would allow, for example, that *someone's being pleased that someone is suffering* is not intrinsically good. If Brentano and Ross are right, we may say that the property of *being pleased that someone is suffering* is not an intrinsically good-making property, that is, the fact that something has it is not intrinsically good. But if *being pleased that someone is suffering* is not an intrinsically good-making property, it hardly follows that the property of *being pleased* is not or that it is only a prima facie good-making property. These are, after all, distinct properties, since one can have the latter without having the former. Similarly, if the fact that *someone's being pleased that someone is suffering* is not intrinsically good, it follows that some pleasures are not intrinsically good (at least when a pleasure is broadly construed as a state of affairs that implies pleasure and no pain). But we cannot infer from these claims that *someone's being pleased* is not intrinsically good or that it is only prima facie good. The fact that *someone is pleased* is different from the fact that *someone is pleased that someone is suffering*. The former state of affairs can obtain even when the latter does not. It is simply mistaken to infer from the fact that some pleasures (some states of affairs that imply pleasure and no pain) are not intrinsically good the conclusion that *someone's being pleased* is intrinsically good in some contexts and not in others, or that the property *being pleased* is not an intrinsically good-making property. The fact that some pleasures are intrinsically bad does not imply that the thesis of universality is false or that the principle of conditionality is true.

If the arguments and examples of the last two sections are sound, then we have some reason to accept the principle of organic unities and the principle of universality. We have reason to believe that there are organic unities, wholes whose intrinsic value is not equal to the value of the sum of their parts. Is it possible to define the concept of an organic unity without making use of the notion of a "sum" of values? Chisholm has sought to do so, but I believe that his proposed definition is inadequate to the variety of organic unities he himself distinguishes. For a discussion of Chisholm's definition and its problems, see Appendix A.

4

Higher goods and the myth of Tithonus

In this chapter, I discuss and defend the existence of "higher goods." In the first section, I explain what such goods would be and consider some examples that tend support their existence. The existence of such goods has been accepted by many philosophers, including Franz Brentano, Blaise Pascal, W. D. Ross, and perhaps Aristotle and John Stuart Mill. In the second section, I consider a problem that arises for the existence of higher goods if we reject certain extravagant claims that some of their defenders, such as Ross, have made about them. I argue that even if such claims are false, the existence of higher goods can be defended. The defense I offer presupposes a principle analogous to the principle of organic unities, a principle I call the "principle of rank." In the third section, I consider briefly the importance of such goods for Mill's distinction between the quantity and quality of pleasures. In the fourth section, I discuss the importance of higher goods and the principle of summation. This discussion of higher goods, organic unities, and summation continues the discussion of these issues from the last chapter.

HIGHER GOODS

In "Overpopulation and the Quality of Life," Derek Parfit imagines a choice between two futures, the *century of ecstasy* and the *drab eternity*. In the former, he would live for another hundred years, with a life of extremely high quality. In the latter, he would live forever a life that was barely worth living. There would be nothing bad in this life, but it would contain only Muzak and potatoes. Parfit says that he would prefer the century of ecstasy to the drab eternity, that it would give him a better future: He writes, "Though each day of the Drab Eternity would have some value for me, no amount of this value could be as good for me as the Century of Ecstasy."[1] According to Parfit, the century of ecstasy contains goods, albeit a finite number of them, that are better than any number of the goods found in the drab eternity.

Many other philosophers have taken seriously the possibility of such classes of goods. In his 1907 essay "Loving and Hating," Franz Brentano writes, "It is quite possible for there to be a class of goods which could be increased *ad indefinitum* but without exceeding a given finite good."[2] Brentano believes that others have held the same view. For example, he attributes to Pascal the view that "there are classes of goods which can be ranked in the following way: the smallest of any of the goods that are to be found in the higher class will always be superior to the totality of goods which are to be found in the lower class."[3] Others have taken a similar stand. In *The Right and the Good*, W. D. Ross endorses a similar view:

With respect to pleasure and virtue, it seems to me much more likely to be the truth that *no* amount of pleasure is equal to any amount of virtue, that in fact virtue belongs to a higher order of value, beginning at a point higher on the scale of value than pleasure ever reaches; in other words, that while pleasure is comparable in value with virtue (i.e. can be said to be less valuable than virtue) it is not commensurable with it, as a finite duration is not commensurable with an infinite duration.[4]

The position of Brentano, Pascal, and Ross pertains to intrinsic goods, to things that are desirable in and for themselves. It is their view that there are certain kinds of intrinsic goods that could be increased ad indefinitum without being intrinsically better than some other, "higher" kind of intrinsic good. Anyone who accepts this thesis accepts the view that some kinds of goods are higher than others.

Aristotle and Mill make similar comments that suggest that they, too, accept the existence of such higher goods. Aristotle writes, "No one would choose to live his entire life with the mentality of a child, even if he were to enjoy to the fullest possible extent what children enjoy."[5] Mill says:

1. Derek Parfit, "Overpopulation and the Quality of Life," in *Applied Ethics,* edited by Peter Singer (New York: Oxford University Press, 1986), p. 161.
2. Franz Brentano, "Loving and Hating," *The Origin of Our Knowledge of Right and Wrong,* translated by Roderick Chisholm and Elizabeth Schneewind (London: Routledge & Kegan Paul, 1969, p. 158.
3. Ibid., p. 157.
4. W. D. Ross, *The Right and the Good* (Oxford: Oxford University Press, 1930). p. 150.
5. Aristotle, *Nicomachean Ethics,* translated by Martin Ostwald (Indianapolis: Bobbs-Merrill Co., 1962), Book X, Chapter 3, 1174a, 1–4.

Few human creatures would consent to be changed into any of the lower animals for a promise of the fullest allowance of a beast's pleasures; no intelligent human being would consent to be a fool. . . . A being of higher faculties requires more to make him happy, is capable probably of more acute suffering, and certainly accessible to it at more points, than one of an inferior type; but in spite of these liabilities, he can never really wish to sink into what he feels is a lower grade of existence.[6]

Aristotle and Mill may be taken to say that most adult human lives involve goods that are better than the goods that are found in the lives of children and animals. Admittedly, Aristotle and Mill do not explicitly say that no amount of the goods found in the lives of children, fools, and animals would be better than the goods found in some finite human lives. Still, it would not perhaps be too far from the spirit of their remarks to say that most finite human adult lives involve the kinds of goods that make such lives better than a life of any length involving nothing but the pleasures of infants and animals. Most people, I suppose, would not think that they would have been better off, that their lives would have been better, had they been born imbeciles, contented with the lowest level of infantile pleasures, with no self-awareness, memory of the past, or expectation of future pleasure, however long such a life lasted.

Are there classes of goods of the sort suggested by Brentano, Pascal, and Ross? Is there a type of good, X, such that no number of instances of another type of good Y would be better than X? Before considering some examples that tend to support the existence of such goods, it is, I think, worthwhile to make some general comments about the notion of one good being higher than another. First, if X is a higher good than Y, then either X is intrinsically better than Y or an instance of X is intrinsically better than an instance of Y. But to say that one kind of good, X, is higher than another, Y, is not merely to say that X is intrinsically better than Y. The fact that a single instance of X is intrinsically better than a single instance of Y does not imply that X is a higher good than Y. It may be the case that a single instance of intense, innocent physical pleasure is intrinsically better than a slightly milder, innocent physical pleasure. But it does not follow that the former is better than any number of instances the latter.

Second, to hold that X is a higher good than Y is *not* to deny that a greater number of instances of Y is intrinsically better than a smaller number of instances of Y. One can consistently hold that X is a higher good

6. Mill, *Utilitarianism,* edited with an introduction by George Sher (Indianapolis: Hackett Publishing Co., 1979), p. 9.

than Y and that a greater number of instances of Y is intrinsically better than a smaller number. Ross, for example, holds that virtue is a higher good than pleasure, but this does not imply that there is no difference in value between a large number of instances of pleasure and a smaller number. Ross's position is that even though a greater number of instances of innocent pleasure is intrinsically better than a smaller number of instances of innocent pleasure, no number of instances of innocent pleasure is intrinsically better than a single instance of virtue.

Third, I am concerned with the notion of higher goods, with one good being higher than another good. But it is worth noting that some thinkers have taken a similar view with respect to evils. Some thinkers have suggested that there are evils such that no number of evils of one kind can ever be worse than a single instance of another kind. This view is suggested by Cardinal J. H. Newman's remark that "if all mankind suffered the extremest agony, this would be less bad than if one venial sin was committed."[7] Other thinkers have thought that there are some evils such that no number of goods can ever compensate for or balance the existence of such evils. Schopenhauer, for example, seems to have thought that any world that contains some suffering is intrinsically bad, no matter how many or what kinds of goods it contains.[8] A similar view is reflected in the following well-known exchange from Fyodor Dostoevsky's *The Brothers Karamazov*:

"Imagine that you are creating a fabric of human destiny with the object of making men happy in the end, giving them peace and rest at last, but that it was essential and inevitable to torture to death only one tiny creature – that baby beating its breast with its fist, for instance – and to found that edifice on its unavenged tears, would you consent to be the architect on those conditions? Tell me, and tell the truth."

"No, I wouldn't consent," said Alyosha softly.[9]

I think we may take Alyosha to hold that no matter how much happiness, peace, and rest such a world might contain, the evil of bringing it about through such suffering would make the entire whole bad, would make it better that such a world not exist at all. Finally, some thinkers appear to

7. J. H. Newman, *Certain Difficulties Felt by Anglicans in Catholic Teaching* (London: Longmans, Green and Co., 1885), quoted in Parfit, "Overpopulation and the Quality of Life," p. 161.
8. Quoted in Chisholm, *Brentano and Intrinsic Value* (Cambridge: Cambridge University Press, 1986), p. 94.
9. Fyodor Dostoevsky, *The Brothers Karamazov*, translated by Constance Garnett (New York: Macmillan and Co., 1923), Bk. V, Ch. IV, p. 258.

suggest that there are some goods such that certain kinds of evils cannot balance or outweigh those goods. According to this view, it is possible for there to be wholes containing such goods that will be good wholes no matter how many instances of certain kinds of evils they also contain. Perhaps a good of this sort is being described in John Hick's remark that "Christian theodicy claims, then, that the end to which God is leading us is a good so great as to justify all the failures and suffering and sorrow that will have been endured on the way to it. The life of the Kingdom of God will be an infinite, because eternal good, outweighing all temporal and therefore finite evils."[10]

I am not especially concerned to defend the existence of such goods or evils or the views of Newman, Schopenhauer, or Hick. Indeed, some of these claims seem implausible. Yet if the existence of higher goods can be supported, then perhaps we should also be open to the sorts of views expressed by these thinkers. In any case, a defense of the existence of higher goods will, I think, remove at least some of the objections faced by their views.

Are some goods higher than others? Parfit's example of the century of ecstasy and the drab eternity seems to support such a view. If we think that we would be better off choosing the former over the latter, this is because we think that the finite number of goods we possess in the former is better than any number of the goods we possess in the latter. A second example, similar to Parfit's, involves a variation on the ancient Greek myth of Tithonus. Tithonus wished for immortality but failed to wish for eternal youth. His wish for immortality granted, he continued to age and eventually withered away into a chirping cricket. Tithonus took on the form of a cricket only after living a normal human life span, but we can easily imagine a variation of the story in which the gods changed him immediately into a cricket, an immortal cricket. Even if we imagine that Tithonus's life as an insect was as pleasant as an insect's life can be, very few of us would choose everlasting life as cricket over a finite human life. No matter how great the number of insect pleasures immortal life as a cricket might hold, very few of us would think it preferable to a full, yet finite, human life. This is not because we think that the life of a cricket is not good, but rather because we think that there are goods in our finite human lives that are such that no number of instances of the goods found in the life of an insect are better.

10. John Hick, "Evil and the Infinite Future Good," in *A Modern Introduction to Philosophy*, 3rd edition, edited by Paul Edwards and Arthur Pap (New York: Free Press, 1973), p. 471.

Leaving aside the possibility of one's metamorphosizing into an insect, very few of us would find it desirable to trade the finite remainder of our normal lives for the indefinitely extended life of a contented imbecile lacking any real self-awareness, with no memory of the past or expectation of future joys. If such were the side effects of the Fountain of Youth, there would be few takers. Again, this is not because the life of the contented imbecile is not good – indeed, it does seem to be good – but because the complex of goods we expect in the rest of our lives seems to be better than any number of instances of contented moments as an imbecile. In Plato's *Philebus*, Socrates likens a life of pleasure without memory, intelligence, knowledge, or true opinion to the life of an oyster and convinces Protarchus that such a life is not desirable.[11] But we do not need to say that such a life is not good in order to agree that it is not preferable to a good, normal human life, even if the former is a very long, oysterlike existence.

One objection to this sort of example is that the reason no one would find the change into an immortal cricket or a very long-lived imbecile desirable is that what exists afterward "would not be me." In other words, such a change would be destructive of the person. One might object, "*I* simply could not be such a thing. Such a change could not be any improvement in my state, for I would no longer exist." It is hard to know what to say in response to such an objection. A fully adequate response might require addressing issues of personal identity beyond the scope of this work. Yet it is worth pointing out that it is not implausible to think that one could be much like a contented imbecile with no real self-awareness or memory of the past or future expectations. This seems the state all of us once enjoyed as newborn infants. If it is logically possible that our consciousness was once like that, I see no compelling reason to think it logically impossible for us to be like that again. Furthermore, I see no good reason to think it logically impossible for some misfortune, some accident or disease, to befall me that would result in my being such a contented imbecile. This is a sad vulnerability we all share. I do not find this objection to the example compelling. In any case, it is an objection to which our next example is not open.

For our second example, imagine that W is a possible world in which there are a million people living pleasant, virtuous lives, engaged in aesthetically and intellectually excellent activities. W is a very good world

---

11. Plato, *Philebus*, translated and with a commentary by R. Hackforth (Cambridge: Cambridge University Press, 1972), p. 34, section 21A.

containing many different sorts of intrinsic goods: pleasure, friendship, morally and intellectually virtuous activity, the appreciation of beauty, and so forth. Now suppose that in a different possible world, W', the sole sentient beings are wormlike creatures that we'll call "O-worms." The O-worms have no self-consciousness, no awareness of the past or future, no friendship or love for one another, and, of course, no moral, aesthetic, or intellectual life whatever. They never feel any pain, but they do feel intense pleasure for a few seconds on the sole occasion in their life cycle when they reproduce. W' is a dull world but it does seem to be a good one, containing a vast number of instances of intense pleasure. When one reflects on these worlds, it does seem plausible to think that no matter how many instances of pleasure W' contains, it is not intrinsically better than W. Speaking roughly, if there were another world just like W', but containing more O-worms and more instances of pleasure, it would be better than W', but it too would not be better than W. If W is intrinsically better than W' no matter how many instances of pleasures we find in W', then it does seem that Brentano, Pascal, and Ross are right about the existence of a higher class of goods. It might be hard to identify exactly what belongs in this higher class, but if W is better than W', we can reasonably think that there are such goods.

These examples tend to support the view that there are certain goods, goods found in human lives, that, are better than any number of instances of another sort of good, namely, certain instances of pleasure. Along with certain instances of pleasure, are there other kinds goods that are such that no number of instances of such goods would be better than some other kind of good, such as the goods found in many human lives or those that make W a very good world? Our answer to this question depends, at least in part, on what else we are willing to count as intrinsically good. Brentano, for example, counts mere consciousness or the having of ideas as intrinsically good. Both he and Ross count instances of knowledge as intrinsically good. Still, other philosophers take mere existence or the fact that something exists as intrinsically good.[12] I will not defend here these claims about the intrinsic value of such things, though I do think that it is plausible that at least consciousness and knowledge are intrinsically good. Yet if any of these claims are true, then I think they represent a class of goods similar in nature to certain instances of pleasure. Consider again our world, W, containing a million people living pleasant, virtuous

12. Panayot Butchvarov, for example, suggests that mere existence is intrinsically good. See his *Skepticism in Ethics* (Indianapolis: Indiana University Press), pp. 88–90.

lives, and compare it to a world containing nothing but wormlike creatures having only the immediate consciousness of their present existence and perhaps of their immediate surroundings. Even if we grant that every such instance of consciousness is intrinsically good, it does not seem that there is any number of such instances of consciousness that would make such a world better than W. If this is so, then it also appears likely that the same is true of certain instances of knowledge. Suppose we grant our wormlike creatures knowledge of their own present existence and that of their immediate surroundings. No number of instances of such knowledge seems better than the existence of W. Finally, if what we have said about these instances of consciousness and knowledge is correct, then it seems that the same is true about whatever good there is in mere existence. No matter how many such beings exist, the goodness of that number of existing beings will never be greater than the value of W.

THE PRINCIPLE OF RANK

I conclude that there is at least a prima facie case for us to think that there are classes of goods of the sort suggested by Brentano, Ross, and Parfit, that there are goods that are such that no number of instances of pleasure, consciousness, knowledge, or mere existence will be intrinsically better than they are. The sorts of examples presented in the first section tend to support the view that there are classes of goods that are such that any number of instances of those goods will not be intrinsically better than a given finite good. I have suggested that the members of this "lower" class of goods include certain kinds of pleasures, but one might also include certain instances of knowledge, consciousness, and mere existence.

In this section, I wish to focus on a problem that arises in connection with Ross's claim that *no* amount of pleasure is equal to any amount of virtue. Let us take this claim to mean that no amount of pleasure is the same in intrinsic value as any number of acts of virtue, and thus to imply that no amount of pleasure is the same in value as a single act of virtue. I must confess that I do not find this particular claim especially persuasive. Ross's claim seems, I think, no more persuasive than Newman's claim about one venial sin and extreme human suffering. By the same token, it does not seem likely that a single act of artistic or intellectual excellence is better than any amount of pleasure. Such views seem extreme, almost fanatical. But rejecting them presents a problem for the existence of higher goods. Roughly, the problem is this: If we reject the view that no amount of pleasure is better than a single act of moral or intellectual virtue, how can we hold that no amount of pleasure is better than a life that involves many, but only a finite number, of such acts? If it is false that no amount of pleasure is better than a single act of moral or intellectual virtue, and if the examples of higher goods presented earlier appear to have whatever plausibility they enjoy at least in part because of the presence of goods such as acts of moral and intellectual virtue, then is it reasonable for us to continue to hold that those higher goods are better than any amount of pleasure? An analogous problem appears to confront Parfit's claims about the century of ecstasy and the drab eternity. Suppose that we are offered the choice between living for another minute in ecstasy or having another thirty drab years of Muzak and potatoes. I, for one, would choose the thirty drab years. I think that it would be better for me to go on for another thirty drab years than to go out in a brief blaze of glory. If we would prefer another thirty drab years to five minutes of ecstasy, if we think that we should be better off that way, then how can it be reasonable for us to think that a century of ecstasy would be better than a drab eternity, or at least a very long, drab life?

In addressing this problem, we should note that although Parfit does not describe the kinds of goods involved in the century of ecstasy, the higher goods in our last two examples are not single, isolated acts of virtue or friendship or artistic and intellectual excellence. They are more complex wholes, such as lives and communities of such lives, that embody these goods as well as others. The sort of virtuous life that a human being might enjoy, and the sort that seems especially valuable, is not *merely* a collection of single acts of virtue. The sort of life that seems especially valuable and a candidate for a higher good involves much more. For example, the sort of life that Tithonus might have enjoyed had he not become an insect would not have been merely a collection of episodes of pleasure and acts of friendship or virtue, even if it would have involved such things. It would have involved the consciousness and knowledge of such acts, as well as the memory and approval of at least some of them and the justified expectation of more to come. Moreover, it would have involved the fact that these episodes of pleasure and acts of virtue and friendship would have belonged to one continuing person, and thus a person with a history of accomplishments and one deserving of goods like pleasure and friendship.

Now even if it is admitted that the sorts of wholes that seem likely candidates for higher goods are not mere collections of isolated acts of virtue or friendship, that they involve and are constituted by a rich, complex variety of other goods, the problem still remains. The temptation might still exist to view the axiological character of such a whole as being no different from the good parts it involves. In other words, one might think that *whatever* good parts constitute one of these so-called higher goods, if those parts are not themselves higher goods, then the whole that they constitute cannot be so either. Consequently, if one accepts this view and finds implausible Ross's claim that a single act of virtue is intrinsically better than any amount of pleasure, then one might also find it implausible to think the value of a life could be a higher sort of good, a good that is better than any number of instances of pleasure.

Yet this temptation should be resisted. The preceding objection rests on the assumption that the axiological character of a whole cannot be different from that of its parts. It assumes that if the parts of some whole are not of a higher order, then that whole cannot be of a higher order. I suggest that there is no good reason to make this assumption. Just as the principle of organic unities tells us that the value of a whole is not nec-essarily the same as the sum of the values of its parts, I suggest that *the axiological "rank" of a whole is not necessarily the same as that of its parts.* Let us call this the "principle of rank." According to this principle, a whole can be a higher good even if none of its parts are themselves higher goods. Thus, even if it is true with respect to every part of some whole that there is some amount of pleasure that is better than it is, it does not follow that there is some amount of pleasure that is better than the whole of which they are parts. There is no logical reason why we should think that a whole consisting of episodes of pleasure, and acts of friendship and virtue, and other familiar sorts of goods had by one continuing subject who is conscious of them, remembering them with satisfaction and approval, does *not* form a higher sort of good even if the parts that comprise it do not.

The view that a good might be a higher good, even if its parts are not, is in some respects similar to Moore's principle of organic unities. In presenting the principle of organic unities, Moore was not concerned with the issue of higher goods. Rather, he was concerned to point out that whether a whole is intrinsically good, bad, or neutral is not necessarily determined by a "mere sum" of the values of its parts. Understood this way, the principle of organic unities tells us, for example, that it is possible for a good whole to have bad parts and no good parts. In a similar fashion, it is suggested here that a given whole might be a higher good even though none of its parts is. Thus, even if we reject Ross's claim that no amount of pleasure is better than a single act of virtue, and reject similar claims about single acts of friendship or intellectual and artistic virtue, it does not follow that we must reject the existence of higher goods. There is no reason why we should think that the axiological character of a whole, whether or not it is a higher good, must be the same as that of its parts. In other words, a whole, X, that consists of A, B, and C, can be a higher good than Y, even if neither A, B, nor C is a higher good than Y.

If the preceding remarks constitute a satisfactory response on behalf of the notion of higher goods, there are several additional points worth making. First, to hold that some good is a higher good than any number of instances of pleasure, consciousness, knowledge, or existence is not to imply that the latter sorts of things are not good or not important. Indeed, many of these latter sorts of things are constituents or parts of some of those wholes that are higher goods. If Tithonus's life is a higher good than any number of instances of mere insect pleasure, it seems that this is so, at least in part, because his life is a whole that contains pleasure, consciousness, and knowledge. Similarly, if a world containing a million people living happy, virtuous lives is better than a world containing only the O-worms, however many it contains, then the former seems better, at least in part, because it does include pleasure, consciousness, and knowledge. Indeed, one might go on to argue that such things are essential to any whole that is a higher good.

Second, what we have said in defense of the existence of higher goods might be relevant to the claims of Newman. Consider again his claim that it is better that all mankind suffer the extremest agony than that one venial sin be committed. Such a claim seems as implausible as Ross's remark that no amount of pleasure is better than a single act of virtue. But even if we reject the view that one venial sin is worse than any amount of human suffering, it is still open for us to hold that there could be great, complex wholes involving many instances of wickedness, depravity, and vice that are worse than any number of instances of, say, the pain of a severe headache. On such a view, the evil of these complex, yet finite, wholes could not be exceeded by any number of the sort of evil involved in a severe headache. Thus, one might endorse a principle similar to that proposed earlier, namely, that an evil, X, might be worse than any number of instances of another evil, Y, and in this respect a lower evil than Y, even if none of the parts of X is a lower evil than Y.

There remain many important unanswered questions about higher goods. For example, some of them are wholes that embody the particular goods found in many human lives, such as virtue, pleasure, and friendship. Are there any goods that a whole must embody in order to be a higher good? Moreover, does temporal duration matter? Would a very short life or a short portion of a long life embodying such goods be a higher good? Undoubtedly, there is much more to say here, but since I do not know how to answer these questions, I shall leave them.

HIGHER GOODS AND MILL'S DISTINCTION

The existence of classes of goods of the kind described previously bears on certain fundamental issues in the theory of value. I discuss two of these. The first concerns how we should or should not understand Mill's distinction between the quantity and quality of pleasures, and the second pertains to the principle of summation.

In *Utilitarianism,* John Stuart Mill makes it clear that the intrinsic value of an episode of pleasure is a function of its *quality* as well as its *quantity*. The quantity of a pleasure is chiefly a function of its duration and intensity. According to Mill, it is possible for pleasures of equal quantity to differ in their intrinsic value. If pleasures of equal quantity differ in their intrinsic value, this is because they differ in their quality. In his introduction to Mill's *Utilitarianism,* George Sher proposes a way of dealing with Mill's distinction between the quantity of a pleasure and its quality.[13] Sher suggests that we might treat higher-quality pleasures as being twice as valuable as lower-quality pleasures and that we might count them twice as much in our calculations. This is not, I think, the best way of interpreting Mill's view. One cannot help wondering why some higher pleasures might not be higher than others, so that some higher pleasures might be, say, three or four times higher than some lower pleasure.

A similar but more promising proposal is made by Fred Feldman in his *Introductory Ethics.* Feldman describes what I think is a fairly common approach to understanding Mill's distinction between the quantity and quality of pleasures.[14] According to this approach, there is a scale for measuring the duration of episodes of pleasure and a scale for measuring their intensity. We can assign a numerical value to the duration and the intensity of every episode of pleasure. For example, if we assign a value of 5 to a pleasure that last for five minutes, we should assign a value of 10 to a pleasure that last twice as long. If we assign a value of 4 to a certain intensity of pleasure, we shall assign a value of 8 to a pleasure that is twice as intense. The *quantity* of a pleasure is the product of its duration ranking

13. Mill, *Utilitarianism,* pp. xii–xiii.
14. Fred Feldman, *Introductory Ethics* (Englewood Cliffs, N.J.: Prentice-Hall, 1978), pp. 30–6.

multiplied by its intensity ranking. Thus, the quantity of a pleasure that lasts for ten minutes and has an intensity of 4 will be 40 and the quantity of a pleasure that lasts for five minutes and has an intensity of 5 will be 25. Feldman proposes that we may also introduce a quality scale, assigning a numerical value to the quality of each episode of pleasure. For example, we might assign one pleasure a quality ranking of 5 and another pleasure a quality ranking of 10. In assessing the intrinsic value of an episode of pleasure, we multiply the quantity of the pleasure by its quality. Thus, the intrinsic value of a pleasure that has a quantity of 10 and a quality of 2 is 20, and the intrinsic value of a pleasure that has a quantity of 5 and a quality of 6 is 30. This last bit of calculation illustrates that one episode of pleasure can be of greater intrinsic value than another even though its quantity is less. Feldman recognizes that there are a number of conceptual problems with this approach – that, for example, it is not clear that it makes any sense to say that the quality of one pleasure is two or three times greater than the quality of another. Moreover, in fairness to Feldman, he is not advocating this approach as anything other than one way in which we might try to understand Mill's distinction between quantity and quality and the use Mill makes of it. Still, such a view reflects Henry Sidgwick's observation, noted by Parfit, that "all qualitative comparison of pleasures must resolve itself in quantitative [comparison]."[15]

Whether or not this is the best way of understanding Mill's distinction, it is not adequate to what we have said about the problem of Tithonus or the comparative values of different worlds. If we calculate the intrinsic value of pleasures this way, and if we can add the values of various episodes of pleasures to achieve a value ranking for their total, then it seems that there is some number of low-quality cricket pleasures that will be better than the finite number of higher-quality pleasures that Tithonus enjoys as a man. According to this view, if Tithonus as a cricket experiences enough low-quality pleasures, then his life as a cricket will be intrinsically better than his life as a man. Similarly, if there are enough O-worms experiencing low-quality pleasures, then the value of such a world will be greater than the value of a world in which a finite number of people experience a finite number of higher-quality pleasures.

I do not know whether Mill would accept what we have said about Tithonus and the comparison of various worlds, or whether he would accept Feldman's interpretation of the quantity–quality distinction. I tend to think that he would do the former. When Mill says that few humans

15. Parfit, "Overpopulation and the Quality of Life," p. 161.

would consent to be changed into any of the lower animals for a promise of the fullest allowance of a beast's pleasures, and when he says that no intelligent human being would consent to be a fool, it seems quite out of keeping with the spirit of such remarks to qualify them by adding "unless, of course, one were to enjoy the pleasures of a beast or a fool for a very, very long time." Although I tend to think that Mill would not accept Feldman's way of dealing with the quantity–quality distinction, I confess that I have no clear account to offer instead. I do think, however, that whatever account one offers should be compatible with what we have said about the problem of Tithonus and the comparison of various worlds.

HIGHER GOODS AND THE PRINCIPLE OF SUMMATION

Let us turn to consider the significance of the classes of goods described previously for the principle of organic unities and the principle of summation. As we saw in the last chapter, Moore states the principle of organic unities as follows: "the value of a whole must not be assumed to be the same as the values of its parts."[16] Let us take this to imply that the value of some wholes is not equal to, or the same as, the sum of the values of its parts. In contrast, the principle of summation tells us that the value of every whole is equal to the sum of the values of its parts. The principle of organic unities and the principle of summation are inconsistent with one another. If the one is true, then the other is false, and vice versa.

In the last chapter, we saw that Chisholm illustrates the principle of organic unities through various examples. For instance, take the state of affairs *Smith's being pleased that Jones is suffering.* Call this state of affairs S. As an instance of *Schadenfreude,* this state of affairs appears to be something that is intrinsically bad. S does have a good part, namely, Smith's being pleased. But does S have any bad parts? Chisholm says no, for the intentional attitude of being pleased that Jones is suffering, like the intentional attitude of believing or fearing that Jones is suffering, does *not* imply that Jones is suffering. Thus, the state of affairs *Jones is suffering* is not a part of S. It is no more a part of S than it is a part of Smith's believing that Jones is suffering. If this is so, then it seems that S is an intrinsically bad state of affairs that has a good part and no bad part. In this respect, the value of S does not appear to be equal to the sum of the values of its parts.

The appeal to such examples does, I think, tend to support the principle

16. G. E. Moore, *Principia Ethica* (Cambridge: Cambridge University Press, 1903), p. 28.

of organic unities. But it may also be supported by the sorts of facts to which Brentano, Pascal, and Ross call our attention and by reflecting on some other difficulties with the principle of summation. Consider, for example, how one might follow the principle of summation in explicating what it is for one possible world to be intrinsically better than another. Let us assume that a possible world is a maximally consistent state of affairs. What is it for one possible world, W, to be intrinsically better than another possible world, W'? The principle of summation would tell us that W is intrinsically better than W' if and only if the sum of the intrinsic values, both positive and negative, of the parts of W is greater than the sum of the values of the parts of W'. Intuitively, the way this approach works is to assign some positive numerical value to every good part of W, and some negative value to every bad part of W, and to sum up the positive and negative values to get a total score for W. If the total score for W is greater than the total score for W', then, according to the principle of summation, W is intrinsically better than W'.

One might attempt to illustrate this approach in the following way. Suppose that some form of simple hedonism is true, so that the only thing that is intrinsically good is pleasure and the only thing that is intrinsically bad is pain. Assume that in W there are only two sentient beings, Adam and Eve. Adam has ten units of pleasure and Eve has ten units of pleasure. Suppose that we assign a positive value of 10 to each of these states of affairs. Now one might think that we can calculate the intrinsic value of W by summing up the values of every good part of W. So, we might say that since the value of Adam's ten units of pleasure is 10 and the value of Eve's ten units of pleasure is 10, the total intrinsic value of W is 20. Similarly, suppose that in W' Adam and Eve each have twenty units of pleasure, and we assign a positive value of 20 to each of these states of affairs. The total score of W' would thus be 40. Since the score for W' is greater than that of W, W' is an intrinsically better world than W.

Quite apart from the problem of higher goods, there are at least two difficulties with this simple way of assessing the value of wholes and possible worlds. The first is that it assumes that the only good parts of W and W' are those mentioned earlier. It assumes, for example, that the only good parts of W are Adam's having ten units of pleasure and Eve's having ten units of pleasure. But aren't there other good parts of W in addition to these? Aren't the following intrinsically good parts of W: Someone's being pleased, Someone's having ten units of pleasure, Adam's having ten units of pleasure and 2 and 2 are 4, Adam's having ten units of pleasure or Eve's having fifty units of pleasure, Adam's being in a world where someone has ten units of pleasure, Adam's having at least nine units of pleasure? It should be clear that there is an infinite number of intrinsically good states of affairs that are parts of W. If we are to calculate the value of a world by summing up the values of its intrinsically good parts, then the intrinsic value of W would be infinitely large. This is surely an undesirable conclusion.

A second problem arises if we consider the following possibilities. Suppose that W' and W'' each have an infinite number of people. Suppose that each person in W' and W'' experiences a pleasant life, but that no person in W'' ever experiences anywhere near the amount of pleasure experienced by a person in W'. Imagine, for example, that each person in W' experiences at least 100 units of pleasure and no person in W'' ever experiences more than 10 units of pleasure. It seems to me that W' is intrinsically better than W''. Unfortunately, it is not clear that the principle of summation would yield this result, for it would require us to sum up an infinite number of intrinsically good states of affairs in each world to arrive at each world's total score. But it is not clear that doing this would yield a total score for W' that is greater than that of W'' or even that one can arrive at a total score for either world. (One might also wonder how such an approach would calculate the value of Tithonus's immortal life as a pleased cricket and the supposedly better life he might have had as an immortal, happy man.)

Let us leave these problems aside and return to the issue of higher goods. We have said that a world, W, that contains one million people living pleasant, virtuous lives, having friendships, and engaged in intellectually and artistically excellent activity is intrinsically better than a world, W', that contains nothing but O-worms and their single experiences of pleasures, no matter how many such experiences it might contain. In other words, if the number of goods contained in the latter world were increased ad indefinitum, it would not be better than the former. This is incompatible with the principle of summation, since if we assign some positive value to the pleasant experience of each O-worm and if the value of W is finite, then it seems that it would be possible to increase the number of instances of O-worm pleasures to the point where the value of such a number of experiences would be greater than W. If what we have said in the first section about such worlds is true, then the value of W and W' cannot be correctly determined by simply assigning some numerical value to each good part and summing up those values. More generally, according to the principle of summation, if we have a whole, W', that contains only instances of the lower sort of good, we can obtain another whole,

W'', with greater value simply by adding more instances of the lower good to W'. This so simply because W'' has all the good parts W' has and more. But if the value of a whole increases by adding instances of the lower kind of good to it, and if any whole containing goods of the higher sort has only a finite value, then it seems that there must be some number of instances of the lower good for which the sum of their value would be greater than the value of the whole consisting of the higher good. Yet this is just what Brentano, Ross, and Parfit deny, and it is incompatible with what we have said about the choice between the century of ecstasy and the drab eternity, the myth of Tithonus, and the value of different worlds.

In *Doing the Best We Can,* Fred Feldman recognizes at least the first of these problems and endorses a modified version of the principle of summation. He suggests that "the intrinsic value of a possible world is equal to the sum of the intrinsic values of the basic intrinsic value states that occur there."[17] We should note two points about Feldman's view. First, Feldman's modified version of the principle of summation refers to the intrinsic value of *worlds* rather than of wholes in general. Thus, it seems compatible with there being some wholes, wholes that are not possible worlds, that are organic unities. Second, Feldman introduces the notion of a "basic" intrinsic value state. But what is a basic intrinsic value state? Unfortunately, as Feldman admits, it is very hard to define precisely. Still, assuming that simple hedonism is true, the intuitive idea would be that a state of affairs such as Adam's having ten units of pleasure at noon on January 1, 1990, is a basic intrinsic value state. Of course, if that state of affairs obtains, then so do the following: someone's being pleased, Adam's having ten units of pleasure or Eve's having fifty units of pleasure, and so forth. But the intuitive idea is that these latter states of affairs are not basic in the way that the former is. "A basic intrinsic value state is one that includes neither more than nor less than the part that is of value. It focusses exclusively on the thing of value."[18] Different axiologies will pick out different states of affairs as basic.

Perhaps Feldman's introduction of basic intrinsic value states is an promising approach to the first problem we've raised about assessing the value of possible worlds in terms of summation. It is less clear how it would deal with the second problem we've raised: the problem of infi-

17. Fred Feldman, *Doing the Best We Can* (Dordrecht: D. Reidel Publishing Co., 1986), p. 218.
18. Ibid., pp. 30–1.

nitely large populations. In any case, it does not seem adequate to the problem of classes of goods to which Brentano, Pascal, and Ross call our attention, since we can increase the number of lower basic intrinsic value states in one world ad indefinitum and sum their values without achieving a value greater than the value of the other world containing a higher good. Neither the principle of summation nor Feldman's modified version of it seems right. It is also worth noting that there seems to be no good reason to assume, as Feldman apparently does, that a possible world cannot itself be an organic unity in the sense that the intrinsic value of a world might be greater or less than the sum of the basic intrinsic value states in that world. If we accept the existence of organic unities, there is no reason to think that some of those wholes that are possible worlds are not also organic unities. If we accept either the principle of organic unities or the existence of higher goods, then we have reason to reject the principle of summation and Feldman's modified version of it, and to reject the view that the value of a possible world is necessarily a sum of its parts or even of its basic parts.

Finally, I would also urge that these same considerations pose a problem for any theory of intrinsic value that assumes that there can be a numerical measure of intrinsic value and that these values can be subjected to the ordinary mathematical operations of adding, subtracting, multiplying, and averaging. Such theories have been held by many philosophers, including, I believe, Gilbert Harman and Warren Quinn.[19] The problem arises if we assume that we can assign some numerical value to the pleasant experience of each O-worm and assume that we can sum the values of such experiences. If the value of W is finite, then it seems that at some point the value of the pleasant experience of the O-worms will be greater than the value of W. But this is incompatible with what we have said about the value of W and the experiences of the O-worms. Similarly, if we think we can assign some numerical value, however small, to the insect pleasures of Tithonus's life as a cricket, then it seems that at some point the sum of the values of his insect pleasures will be greater than the finite value of his life as a man. But again, this is incompatible with what we have said about the relative values of his normal human life and insect pleasure. (One might think that the problem could be solved by assigning smaller and smaller numerical values to each episode of pleasure. But why should

19. Gilbert Harman, "Toward a Theory of Intrinsic Value," *The Journal of Philosophy* 64 (December 1967), pp. 792–804; Warren Quinn, "Theories of Intrinsic Value," *American Philosophical Quarterly* 11 (1974), pp. 123–32.

we think that pleasures that are qualitatively identical should be given a different value?) If the sorts of examples presented in this chapter are plausible, then we should reject both the principle of summation and the assumption that there is a numerical measure of intrinsic value whose values can be subjected to ordinary mathematical operations, such as addition, subtraction, and multiplication.

5

Pleasure and its intrinsic value

What kinds of things are intrinsically good? Traditionally, a variety of things have been thought to be intrinsically good: pleasure, morally good emotions, the satisfaction of desire, correct judgment, knowledge, understanding, consciousness itself, beauty, and, in at least some cases, the flourishing of nonsentient life. In this chapter and the next, I defend the view that most of these things are intrinsically good. In this chapter, however, I focus on the nature and value of pleasure and hedonism in general.

SENSORY AND NONSENSORY PLEASURE

I wish to consider briefly three views on the nature of sensory and nonsensory pleasure. These views are those of Butchvarov, the Chisholm–Brentano view, and a recent proposal by Fred Feldman. Examples of sensory pleasures are gustatory and olfactory pleasures and the pleasures of a warm bath or massage. Examples of nonsensory pleasure are being pleased that one's work is going well, being pleased that one's newborn child is healthy, and being pleased that one's spouse has won the lottery. In earlier chapters, we have used examples of nonsensory pleasures to illustrate the principle of organic unities.

With respect to sensory pleasures, there seems to be no common distinctive sensation or sense content that we can point to as *the* pleasure. The pleasures of a warm bath, a massage, and a fragrant odor are very different, yet each of these is a sensory pleasure. As different as these pleasures are, they seem to have more in common with one another than they have with nonsensory pleasures. Some philosophers, such as Butchvarov, suggest that the only clear phenomenologically distinctive sense of pleasure is that of sensory or "bodily" pleasures, and that the "so-called higher pleasures, for example, those of intellectual work, as well as some others not describable as 'higher' yet also not 'bodily,' are best understood as one's consciousness of the goodness of the state or activity described as pleasant."[1] This view casts the difference between sensory and nonsensory pleasures in such a fashion that it becomes unclear why anyone should think that the nonsensory states are properly thought pleasures at all.

In spite of the admitted and recognizable differences between the two phenomena, there does seem to be some point in thinking of the so-called higher pleasures as genuine pleasures. There are several reasons to think that Butchvarov's view does not do justice to the notion of real nonsensory pleasures. Before considering these reasons, however, it is worth pointing out that there are two different ways in which we can understand Butchvarov's view. Butchvarov says that higher pleasures are best understood as one's consciousness of the goodness of the state or activity described as pleasant. Now, in general, the consciousness of something's being F can be taken as either (1) a belief to the effect that something has F or (2) a nondoxastic awareness that something is F. Thus, my being conscious that an apple is yellow could be either a belief to the effect that it is yellow, a belief I could have when I am not looking at the apple, or it could be my seeing it as yellow. Similarly, one's consciousness of the goodness of the state or activity could be understood as either (1) a belief about the goodness of the state or activity or (2) a nondoxastic awareness of the goodness of the state or activity. Let us consider first the view that higher pleasures are best understood as beliefs about the goodness of the thing described as pleasant.

One problem with this view is that it seems that one can believe that something is good without being pleased by it. For example, one can believe that a stranger is happy and healthy, and that his being so is good, without being pleased by it. Of course, not being pleased by the other's health and happiness does not imply that one wishes the stranger were not healthy and happy or even that one is indifferent to his being so. Indeed, we should allow that one can be favorably disposed toward, have a "pro" attitude toward, a stranger's well-being without taking pleasure in it. But consider the difference between hearing the doctor state that one's newborn child is healthy and the "cool" surmise that a particularly impressive athlete is healthy. In each case, there might be a belief about the goodness of health, but in the former there is often a particular experience of delight and pleasure in hearing the good news, a feeling that is typically lacking in the latter. The view that the higher pleasures are merely attributions of goodness ignores the difference between these two

1. Panayot Butchvarov, *Skepticism in Ethics* (Indianapolis: Indiana University Press, 1989), p. 90.

sorts of experiences, and only by ignoring them does the assimilation of higher pleasures to attributions of goodness seem plausible.

We may also note that the envious man can believe, for example, that another's work or activity is good without being pleased by that work or activity. This is typical of the experience of envy. The envious man might well be aware that another's work is good, yet take no pleasure in the other's accomplishment. Indeed, the envious man might say, "Her work is so much better than mine – that's why I'm unhappy." Of course, it is not the mere recognition of the other's achievement as superior that makes the envious man unhappy. The causes of his displeasure are surely more complex, and the judgment that the other's work is better is only part of the reason that the envious man is displeased. But whatever the whole story, the envious man takes no pleasure in the other's work even though he believes it is good.

Along these same lines, nonsensory or nonbodily pain or displeasure involves more than the mere attribution of badness, the mere belief that something is bad. Consider the difference between reading about the death of a stranger in the obituary column of the newspaper and learning about the death of one's mother. In each case, there can be an attribution of badness, but in the latter there is also a experience of pain and grief brought on by hearing the terrible news. In each case, one might hate or have an "anti" attitude toward the death in and for itself, but in one case there is an experience of pain that is not present in the other.

There is, I think, no compelling reason why we should think that higher pleasures are best understood as the consciousness of the goodness of an activity or state, where this consciousness is construed as a belief that the state or activity is good. Such a view does not do justice to the difference between merely believing that something is good and taking pleasure in it. But what if we construe the consciousness of goodness as a nondoxastic awareness of goodness? Is this view more plausible? I do not think so. First, the notion of a nondoxastic awareness of goodness is phenomenologically problematic. I am not sure what a nondoxastic awareness of goodness would be. Second, and perhaps more important, is that many of the same objections raised earlier also appear applicable to this view. Even if we concede that there is such a thing as a nondoxastic awareness of goodness, it would seem possible, for example, for the envious man to have a nondoxastic awareness that someone's work or activity was good without taking pleasure in it. Moreover, if there is such an awareness of the goodness of health, it seems that one could be aware that an athlete was healthy without taking pleasure in that fact. One might be aware of the goodness of a stranger's health without experiencing the pleasure that comes from learning that one's child is healthy. There is no compelling reason why we should think that this latter sort of pleasure is nothing more than a nondoxastic awareness of goodness.

Let us turn to the views of Brentano and Chisholm on sensory and nonsensory pleasures. Brentano explicates the concepts of sensory and nonsensory pleasure and pain in terms of the fundamental concepts of love and hate. "When one experiences sensory pleasure," Chisholm writes, "then (1) there is a sense content a that is the primary object of a certain sensing, and (2) this sensing is in turn the primary object of an act of love."[2] This fact, says Chisholm, can be expressed as Sa & $L(Sa)$. According to this view, sensory pleasure involves taking an act of sensing, Sa, as the object of an act of love, $L(Sa)$. For example, if one experiences the sensory pleasure of a warm bath, then there is some sense content such that one senses it and one loves the act of sensing it. If one attends to this experience, it too can become an object of love. We may express this additional fact as $L[Sa$ & $L(Sa)]$. Sensory pain is similar to sensory pleasure, as it involves (1) a sense content, which is the primary object of an act of sensing, and (2) this act of sensing is the primary object of an act of hate. This fact can be expressed as Sa & $H(Sa)$. As with sensory pleasure, when this fact is attended to, it becomes an object of hate, $H[Sa$ & $H(Sa)]$.

How are nonsensory pleasures related to sensory pleasures? Brentano writes:

There are two senses in which a man may be said to be pleased with an object or to take pleasure in it, and two senses in which he may be said to be displeased with an object or to take displeasure in it. In the first case, he may simply find the object to be agreeable. In the second, he finds the object to be agreeable, or disagreeable, and then because of this fact he also takes pleasure in *another* object. As a result of his being pleased or displeased, with the first object, there redounds a sensuous pleasure or displeasure.[3]

If, unlike Brentano, we accept the concept of a state of affairs, we may express his view in the following way. In the case of a nonsensory pleasure, there is a state of affairs (1) that one contemplates or believes to obtain; (2) one loves or has a pro attitude toward that state of affairs, and (3) the experience of love toward that state of affairs *causes* the experience of

2. Roderick Chisholm, *Brentano and Intrinsic Value* (Cambridge: Cambridge University Press, 1986), p. 26.
3. Franz Brentano, *The Origin of Our Knowledge of Right and Wrong,* translated by Roderick Chisholm and Elizabeth Schneewind (London: Routledge & Kegan Paul, 1969), pp. 154–5.

certain sensory pleasures. As Brentano says, the sensory pleasure "redounds" on the experience of love directed toward the contemplated or accepted state of affairs. Chisholm points out that the nonsensory pleasure is not merely the experience of the pro attitude or the resultant sensory pleasure. I take Brentano to hold that the nonsensory pleasure is the combined experience of loving a contemplated or accepted state of affairs and the resultant sensory pleasure. As with sensory pleasure, if one attends to the nonsensory pleasure, it itself can be an object of love. Nonsensory pain or displeasure is similar to sensory pleasure. The former involves a state of affairs (1) that one contemplates or accepts; (2) one hates or has an anti attitude toward that state of affairs, and (3) the experience of hate toward this state of affairs causes the experience of sensory pain. In illustrating the relation between sensory and nonsensory pleasure, Brentano writes:

When Newton read that his astronomical hypotheses had been confirmed by new measurements, his joy became more and more intense and he was finally so overcome that he could no longer continue reading. He succumbed to the intensive sensuous pleasure which had redounded from his higher feelings. The same was true of Archimedes when he cried out "Eureka!" as though intoxicated. Even those pleasures one may take in the awareness of virtue and vice may give rise to violent sensuous passions.[4]

What makes nonsensory pleasures *pleasures* is the sensory pleasure that redounds on certain other psychological states, and what makes nonsensory pains *pains* is the sensory pain that redounds on other mental states.

The Chisholm–Brentano view is something of an improvement over that suggested by Butchvarov, but it appears open to the following objections raised by Feldman. The first objection may be stated as follows: "This account is phenomenologically inaccurate. There have been times when I have been introduced to someone and I was genuinely pleased to meet them, but I did not experience anything I would call a sensory pleasure. One can therefore have a non-sensory pleasure without experiencing any sensory pleasure at all."[5] A second objection is: "We can imagine a man who has had a motorcycle accident and is now thoroughly anesthetized so that he can feel neither sensory pleasures nor pains. He may nonetheless feel non-sensory pleasure that he is alive."

I think that both of these are serious objections to the Chisholm–Bren-

4. Ibid., p. 155.
5. Both of the objections I consider here are raised by Fred Feldman. See Feldman, "Two Questions About Pleasure," *Philosophical Analysis: A Defense by Example,* edited by David F. Austin (Dordrecht: Kluwer Academic Publishers, 1987), p. 69.

tano account. But let us consider what might be said on their behalf. First, we should recall what we have said in response to Butchvarov's view, namely, that one can look favorably on something, such as the good health of an athlete, without taking pleasure in it. Thus, we must distinguish between liking something or having a favorable attitude toward it and taking pleasure in it. One might very much like or have a strong pro attitude toward meeting someone or toward discovering that one is alive without experiencing any sensory pleasure. Given this distinction between merely liking something and taking pleasure in it, perhaps the defender of the Chisholm–Brentano view could insist that the subjects in the first two objections are not really pleased about anything. It is simply the case that they very much like meeting someone or discovering that they are alive.

I am not sure that this response is convincing. Feldman might still insist that we often do take ourselves to be pleased in some situations where we are experiencing no sensory pleasure. I am not sure how one would settle such a dispute, but it is not entirely persuasive to tell someone in such a situation that he is not really pleased, but only that he likes something. A more important difficulty is that if one introduces a sharp distinction between liking something and taking pleasure in it, then the Brentano–Chisholm account of sensory pleasure seems less satisfactory. If one can like the obtaining of a state of affairs, such as meeting a famous person, without this being an instance of pleasure, then it is unclear why one's liking to have a certain sense content should be any more plausibly thought a pleasure. Why should we count the having of a sense content and liking the having of it as a sensory pleasure if the liking of other things is not ipso facto a kind of pleasure?

A more promising account than the two considered so far is suggested by Feldman. Chisholm and Brentano analyze nonsensory pleasure in terms of sensory pleasure. Feldman does the reverse, suggesting instead that we can understand sensory pleasure in terms of nonsensory pleasure. He holds roughly that we can understand sensory pleasure in terms of taking intrinsic nonsensory pleasure in having a certain sensation. To take intrinsic nonsensory pleasure in something is to be pleased with that thing in and for itself or for its own sake.

Let $[Fs,t]$ be the state of affairs of s feeling F at t. Feldman proposes:

(D3) $[Fs,t]$ is a sensory pleasure iff $[Fs,t]$ is a sensation, $[Fs,t]$ occurs, and s takes intrinsic *de se* propositional pleasure in $[Fs,t]$ at t.[6]

6. Ibid., p. 75.

According to (D3), when a person has a sensory pleasure, he is taking intrinsic propositional pleasure (nonsensory pleasure) in the fact that he is having a certain sensation. Following Feldman, we may illustrate this approach by considering the case of a sunbather experiencing a sensory pleasure of warmth: "There is a certain sensory property, W, which characterizes people if and only if they are feeling warmth in a certain way. The sunbather, s, is characterized by W at t. The state of affairs, $[Ws,t]$ is a sensation. At t, the sunbather is intrinsically pleased to be characterized by W."[7]

Feldman analyzes sensory pleasure in terms of *de se* propositional pleasure. In some cases of *de se* propositional pleasure, one is aware of the identity of the person having the sense quality. There is no confusion or doubt about *who* is experiencing that quality. But Feldman also assumes that one can have *de se* attitudes without be self-conscious, without thinking, for example, about *who* is characterized by a certain sensory property. "Suppose I am drowsy and non–self-conscious. I am pleased to be feeling this lovely warmth, but I am not giving any thought to the identity of the feeler of the warmth. I am not consciously taking him to be me, and I am not consciously taking him to be anyone else. I'm just not thinking of him."[8] Even though one is not giving any thought to the identity of the feeler of the warmth, one is still pleased that he himself is warm. Perhaps we may express part of Feldman's point by saying that one can be pleased that he himself is warm even though one is not *entertaining* or *attending* to the state of affairs that he himself is warm.

Whether or not Feldman's view of sensory and nonsensory pleasure is correct, it does seem to have certain advantages over the other two views considered here. It is plausible enough to take as a working account of sensory and nonsensory pleasure. Let us turn to the value of pleasure.

PLEASURE AND DISPLEASURE IN THE GOOD, BAD, AND NEUTRAL

In assessing the intrinsic value of a nonsensory pleasure, at least two features appear relevant. First, we can ask whether the intentional object of a pleasure is intrinsically worthy of love, hate, or indifference. In other words, we may consider the intrinsic value of its object in assessing the intrinsic value of a nonsensory pleasure. Second, we can ask whether the

7. Ibid., p. 76.
8. Ibid., p. 75.

pleasure is directed to a state of affairs that obtains, whether the pleasure is true or false. As we noted in Chapter 3, one can take pleasure in states of affairs that do not obtain, as well as in those that do.

In this section, I focus on the importance of a nonsensory pleasure's object. I wish to consider the intrinsic value of taking pleasure in states of affairs that are intrinsically worthy of love, intrinsically worthy of hate, and the four forms of neutrality distinguished in Chapter 1. In the next section, I consider the importance of whether or not the object of that pleasure obtains.

Let us recall the following principles:

(P2) p is intrinsically worthy of love if and only if p is necessarily such that, for any x, the contemplation of just p by x requires that x love p and not hate p.

(P3) p is intrinsically worthy of hate if and only if p is necessarily such that, for any x, the contemplation of just p by x requires that x hate p and not love p.

(P4) p is strictly neutral if and only if p is necessarily such that, for any x, the contemplation of just p by x requires that both x not love p and x not hate p.

(P5) p is merely neutral if and only if p is necessarily such that, for any x, the contemplation of just p by x does not require that x love p and does not require that x hate p.

(P6) p is positively neutral if and only if p is necessarily such that, for any x, the contemplation of just p by x requires that x not hate p and the contemplation of just p by x does not require that x love p.

(P7) p is negatively neutral if and only if p is necessarily such that, for any x, the contemplation of just p by x requires that x not love p and the contemplation of just p by x does not require that x hate p.

Let us consider the following theses:

(1) Pleasure in what is intrinsically worthy of love is good.
(2) Pleasure in what is intrinsically worthy of hate is bad.
(3) Displeasure in what is intrinsically worthy of love is bad.
(4) Displeasure in what is intrinsically worthy of hate is good.

In discussing the principle of organic unities, we have already touched on the subject of pleasure and displeasure in what is intrinsically good or bad. We have seen, for example, that Brentano holds that pleasure in what is intrinsically bad is bad and displeasure in what is intrinsically bad is good. If Brentano is right about these claims, then both (2) and (4) are true. If pleasure in the bad is bad, then surely taking pleasure in what is intrinsically worthy of hate is bad as well. Similarly, if displeasure in the bad is good, then being displeased with what is worthy of hate must be good.

Principles very similar to these have been endorsed by others.[9] It is hard to see how one might argue for these claims from any premises that are more evident than they are. Many claims about intrinsic value seem to share a similar status. Each of them seems reasonable enough on reflection. Each of them, I believe, is such that if one understands and considers them, then one has at least a prima facie reason to believe them. I shall say more about our warrant for believing such claims in Chapter 8.

In *Brentano and Intrinsic Value,* Chisholm suggests that the following "would seem to be obvious:"[10]

(5) Pleasure in the neutral is intrinsically good.
(6) Displeasure in the neutral is intrinsically bad.

Chisholm suggests that (5) and (6) are accepted by Brentano. The same view of pleasure and displeasure in the neutral is adopted by Tom Carson.[11]

I believe that (5) is neither obvious nor true. Consider the state of affairs *there being no one who is wise and happy.* This state of affairs is a negative neutral, and I suggest that it is not intrinsically good for someone to take pleasure in it. On the contrary, such pleasure seems intrinsically bad. There are other neutral states of affairs that are such that it is intrinsically bad to take pleasure in them. These include *no one's being happy, no one's experiencing pleasure,* and *there being no happy unicorns.* Such neutral states of affairs can be considered "absences" or "privations" of what is intrinsically good.

Taking pleasure in no one's being happy should not be confused with taking pleasure in someone's being unhappy. The intentional object of these pleasures is different. The object of the latter is intrinsically bad. Similarly, taking pleasure in no one's being happy should not be confused with being displeased that someone is happy. In the latter case, the intentional object is different, and so is the attitude toward that object.

If pressed to defend the claim that pleasure in a negative neutral is intrinsically bad, it is not clear how one might argue for it from premises that are more evident. Yet it seems at least as reasonable as the claim that taking pleasure in the bad is bad. In particular, it is at least as reasonable to hold that it is intrinsically bad for someone to be pleased that no one

9. See Chisholm, *Brentano and Intrinsic Value,* pp. 63–6; Tom Carson, "Happiness, Contentment, and the Good Life," *Pacific Philosophical Quarterly* 62 (October 1981), pp. 378–92.
10. Chisholm, *Brentano and Intrinsic Value,* p. 66.
11. Carson, "Happiness, Contentment, and the Good Life," pp. 378–92.

is happy as it is to claim that it is intrinsically bad for someone to take pleasure in someone's being unhappy.

Proposition (5) is false. Some cases of pleasure in the neutral are not intrinsically good. Given our distinctions between the four forms of neutrality, what can we say about pleasure in the neutral? I propose the following:

(7) Pleasure in the merely neutral is intrinsically good.
(8) Displeasure in the merely neutral is intrinsically bad.

Examples of merely neutral states of affairs are *there being stones* and *the sky's being blue*. Pleasure and displeasure in the merely neutral violates no ethical requirement, but since (7) involves pleasure and (8) involves displeasure, we may hold that the former is good and the latter is bad.

(9) Pleasure in the positively neutral is intrinsically good.
(10) Displeasure in the positively neutral is intrinsically bad.

The state of affairs *no one's being in pain* is a positive neutral. Positive neutrals include the absence of an intrinsic evil. Pleasure in the positively neutral violates no ethical requirement, and since it involves pleasure, it would seem to be good. Being displeased that no one is in pain violates an ethical requirement, and since it also involves displeasure, it is bad.

(11) Displeasure in the strictly neutral is intrinsically bad.
(12) Pleasure in the strictly neutral is intrinsically bad.

In Chapter 1, I suggested that a state of affairs in which goods and evils are balanced is strictly neutral. Such a state of affairs is *Smith's having five units of pleasure and Brown's having five units of pain*. Displeasure in a strictly neutral state of affairs, like (10), involves the violation of an ethical requirement, and is also an instance of displeasure; as such, it is bad. Even though (12) involves someone's being pleased, it is taking pleasure in something that there is an ethical requirement not to love. In this respect, taking pleasure in the strictly neutral is like taking pleasure in what is intrinsically bad.

(13) Pleasure in the negatively neutral is intrinsically bad.
(14) Displeasure in the negatively neutral is intrinsically bad.

Negative neutrals include the absence of a good, for example, *no one's being happy*. Even though (13) involves pleasure, it is pleasure in something that there is an ethical requirement not to love. It is like taking pleasure in what is bad; as such, it is intrinsically bad. Being displeased in the

76

negatively neutral violates no ethical requirement and resembles displeasure in the merely neutral (which is bad). It is also an instance of displeasure, so it would seem to be bad.

Of course, some might argue that (14) is false. It could be held that displeasure in the negatively neutral is like displeasure in the bad. But even if displeasure in the bad is good, there is an important difference from displeasure in the negatively neutral. There is an ethical requirement that one hate or have an anti attitude toward what is bad, but there is *no* requirement that one hate or be displeased about the negatively neutral. There is merely a requirement that one not love it.

If (13) and (14) are true, then it is bad to take pleasure or displeasure in the negatively neutral. Thus, it is bad to be displeased or pained that no one is perfectly wise or that there are no happy unicorns. If one considers these things, it is better simply to accept them and, in some cases, where it is possible, do what one can to make things otherwise. Of course, even if it is bad to be displeased that no one is perfectly wise, it does *not* follow that one should not prefer someone's being perfectly wise to no one's being so. In some cases, it is appropriate to prefer *A* to *B,* even if it is not appropriate to hate *B* in and for itself. Suppose, however, that I am wrong and (14) is false. If (14) is false, then (6) is false. Recall that (6) was the claim, taken by some to be obvious, that displeasure in the neutral is bad.

TRUE AND FALSE PLEASURES

Let us turn to the issue of "true" and "false" pleasures and to an assessment of their intrinsic value. Let us say that S's being pleased that p is true if and only if S is pleased that p and p obtains. S's being pleased that p is false if and only if S is pleased that p and p does not obtain. The truth or falsity of a nonsensory pleasure is a function of whether the state of affairs that is the intentional object of that pleasure obtains. The truth or falsity of a nonsensory pain or displeasure may analogously be taken as a function of obtaining or nonobtaining of its intentional object.

In addition to true and false pleasures, we may distinguish between "acceptance" and "contemplative" pleasures. The distinction between these two sorts of pleasure is suggested by Moore's discussion of aesthetic experience in the last chapter of *Principia Ethica*.[12] Often when one is pleased that *p,* one believes that *p* obtains. In such cases, the pleasure that one experiences toward a state of affairs is partially a result of one's be-

---

12. G. E. Moore, *Principia Ethica* (Cambridge: Cambridge University Press, 1903), p. 198.

lieving that it obtains. Let us call pleasures of this sort "acceptance pleasures." In some cases, however, one can take pleasure in a state of affairs without believing that it obtains. In cases of this kind, the pleasure that one experiences toward a state of affairs is not a result of one's believing it to obtain, but rather is dependent on one's contemplation or entertaining of it. Let us call such pleasures "contemplative pleasures." Contemplative pleasures are illustrated by pleasant daydreams and reveries, but also by the pleasures one experiences in watching a movie or in reading what one knows to be works of fiction. (Such examples suggest that "entertainment pleasures" might be a more apt term.) Unlike acceptance pleasures, if one has a contemplative pleasure toward *p*, one does not believe that *p* obtains.

Given these distinctions, we can distinguish between true and false acceptance pleasures and true and false contemplative pleasures. If one has a true acceptance pleasure, then one has a true belief. If one has a false acceptance pleasure, then one has a false belief. But true and false entertainment pleasures imply nothing about the possession of true or false beliefs.

We are now, at last, in a position to say something about the intrinsic value of true and false pleasures. What is the value of a false acceptance pleasure that has an object that is worthy of love? According to Chisholm, Brentano would say that such pleasures are bad:

Suppose I believe, incorrectly, that my father has performed certain magnificent deeds and suppose I take pleasure in what I believe he has done. Brentano says that in such a case "the love is correct, but the form that the pleasure takes is not correct." Or, as we may put it, the pleasure is correct but false. Brentano is clear that such a false but correct pleasure is one that it would be better not to have – this because of the intrinsic evil that error involves.[13]

Presumably, Brentano's negative evaluation of correct but false acceptance pleasures would not apply to correct but false contemplative pleasures, since the latter involve no errors, no mistaken beliefs.

I believe that Brentano's assessment of correct false acceptance pleasures is a bit harsh. Perhaps such pleasures have little positive value, but they do not seem to be intrinsically bad. Consider a pleasant dream in which one takes pleasure in someone's having performed a good deed or in which one has made an important discovery. Such dream experiences involve correct yet illusory pleasures, but it seems extreme to say that they are, for that reason, bad or that it would be better not to have such dreams.

13. Chisholm, *Brentano and Intrinsic Value*, p. 67.

Of course, even if we allow that correct false acceptance pleasures have some positive intrinsic value, it might still be true that they are often instrumentally or extrinsically bad because of the errors they involve; that the false beliefs they involve lead one to act inappropriately. When this is so, we may hold that, all things considered, it would be better not to have them. Still, a dream that involves illusory pleasures is hardly ever instrumentally bad for this reason simply because, on waking, we realize that it was just a dream.

If the preceding remarks are right, then false acceptance pleasures having objects worthy of love are intrinsically good. If such pleasures are intrinsically good, even though they imply the existence of error, then it is reasonable to think that contemplative pleasures whose objects are worthy of love are also intrinsically good, for such pleasures do not imply the existence of any error. If this is right, then we should conclude that whether a pleasure is true or false, it is intrinsically good if the object of that pleasure is intrinsically worthy of love.

Which is intrinsically better, a true acceptance pleasure that p or a true contemplative pleasure p, where p is a state of affairs that is worthy of love? Moore writes, it "appears to me certain, that the case of a person, merely imagining, without believing, the beautiful objects in question, would, *although these objects really existed,* be yet inferior to that of the person who also believed in their existence."[14] What Moore says about aesthetic appreciation can also be applied to contemplative and acceptance pleasures. Let X be: S contemplates p and S is correctly pleased that p. Let Y be: S believes that p and S is correctly pleased that p. Following Moore, we may say that the whole that consists in X *and p's obtaining* has less intrinsic value than the whole that consists in Y *and p's obtaining.* Presumably, the latter is better because it implies true belief. If this is right, then we may say that a correct true acceptance pleasure that p is intrinsically better than a correct true contemplative pleasure that p. And we may add that the latter is better than a correct false acceptance pleasure that p.

If correct false acceptance pleasures have some small degree of goodness, their presence as parts of certain wholes often renders those wholes *less* intrinsically valuable than would the presence of certain other attitudes that involve no pleasure at all. Imagine, for example, that Jones is suffering and Smith has the false acceptance pleasure that Jones is happy. Such a state of affairs seems to have less intrinsic value than Jones's suffering and Smith's believing and being displeased that Jones is suffering. This instance

---

14. Moore, *Principia Ethica,* p. 198.

of true *Mitleid* is intrinsically preferable to the instance of false *Mitfreude*. Of course, the former attitude is often instrumentally more valuable than the latter, since it might prompt some action to relieve the suffering. Still, the former has greater intrinsic value than the former, and its intrinsic value is not affected whatsoever by Smith's power or actions to help Jones. Consider also someone who is to die after a long, painful illness. Suppose that she believes falsely that she will get well and that she takes pleasure in getting well. This whole, involving a correct but false acceptance pleasure, seems intrinsically less valuable than one involving a courageous recognition and acceptance of her true fate. Facing a long, painful, terminal illness and being pleased that one will get well seems intrinsically less valuable than facing such an illness and responding to it courageously, taking correct displeasure in one's own suffering.

HEDONISM

We are now in a position to evaluate the truth of value hedonism. I take value hedonism to accept the following propositions:

(15) Someone's feeling sensory pleasure is intrinsically good.
(16) Someone's feeling sensory pain is intrinsically bad.
(17) A state of affairs, X, is intrinsically better than a state of affairs, Y, if and only if X implies a greater balance of pleasure over pain than Y.
(18) Every state of affairs that implies pleasure and no pain is intrinsically good.
(19) Only states of affairs that imply pleasure are intrinsically good.

Of these five claims, only the first and second are true. Every instance of sensory pleasure is, as such, intrinsically good, and every instance of sensory pain is, as such, intrinsically bad. In Chapter 3 we considered some reasons for thinking that sensory pleasure is not intrinsically good. The rationale for denying (15) on the basis of considerations raised by Ross and suggested by Kant is unpersuasive and, in some respects, is contrary to what we recognize as bad about the prosperity and happiness of the wicked.

There are several reasons to reject (17). First, it is incompatible with a correct assessment of the value of *Schadenfreude, Mitfreude,* and *Mitleid.* Taking pleasure in another person's pain is not intrinsically better than being displeased at another's pain, even though the former implies a greater balance of pleasure over pain. Thus, implying a greater balance of pleasure over pain is not a sufficient condition for one state of affairs being better than another. It is also not a necessary condition, since being pleased

80

at another's joy is intrinsically better than taking pleasure in another's sorrow, even though the former does not imply a greater balance of pleasure than pain. Second, recall the suggestion about retribution and requital from Chapter 2. If Paul is wicked and Tom is virtuous, W, then the state of affairs *W and Tom is happy* is intrinsically better than *W and Paul is happy*. If this is so, then (17) is false. Third, we have said that a correct true acceptance pleasure that *p* is better than a correct true contemplative pleasure that *p* and that each of these is better than a correct false acceptance pleasure. If this is so, then again, the intrinsic superiority of a state of affairs does not depend on its implying more pleasure than pain. Fourth, if what we have said about pleasure in the neutral is right, then (17) is false. Taking pleasure in what is strictly or negatively neutral is intrinsically worse than taking the same degree of pleasure in what is merely or positively neutral.

The correct assessment of *Schadenfreude* and pleasure in the strictly and negatively neutral is also incompatible with (18). Against this view, however, William Frankena writes:

non-hedonists usually argue that there are bad pleasures – pleasures that are bad, not only because of their consequences, but in themselves. But, so far as I can see, the non-hedonists never really show this. I agree that malicious pleasure and the enjoyment of cruelty and ugliness, if they really occur, are bad, but are they bad *qua* pleasures and enjoyments? They may be *morally* bad in themselves or bad because they are symptoms of some defect or deranged personality, but their being bad in these senses must not be confused with their being bad *qua* pleasures and enjoyments. Non-hedonists never make clear that they are not confusing these kinds of badness.[15]

There are several points worth making about this passage. First, even if nonhedonists never *show* that malicious pleasures are intrinsically bad, this implies nothing whatsoever about the truth of their view or about the reasonableness of their believing it to be true. There are a great many things that one can be justified in believing, even if one cannot show them to be true or deduce them from premises that are more evident. It is also fair to note that the hedonist never *shows* that sensory pleasure is intrinsically good or that sensory pain is intrinsically bad. Second, the nonhedonist does not need to hold that malicious pleasures are bad qua pleasures, whatever that might involve. It is not the fact that they are pleasures that makes malicious pleasures bad; rather, it is because of their

15. William Frankena, *Ethics,* 2nd edition (Englewood Cliffs, N.J.: Prentice-Hall, 1973), p. 90.

whole nature, because they are pleasures in a certain kind of thing, because they are pleasures having a certain kind of object. Smith's being pleased that Jones is suffering is not bad because it implies that someone is pleased; it is bad because Smith is taking pleasure in another's suffering. Third, malicious pleasures are morally bad, at least insofar as they are marks of a morally bad character and to the extent that they might lead to morally wrong actions. But the nonhedonist may clearly assert that they are intrinsically bad or bad in themselves. He holds that it is ethically fitting for anyone who contemplates malicious pleasures to prefer simpliciter their nonoccurrence to their occurrence. If we are right about what we have said about the nature of intrinsic value in Chapter 1, then we may let the question about the value of such pleasures rest with our reflective judgment about whether such a preference is correct or fitting.

Frankena's remarks suggest another counterexample to (18). He says that taking pleasure in ugliness, where the ugliness is real, is bad. It is plausible to think that along with malicious pleasures, we should count pleasure and admiration of the ugly as an intrinsic evil. This is also Moore's view. He holds that among intrinsic evils we should count "an enjoyment or admiring contemplation of things which are themselves either evil or ugly."[16] If this is so, then we have yet another sort of evil that implies pleasure and no pain.

Finally, let us consider (19), the claim that only states of affairs that imply pleasure are intrinsically good. Moore concedes that "Pleasure does seem to be a necessary constituent of most valuable wholes."[17] Yet even to concede this much is still not to endorse (19). In contrast to Moore, Frankena writes, "I still think that an experience or activity is not good in itself unless it is pleasant or satisfactory or, in other words, that some kind of satisfactoriness is a necessary condition of something's being intrinsically good."[18] Frankena distinguishes pleasantness from satisfactoriness. The former is a kind of satisfactoriness, as are happiness, contentment, and beatitude. Yet is spite of this remark, Frankena says, a few pages earlier, that "The experience of acting virtuously and of feeling morally good emotions, however, may be intrinsically good as far as it goes. I shall argue that it is."[19] This latter claim seems true, but I think it cannot be reconciled with an endorsement of (19) or of Frankena's remarks about the importance of pleasure or satisfactoriness. This is because there are

16. Moore, *Principia Ethica*, pp. 208–9.
17. Ibid., p. 93.
18. Frankena, *Ethics*, p. 91.
19. Ibid., p. 91.

instances of acting virtuously and feeling morally good emotions that do not involve any form of satisfactoriness, that do not imply pleasure, contentment, beatitude, or happiness (where happiness is construed as a form of satisfactoriness). Consider, for example, what Aristotle says about righteous indignation – feeling pain when someone suffers undeservedly. If we agree with Aristotle that righteous indignation is a morally good emotion, then some morally good emotions imply pain and anger rather than pleasure or satisfactoriness. Moreover, Aristotle writes:

we can experience fear, confidence, desire, anger, pity, and generally any kind of pleasure and pain either too much or too little, and in either case not properly. But to experience all this at the right time, toward the right objects, toward the right people, for the right reason, and in the right manner – that is the median and best course, the course that is the mark of virtue.[20]

Aristotle recognizes that virtuous activity and emotion can sometimes be a matter of experiencing fear, anger, and pity appropriately. If this is so, then again, the experience of some morally good emotions implies pain or displeasure without implying or involving the experience of some form of satisfactoriness. If such experiences are intrinsically good, then it follows that some intrinsically good experiences do not imply or involve pleasure or satisfactoriness.

It is not necessary to look only at those morally good emotions involving negative attitudes such as fear, pity, anger, pain, or displeasure to see that (19) is false. Consider such things as correct or fitting love and preference. To love what is intrinsically good is a morally good emotion and is itself intrinsically good.[21] Someone's loving correctly does not imply that he is pleased, and therefore, (19) is false. The same is true for every act of correct preference. Similarly, every correct desire in which one desires for its own sake what is worthy of love is intrinsically good, but correct desire is not itself a pleasure or any form of satisfactoriness. One can, for example, correctly desire that Smith be happy without being pleased that he is, and one can prefer everyone's being happy to its opposite without any experience of pleasure or satisfactoriness.

Distinguishing love, preference, and desire from pleasure and other

---

20. Aristotle, *Nicomachean Ethics,* translated by Martin Ostwald (Indianapolis: Bobbs-Merrill Co., 1962), Bk. II, Chapter 6, 1106b 18–22.
21. Brentano is clear about this point. He writes, "Every act of high-minded love is also something that is good in itself." *The Origin of Our Knowledge of Right and Wrong,* p. 29. And again, "The correctness and higher character of these feelings – like the correctness and evidence of certain judgments – is itself to be counted as something good. And the love of the bad is something that is itself good." Ibid., pp. 22–3.

forms of satisfactoriness is important because it reveals a class of morally good emotions that do not imply pleasure or satisfaction. The distinction is important for another reason as well. Suppose that one believes and is pleased that God exists or that there is a supremely wise and good being, but suppose that there is no such being. This would be a correct false acceptance pleasure. We may hold, contrary to Brentano, that the value of such a pleasure is intrinsically good. But what of the attitudes of loving, desiring, and hoping as such that God exists, where such attitudes are not understood to imply a belief in his existence? Such attitudes seem to be intrinsically good, insofar as they involve an intrinsic love or pro attitude toward something that is intrinsically worthy of love. These attitudes are correct whether or not God exists, and if he does not exist, they would be perhaps intrinsically superior to the correct false acceptance pleasure of the religious believer.

THE VALUE OF DESIRE SATISFACTION

What is the value of desire satisfaction? One way of formulating this question is to ask whether the state of affairs *S's having a satisfied desire* is intrinsically good. In asking this question, we are considering the satisfaction of desire as such, in abstraction from any consideration of what S actually desires. In this respect, our question is similar to asking whether it is intrinsically good that someone is pleased, where we consider someone's being pleased in abstraction from any consideration of what S is pleased about.

The notion of desire satisfaction requires some clarification. First, when we talk of having our desires satisfied, we sometimes mean that obtaining the object of our desire produces a feeling of satisfaction or pleasure or contentment. But it is also true that sometimes, getting what we want or desire does not please or satisfy us, and in some cases it disappoints or displeases us. Consequently, we should distinguish getting what we desire from the pleasure, satisfaction, or contentment that often, but not always, results. As Butchvarov observes, "Pleasure may but need not accompany the satisfaction of desire. It may occur even if there is no relevant desire, and a desire may be satisfied even if no pleasure is experienced."[22] Second, I shall assume that one's desire can be satisfied even though one is unaware that it has been satisfied. If I desire that John have a safe trip home, my desire is satisfied as soon as John arrives home safely, even though I might

22. Butchvarov, *Skepticism in Ethics*, p. 93.

84

be unaware of that fact. Once he is home, I've got what I desired, whether or not I know it. Thus, having a satisfied desire does not imply that one has a true belief that the object of that desire obtains. Bearing these points in mind, let us say:

(D4) *S*'s desire that *p* is satisfied at *t* = *df.* S desires that *p* and *p* obtains at *t*.
(D5) *S*'s desire that *p* is unsatisfied at *t* = *df.* S desires that *p* and *p* does not obtain at *t*.

These definitions pertain to desire *de dicto,* to desiring certain states of affairs. What I say subsequently about the value of desire satisfaction concerns desire *de dicto* but applies as well, I believe, to desire *de se* or *de re.*

If we understand desire satisfaction this way, as implying neither pleasure nor knowledge, then it is not clear that someone's having a satisfied desire has any more than a slight positive intrinsic value. Indeed, if we are to attribute any intrinsic goodness to desire satisfaction, it would appear to have only as much intrinsic value as certain other forms of consciousness, such as believing or conceiving of something or simply desiring something. If this is so, then whatever intrinsic value there is in someone's having a satisfied desire is due to that state of affairs involving someone's having a desire. The fact that the desire is satisfied would not appear to make any difference to its intrinsic value. Of course, even if desire satisfaction has little, if any, positive intrinsic value, having a satisfied desire or knowing that one's desire is satisfied can have instrumental value to the extent that it results in pleasure or a feeling of satisfaction. Similarly, having an unsatisfied desire or knowing that one has an unsatisfied desire can be instrumentally bad to the extent that it results in a feeling of frustration, pain, or anger. In general, it seems reasonable to think that having or knowing that one has a satisfied desire is instrumentally better than having or knowing that one has an unsatisfied desire. Like most claims about instrumental value, this is a contingent, empirical claim.

But shall we say that having a satisfied desire is intrinsically better than having an unsatisfied desire? Shocking as this might seem, I think the answer is "no." In considering this question, we must be careful to distinguish the pleasure and pain that are the results of satisfied and unsatisfied desires. But having carefully distinguished these things from one another, it is not clear that there is any reason to think that a satisfied desire is intrinsically better than an unsatisfied desire. Moreover, if the value of desire satisfaction stems only from its being an instance of consciousness or from its implying that someone desires something, then whatever intrinsic value there is in satisfied desire would also belong to unsatisfied desires insofar as they too are instances of consciousness. If we are to attribute some slight positive intrinsic value to satisfied desires, I suggest that the same value holds for unsatisfied desires.

There is, however, an important objection to this view that is worth considering. It concerns the value of satisfying postmortem desires. "Suppose, for example, that Albert is dying and desires that after his death his ashes be scattered in a particular region of Long Island Sound. In light of this, it would be a good thing to scatter Albert's ashes over that part of Long Island Sound. If this is so, then isn't the obvious explanation of why it is good to scatter Albert's ashes is that it is necessary for the satisfaction of Albert's desire and that the satisfaction of his desires is intrinsically good?"[23] According to this objection, it would be good to scatter Albert's ashes, and the reason this is good is that the satisfaction of Albert's postmortem desire is intrinsically good.

If we think that it is at least sometimes good to carry out the wishes of the dead, can we explain why this is the case without attributing intrinsic value to the satisfaction of the desire as such? I think we can. In satisfying Albert's desire, we show respect or love for Albert, and we may hold that it is this act of respect or love that is intrinsically good. The scattering of Albert's ashes is good because it is an act of love or respect for Albert and not because the satisfaction of Albert's postmortem desire as such is intrinsically good. The fact that Albert desired that his ashes be scattered in this way provides an especially appropriate and conventional way of demonstrating one's love or respect. But we do not need to hold that the scattering of his ashes is good because it satisfies Albert's postmortem desire.

Locating the goodness of scattering Albert's ashes in the love and respect of those carrying out his wishes rather than in the mere satisfaction of his postmortem desire might seem even more reasonable if we consider a small variation on Albert's case. Imagine that young Albert is an avid sailor who has never given any thought to or made any request about his funeral arrangements. He hasn't formed any desire about what should be done with his remains. When Albert dies suddenly in a boating accident, his friends and family decide that they will scatter his ashes in that part of Long Island Sound of which he was particularly fond. Scattering Albert's ashes in the Sound in this case seems no less good than scattering them in the previous case. If this is so, then the goodness of scattering his ashes in this case can be, and indeed must be, explained without holding that there

23. I am indebted to William Tolhurst for this objection.

is something intrinsically good about the satisfaction of Albert's postmortem desires. It does not seem that one must appeal to the goodness of satisfying postmortem desires to explain what is good about scattering Albert's ashes in either example.

If these remarks about the value of desire satisfaction are correct, then any theory of conduct that takes desire satisfaction as its sole ultimate end is aiming at something that has little or no intrinsic value. Such a theory would be about as plausible as a theory that took as it is ultimate aim the maximization of consciousness itself.

6

Consciousness, knowledge, and the consciousness thesis

Many philosophers have held that knowledge, understanding, and wisdom are intrinsically good. This is the view of Plato, Aristotle, St. Thomas, Brentano, and W. D. Ross. Yet many have questioned the intrinsic value of knowledge. Would it really be intrinsically good if someone knew how many lunar mountains are over 4,000 feet or knew every brand of peanut butter made in North America? Such knowledge strikes us as trivia, which is to say that we don't take it to be very valuable. In contrast to the views of many philosophers, Moore writes, "it appears that knowledge, though having little or no intrinsic value in itself, is an absolutely essential constituent in the highest goods, and contributes immensely to their value."[1] For Moore, knowledge is an element in certain great goods, but it has "little or no value in itself."

What are we to say about the value of knowledge? It is clear that having correct beliefs or knowledge is intrinsically better than having incorrect beliefs. No one could fittingly prefer having incorrect beliefs to correct beliefs. Brentano tells us that preferring error for its own sake to correct belief is simply perverse.[2] It is clear that having knowledge or correct beliefs is not intrinsically bad. No one could fittingly hate as such the having of knowledge or correct beliefs. Knowledge or correct belief must be either something intrinsically good or neutral. If either knowledge or correct belief is neutral, then each is most likely a positive neutral. If either were a negative or strict neutral, then, given what we've said in the last chapter, it would be intrinsically bad for anyone to take pleasure in someone's knowing something. If either were merely neutral, then the contemplation of either would not require that one not hate it in and for itself. But it seems that no one could fittingly hate as such the fact that

1. G. E. Moore, *Principia Ethica* (Cambridge: Cambridge University Press, 1903), p. 199.
2. See Franz Brentano, *The Origin of Our Knowledge of Right and Wrong,* translated by Roderick Chisholm and Elizabeth Schneewind (London: Routledge & Kegan Paul, 1969), p. 22.

someone knows something or has a true belief. In other words, the contemplation of either appears to require that one not hate or have an anti attitude toward either one. If this is right, then knowledge or correct belief must be a positive neutral, if it is neutral at all.

Knowledge or correct belief is either a positive neutral or intrinsically good. Of these two alternatives, I think one may reasonably take the stronger stand that it is good in itself. This view may be supported by the following considerations. First, the state of affairs *someone's not having any beliefs, p,* is neutral. If *someone's knowing something, q,* were also neutral, then it would have the same intrinsic value as *p.* But this seems false. Q seems preferable to *p.* For one thing, the former, unlike the latter, implies that something is conscious and thinking, and the mere possession of consciousness and thought seems preferable to their absence. But quite apart from this appeal to the value of consciousness as such, a view defended later, it appears reasonable to think that it is better to know something than not to have any beliefs whatever. If so, *p* and *q* are not the same in value and, therefore, *q* is better than *p.* Second, the state of affairs *someone's not knowing anything, r,* is a neutral and, more precisely, a negative neutral like *no one's being happy.* It is bad to take pleasure in *r,* and the contemplation of it seems to require that one not love it and not to require that one not hate it as such. It is bad to take pleasure in *r,* and there is nothing inappropriate about hating that state of affairs in and for itself. But if *r* is a negative neutral like *no one's being happy,* isn't this because it, like this latter state of affairs, is the absence of a good? The absent good is surely the good of knowing something. I conclude that even if we regard some instances of knowledge or correct belief as trivial or unimportant, we should not hold that they have no intrinsic goodness at all.

We may hold, then, that it is intrinsically good to know how many lunar mountains are over 4,000 feet. Clearly, this does not imply that one ought to go about amassing knowledge of trivia, such as memorizing the contents of the local telephone directory. From the standpoint of maximizing value, there are far more productive activities. Moreover, this stance about the value of knowledge does not prevent us from saying that it is sometimes more instrumentally valuable not to know certain things, for example, when it would spoil the enjoyment of a novel to know too soon the identity of a villain or ruin the thrill of a game by knowing the outcome in advance.

Even if we hold that every instance of knowledge or correct belief is intrinsically good, shall we say, as Moore does, that knowledge has little intrinsic value, that no kind of knowing is very important or a great intrinsic good? I don't think so. Certain forms of knowledge may readily be seen, I think, to have great intrinsic value. Consider, for example, the sort of knowledge that consists in having a clear account or an illuminating philosophical analysis of some concept or property, the sort of account appropriately taken to answer the question "What is *F?*". To have such an account of honesty, beauty, democracy, color, or material objects may plausibly be taken as something of great value in itself, far greater than knowing the contents of the telephone directory.

This sort of philosophical understanding is different from knowing that a particular man is honest or that a particular society is democratic. One can believe or know that someone is honest or beautiful without quite being able to say what honesty or beauty is, without having a philosophical analysis of such things. Of course, if one knows that a particular person is honest, then one grasps the property of being honest, but the sort of grasping or understanding that is required to attribute that property must be distinguished from having a philosophical analysis of it. One could not even ask oneself the question "What is *F?*" or "What is the most illuminating account of *F?*" unless one has already grasped the concept or property of being *F.* Yet clearly, one can ask oneself that question without knowing the answer. Furthermore, one might have an account of honesty or democracy without knowing whether it is exemplified by anything at all. To the extent that theoretical wisdom is thought to involve this sort of understanding of properties or concepts, and not the knowledge of what particulars exemplify them, there is perhaps some justification for the ancient complaint that such knowledge is useless as a means to achieving one's other ends.[3] Achieving a sound philosophical understanding of causes, properties, numbers, or material objects is not really likely to make one a more effective agent in the world. The great value of understanding in these cases does not rest, then, on its being instrumentally useful.

The difference between knowing that a particular thing has some property and having an illuminating account of that property is at least as old as Plato, and its importance should not be overlooked. Concerning the importance of the difference, Butchvarov writes:

As long as by knowledge we mean mere information, for example, knowledge of the contents of a telephone book, we might be inclined to agree with Moore that it is good almost solely as a means or as a contributory factor in organic unities

---

3. See Aristotle, *Nicomachean Ethics,* translated by Martin Ostwald (Indianapolis: Bobbs-Merrill Co., 1962), Bk. VI, Chapter 7.

that are good. But we are not likely to be so inclined with respect to knowledge as understanding.[4]

To know what something is in the sense of having an illuminating philosophical account of it, to have this sort of understanding of it, is in some cases a great intrinsic good. As Butchvarov points out, such understanding is a kind of wisdom. "When we come to philosophy, where the aim is almost always understanding and the topics are by definition the most fundamental ones, the value of such understanding becomes evident. For on those levels understanding becomes indeed describable as wisdom, which was described as the good of the intellect in classical philosophy."[5] It is not clear precisely how one might characterize those concepts or properties that are "fundamental," yet the understanding of what it is for something to be a property, a material object, an event, or a category would be examples of the sort of understanding that has value and is a mark of wisdom. We should also include the understanding of the basic concepts of the arts and the practical and theoretical sciences as intrinsically good. We may count as good such things as the understanding of a proton, gravity, virtue, goodness, beauty, and harmony.

Let us turn from the heights of understanding that are marks of wisdom to the simple having of an idea, to the mere consciousness of something. Some philosophers, Brentano for example, have defended the view that mere consciousness as such is intrinsically good. In discussing the values of desire satisfaction and knowledge, I have already suggested that consciousness of something is intrinsically good, but let us consider more closely whether simply entertaining a proposition, being aware of something, or having something as an object of thought is good in itself. Brentano writes:

Certainly ideas belong to what is intrinsically valuable; indeed, I venture to declare that each and every idea is of value, taken in itself. . . . Certainly, anyone who had to choose between a condition of unconsciousness and the possession of at least some ideas would welcome even the most trivial of these and would not envy inanimate objects. Thus, every idea appears to constitute a valuable enrichment of our lives.[6]

Someone's not being conscious or someone's not entertaining anything are neutral states of affairs. The mere absence of consciousness is neither

4. Panayot Butchvarov, *Skepticism in Ethics,* (Indianapolis: Indiana University Press, 1989), p. 101.
5. Ibid., p. 101.
6. Franz Brentano, *The Foundation and Construction of Ethics,* translated by Elizabeth Schneewind (New York: Humanities Press, 1973), p. 173.

intrinsically good nor bad. Brentano appears to hold that it is better to entertain or be conscious of something than not to entertain or be conscious of anything. If this is so, then someone's entertaining something is intrinsically good.

One objection to this view is that there are some things that it is bad to entertain. One might say that it is bad to entertain one's doing something wrong or to entertain or contemplate the suffering of others. There are, however, two responses to this objection. First, in considering the value of someone's entertaining something, we are to consider the value of just that state of affairs and not the "richer" state of affairs, someone's entertaining his doing evil. This is a satisfactory response if we are concerned simply with the value of someone's entertaining something. Still, it is not completely adequate if we are concerned with defending Brentano's view that *every* idea is good in itself. A second and better response is simply that there is nothing bad about one's entertaining either wrongdoing or the suffering of others. What is bad is taking pleasure in or loving simpliciter such things, or taking certain attitudes toward them beyond merely thinking of them.

There is some plausibility to Brentano's position. The grasping and entertaining of complex metaphysical or mathematical propositions, whether or not one knows them to be true, is an exercise of intelligence, and as such seems to be something that is intrinsically good and to have more than instrumental value. To grasp or entertain a proposition is not the same as knowing that it is true or having a philosophical analysis of it. Grasping and entertaining a proposition is a good distinct from knowledge or the sort of philosophical understanding described earlier. If the entertaining of such things as complex mathematical propositions is good in itself, there is, I think, no good reason for us to think that the entertaining of more mundane and commonplace propositions is not good in itself. Of course, the inability to entertain more commonplace propositions, such as those concerning the weather and the shapes of things, would probably be instrumentally disastrous, and it is easy to think that the value of such ideas is purely instrumental. But if Brentano is right, and I think he is, this diminishing of the richness of our mental life would be the loss of something valuable in itself.

If consciousness as such is intrinsically good, if it is good in itself to have some object before the mind, then as Brentano points out, a great many evils are necessarily such that they imply the existence of some good. Being in pain or error, or having an incorrect love or hate, is necessarily such that if something has those properties, then something is conscious.

Nothing can be in pain or make an incorrect judgment without being conscious of something.

THE CONSCIOUSNESS THESIS AND THE VALUE OF NONSENTIENT LIFE

Among the sorts of things that seem to be intrinsically good are various kinds of pleasure, knowledge, understanding, the entertaining of a proposition or the having of an idea, and morally good emotions, including loving as such what is intrinsically worthy of love. Each of these goods is such that if they obtain, then something is conscious. The "consciousness thesis" tells us that nothing can be intrinsically good or bad unless something is conscious. According to this view, something must be conscious if any intrinsically good state of affairs obtains. This thesis has been endorsed by many philosophers. Brand Blanshard, for example, writes, "Take any example of what we ordinarily regard as good or bad, imagine consciousness away, and the values vanish with it."[7] If this thesis is true, then it seems that such things as beauty, existence, and certain kinds of flourishing, such as the flourishing of an oak tree, are not intrinsically good, for something can be beautiful, exist, or flourish without anything's being conscious. The consciousness thesis is accepted by all forms of hedonism, by any theory that takes intrinsic value to be conferred on things in virtue of their being the object of desire or some related pro attitude, and by many other views as well.

It is important that we be as clear as possible about what the consciousness thesis says. First, the thesis does not tell us that in order for X to be intrinsically good, someone must be conscious of X. Such an interpretation would surely render the thesis false. It can be intrinsically good that John is happy and Paul is happy, even though no one is conscious of that fact or the existence of both John and Paul. Second, the thesis does not tell us that the only things that are intrinsically good are states of consciousness or mental states. The fact that John is happy and Paul is happy is not, strictly speaking, a mental state, though it implies something about the mental states of John and Paul. The fact that John is happy and there are stones is intrinsically good, but this whole is no more a state of consciousness than the fact that there are stones. Finally, the consciousness thesis does not imply that nothing can be intrinsically worthy of love unless someone is conscious. Someone's being happy is worthy of love

7. Brand Blanshard, *Reason and Goodness* (New York: Humanities Press, 1978), p. 273.

whether or not anyone is conscious of it or conscious at all. The thesis is not about what is worthy of love, hate, or preference, but rather about what things are intrinsically good or bad. It is about the obtaining of those states of affairs that are worthy of love and hate, since it those states of affairs that are intrinsically good or bad.

In *Principia Ethica,* Moore implicitly rejects the consciousness thesis insofar as he holds that the existence of a beautiful, yet unperceived and unknown, world is intrinsically better than that of an ugly, unperceived, and unknown world. Yet in his latter work, *Ethics,* Moore writes, "it does seem as if nothing can be intrinsically good unless it contains *both* some feeling and *also* some other form of consciousness."[8] This shift in Moore's views was welcomed by Blanshard:

Moore's final conclusion was, then, that a universe without consciousness would be a universe without value. With this I think we must agree. . . . Of course, there are persons who would answer this differently. Thomists, for example, continue to hold the obscure view of Aristotle that each material thing is a more or less complete actualization of what it is potentially, a more or less perfect embodiment of its special form, and is, so far, good. The disappearance of a boulder on some unheard of dark star would therefore be a loss of value to the world. Of course, one may conceive of value in this way if one wishes, but it carries one quite out of touch with ordinary meaning; most men would say it made no difference whatever to the amount of good in the world whether such a boulder existed or not.[9]

Reflection on Blanshard's boulder tends to support the view that the mere fact that something exists is not intrinsically good. It hardly seems that the disappearance or appearance of a boulder would matter to the overall value of the world.

Still, even if mere existence is not intrinsically good, there are more plausible examples of intrinsic goods that do not imply the existence of consciousness. Among these are the existence of flourishing nonsentient life, such as the flourishing of plants and trees, and the existence of unperceived beauty. The rise and growth of the environmental movement has been accompanied by the belief that the existence of at least some nonsentient living things is good in itself and not merely as a means of sustaining sentient, conscious life. That the flourishing of some nonconscious living things is good in itself does not seem silly or implausible. It

8. G. E. Moore, *Ethics* (Oxford: Oxford University Press, 1912), p. 107.
9. Blanshard, *Reason and Goodness,* p. 273; see W. D. Ross, *The Right and the Good* (Oxford: Oxford University Press, 1930), p. 122.

does not seem absurd that one should fittingly prefer as such there being thriving oak trees to there not being any.

In considering the intrinsic value of flourishing nonsentient life, there are several possible positions one could take. One could hold that the obtaining of that state of affairs is intrinsically good, neutral, or bad. Of these views, the last does not seem plausible, and there seem to be no contemporary philosophers who take this view. This leaves us with the possibilities that the flourishing of nonsentient life is intrinsically good or that it is neutral. Since we have distinguished four forms of neutrality, there are at least these four possibilities concerning the flourishing of non-sentient life: (1) it is negatively neutral, (2) it is strictly neutral, (3) it is merely neutral, or (4) it is positively neutral. Of these four, (1) seems to be the least plausible and (4) the most plausible. Possibility (1) seems the least likely to be true. To say that the flourishing of nonsentient life is negatively neutral is to say that the contemplation of that state of affairs requires that one not love it in and for itself. But there simply seems to be no such ethical requirement. Moreover, we have said in the last chapter that it is intrinsically bad to take pleasure in what is negatively neutral, but taking pleasure in the existence of flourishing nonsentient life does not seem to be intrinsically bad. For similar reasons, (2) does not seem very plausible. To say that something is strictly neutral is to say that the contemplation of that state of affairs requires that one not love it in and for itself; furthermore, we have said that taking pleasure in the strictly neutral is not intrinsically good. But there seems to be no ethical require-ment that one not love as such the flourishing of nonsentient life, and taking pleasure in it does not seem to be intrinsically bad. Could the flourishing of nonsentient life be merely neutral? Although this is a more plausible view than the other two, it still does not seem adequate. To say that something is merely neutral is to say that the contemplation of it does not require either that one hate or love it in and for itself. The contem-plation of the merely neutral does not require that one not hate it, and it does not require that one love it. In short, either love or hate is appropriate to what is merely neutral. But this does not seem to be true of the flour-ishing of nonsentient life, for hatred of the flourishing of nonsentient life seems to be an ethically inappropriate attitude. On the contrary, the con-templation of flourishing nonsentient life seems to require that one not hate it in and for itself. If so, then this state of affairs is not merely neutral. If the flourishing of nonsentient life is a neutral state of affairs, then it is most plausibly taken to be a positive neutral. To say that it is a positive neutral is to commit oneself to some modicum of respect for nonsentient life insofar as this implies that the contemplation of it requires that one not hate it as such.

The flourishing of nonsentient life is either a positive neutral or intrinsically good. Of this much we can be reasonably confident. Yet I tend to side with those who take the bolder position of claiming that at least some flourishing nonsentient life is intrinsically good. Following Brentano, I have urged that consciousness as such is intrinsically good, and contrary to Moore, I have said that every instance of knowledge is, as such, intrinsically good. Now value theories that recognize a plurality of intrinsic goods often face difficult questions about the comparative values of things, and we should always be ready to admit that there are questions of intrinsic value to which we simply do not know the answers. Yet if we are right about the value of consciousness and knowledge, then it seems that we might also hold that some flourishing nonsentient life is also good. For it seems reasonable to think that the existence of, say, a thriving forest of oaks is better in itself than someone's knowing how many phone numbers are in the local phone book or someone's entertaining the proposition that there are unicorns. If these little instances of knowledge or consciousness are intrinsically good, and if it is better that there be a thriving oak forest than that these states of affairs obtain, then it follows that the existence of a thriving oak forest is itself something that has intrinsic value. It does not seem in the least unreasonable that one should prefer in itself the continued existence of a thriving forest or even of one magnificent tree to one's having some bit of trivial knowledge or entertaining some commonplace proposition. Even if one questions the intrinsic goodness of these minor cognitive acts, the same sort of argument can be used with an appeal to minor sensory pleasures that also seem to be intrinsically good. It does not seem at all unreasonable that one should think it intrinsically better that there be a thriving forest than that one enjoy some small sensory pleasure. If this is right, then again, it follows that the existence of such a forest is intrinsically good. If these arguments are sound, then at least the flourishing of some forms of nonsentient life is intrinsically good. It follows that the consciousness thesis is false. Some things are intrinsically good, even though they do not imply that someone is conscious.

I have argued that some forms of flourishing life are intrinsically good, specifically, the existence of a thriving oak forest or even a single magnificent tree. But we may ask whether this is true of flourishing geraniums, patches of Kentucky bluegrass, and bacteria. The argument used previously admittedly loses some of its persuasive force when it is applied to geraniums and microflora. I, for one, would prefer many trivial cognitive states, such as knowing how many phone numbers are in the local phone book, to the existence of one bacterium. Still, once we are convinced that the consciousness thesis is false, it is not clear why we should not think that the flourishing of any form of nonsentient life is not intrinsically good. Once we recognize the good in the flourishing of oaks, what good reason is there not to see it in every instance of thriving life?

BEAUTY

Like the flourishing of nonsentient life, the existence of beautiful objects has often been taken as a challenge to the consciousness thesis. But the seriousness of this challenge is a more difficult matter in part because the relationship between beauty and consciousness is not as clear as one might hope. Consider, for example, the sort of beauty involved in seeing a spectacular sunset. Now, on some plausible views of the nature of colors, the colors that we find beautiful are secondary qualities whose existence is mind dependent, whose *esse est percipi*. If the phenomenologically experienced colors are indeed dependent on a conscious perceiver, then it is not implausible to hold that the beauty one experiences in seeing a sunset is itself dependent, at least in part, on the existence of a conscious perceiver. The same point can be raised about the experience of beauty in fragrances and sounds. If the beauty one experiences in smelling and hearing are dependent on qualities that are themselves dependent on conscious perceivers, then it seems that the beauty itself is consciousness dependent. Thus, on certain views about colors, fragrances, and sounds, if we imagine consciousness away, to paraphrase Blanshard, a great many varieties of beauty vanish with it. Of course, even if we think that a great many forms of beauty are consciousness dependent, it is not clear that all of them are. For instance, one might hold that there are certain shapes that are beautiful, and the existence of these shapes is in no way dependent on consciousness. I am not inclined to doubt that some things can be beautiful in virtue of their shape or to doubt that some things can be beautiful in the absence of consciousness. Still, the appeal to beauty makes for a weaker case against the consciousness thesis if we must appeal to the beauty of pure form or shape, since there are many who would question whether anything can be (very) beautiful in virtue of shape alone.

In spite of the preceding remarks, let us suppose, for the sake of argument, that at least some forms of beauty do not imply the existence of consciousness. What is the intrinsic value of states of affairs of the form "*X* is beautiful"? We can be reasonably confident that such states of affairs are not intrinsically bad, and that they are either neutral or intrinsically good. Like the flourishing of nonsentient life, the existence of beautiful objects would seem to be neither a negative nor a strict neutral, since someone's taking pleasure in the fact that X is beautiful is not intrinsically bad. Furthermore, the existence of beautiful objects would not seem to be merely neutral, since it does seem ethically inappropriate for someone to hate as such the existence of beautiful objects or to prefer as such the nonexistence of a beautiful object to its existence. The desire to destroy beautiful objects as such, simply because they are beautiful, is a form of wickedness. The desire to destroy a work of art, such as Michelangelo's "Pieta," simply because it is beautiful would be a wicked desire. If this is so, then we can be reasonably confident that the existence of beautiful objects is either a positive neutral or intrinsically good.

I think we may reasonably take the bolder position that the existence of beautiful objects is intrinsically good. I assume that *there being no beautiful objects, p,* is a neutral state of affairs. Consequently, if *there being beautiful objects, q,* is intrinsically better than *p,* then *q* is intrinsically good. But is *q* better than *p?* I am inclined to think so. The contemplation of each of these states of affairs seems to require that we prefer the former as such to the latter. It appears ethically inappropriate for anyone to prefer as such *p* to *q* or to be indifferent between them. Moreover, if *p* is a neutral state of affairs, then what kind of neutral is it? *There being no beautiful objects* seems to be a negative neutral. As with other negative neutrals, such as *there being no happy people,* it would be intrinsically bad to take pleasure in there being no beautiful objects. Furthermore, the contemplation of *p* requires that one not love it as such, but it does not require that one not hate it. But if *there being no beautiful objects* is a negative neutral, isn't this because it is the absence of a good, specifically, the intrinsic good of beauty? If this is so, then we have some reason to think that there being beautiful objects is intrinsically good. Furthermore, if we may assume that the existence of beautiful objects does not imply that someone is conscious, and that the existence of beautiful objects is intrinsically good, then it follows that the consciousness thesis is false.

Many persons sympathetic to the environmental movement believe that there is some intrinsic good in the existence of beautiful tracts of wilderness. They hold that it is intrinsically good that such areas exist and that the good in their preservation is not dependent solely on its conduciveness to human or sentient welfare. On such a view, the despoilment of pristine wilderness is the loss of something intrinsically good. The loss of such beauty, and the sheer ugliness of despoilment, quite apart from our knowledge or perception of it, is a bad consequence to be weighed alongside the sadness or offense felt toward the loss of natural beauty and a result that must be justified by some overall gain in value. Those who value the beauty of nature are saddened by the belief that some starkly beautiful area has been lost. Indeed, we can imagine someone saddened on hearing that some beautiful, remote, not easily accessible Antarctic or desert region had become quite ugly. Such sadness need not rest on the belief that lovers of beauty will never enjoy the area, since it is so remote. I am not sure that most reflective people will feel toward the loss of remote natural beauty what Blanshard suggests that they would feel toward the loss of a boulder on some dark star – that it makes no difference whatever. When we are shown pictures of despoiled areas, the sadness that we feel is not due to the fact that we have seen ugly pictures. We are not sad because we now have the experience of ugliness. Rather, we are saddened that the region is no longer beautiful but ugly. What strikes us as bad is not our experience of ugly photographs but the loss of beauty. If the conclusions of this section are sound, such an attitude is reasonable and appropriate.

VALUE PLURALISM AND ITS PROBLEMS

In this chapter and the last, I have tried to defend the view that there are a plurality of things that are intrinsically good. Knowledge, understanding, consciousness, sensory pleasure, certain kinds of nonsensory pleasure, various morally good emotions, the flourishing of some forms of nonsentient life, and beauty may plausibly be thought of as intrinsically good. This list should not be assumed to be complete. It is likely that there are other kinds of things that are intrinsically good as well. Unfortunately, practical and moral problems often require more than mere a knowledge of what is intrinsically good. They often require an assessment of which of several outcomes are intrinsically better than others. For example, would the consequences of opening some beautiful wilderness area to logging and mining operations, with its attendant destruction of natural beauty and wildlife, be intrinsically better than those of not doing so? The consequences or outcomes of these alternatives are hard to know, but so is the comparative value of each. Now I am not concerned here with the theory of right action, but I am skeptical that the intrinsic value of outcomes is the sole right-making property, though I do think it is a relevant consideration. This is one main reason why the study of intrinsic value has a place in ethical theory. Yet value pluralism makes the assessment of outcomes a very messy business. It is even messier if the principle of organic unities is true and if we are right to believe that some goods are higher than others. One cannot simply assume a correct assessment by summing the valuable parts of various wholes. Such moral mathematics are simply out of place here. In comparing outcomes, one must rely to some extent on the same sort of basic judgment of value involved in judgments about what is intrinsically good or bad, and this involves trying to be as clear as possible about what the various states of affairs involve. When outcomes become complex, as they invariably do in real life, this becomes an increasingly difficult task. As this task becomes more difficult, agreement diminishes, even among those who agree on what kinds of things are intrinsically good. Moreover, as it becomes more difficult, reasonable confidence in one's own judgments diminishes. This is an apparently inescapable fact. Simplifying assumptions and models have some use in sharpening our intuitions and focusing on what seems to be relevant. But they also have the inherents risk of oversimplifying and of ignoring complex and relevant features. We must be ready to admit that our judgments about the intrinsic preferability of various complex outcomes are often blind, that our preference for some outcomes over others is not based on any insight or warranted judgment about which is better. About some questions of intrinsic preferability, the most reasonable stance in some cases is to withhold judgment. To hold that we have some knowledge or warranted belief about value is, of course, not to claim that we can know the answer to every question about value.

If it is not to lead to complete moral pessimism and paralysis, this gloomy fact must be appreciated in the light of others. First, if the intrinsic value of outcomes is not the sole relevant consideration for right action, we may know or reasonably believe enough about other considerations to form warranted beliefs about what we ought to do. Even if we cannot know which of two outcomes, A or B, is intrinsically preferable, we might know that there are weightier moral considerations in favor of pursuing A. These considerations might include such things as loyalty, gratitude, and promise keeping. Moral philosophy can be of help in identifying these additional factors. Second, even if we are ignorant about the comparative value of various outcomes, it is our moral responsibility, our duty, to do the best we can by our best lights at the moment. Acting in this way is compatible with a certain amount of ignorance about value and even with acting wrongly, but it constitutes a kind of moral goodness and dignity that puts one beyond any significant reproach.

Part II

Naturalism, nonnaturalism,
and warrant

7

The distinctiveness of intrinsic value

If there is mathematical knowledge, then there is knowledge of mathematical facts and there are mathematical states of affairs that obtain. Similarly, if there is psychological knowledge, some psychological facts are known and there are psychological states of affairs that obtain. According to the traditional view described at the beginning of Chapter 1, there is knowledge of intrinsic value. We know that some things are intrinsically good, others intrinsically bad, and that some things are intrinsically better than others. If there is such knowledge, there are ethical facts and if there are ethical facts, some ethical states of affairs obtain. Ethical knowledge implies the existence of ethical facts and states of affairs, just as mathematical and psychological knowledge implies the existence of mathematical and psychological facts and states of affairs.

THE OBJECTS OF ORDINARY ETHICAL BELIEF AND KNOWLEDGE

If we know that some things are intrinsically good, then presumably there are facts and states of affairs of the form "*X* is intrinsically good." Thus, if we know that someone's being pleased is intrinsically good, presumably there is a state of affairs, *someone's being pleased is intrinsically good,* that obtains. I assume that if there are ethical states of affairs, there are also ethical properties and relations. I assume that whenever a state of affairs of the form "*X* is intrinsically good" obtains, there is a property of being intrinsically good that is exemplified. In any case, we may say that according to the traditional view, if there is ethical knowledge, then there are objects of that knowledge, ethical objects or entities, that are known.

If ethical knowledge implies that there are ethical facts, states of affairs, or properties, I suggest that the same is true of ordinary ethical *belief* or *judgment.* In other words, the objects of ordinary ethical belief are certain abstract objects, states of affairs and properties. Thus, when one makes the ordinary ethical judgment that someone's being pleased is intrinsically good, one is accepting an ethical fact or state of affairs or attributing to something the property of being intrinsically good. In this respect, our ordinary ethical beliefs are like other sorts of beliefs, such as the belief that something is red or that the tallest man is wise. When someone believes that something is red or that the tallest man is wise, he is attributing, respectively, the properties of being red and being wise. He may also be said to accept certain states of affairs, something's being red or the tallest man's being wise. Our ordinary ethical beliefs are like mathematical and psychological judgments. When one makes a mathematical judgment that 7 is a prime number, then presumably there is a mathematical state of affairs one accepts, namely, 7's being a prime number. When one judges that someone is sad, there is a psychological state of affairs one accepts, namely, someone's being sad. When one judges that something is intrinsically good, one accepts a certain ethical state of affairs or attributes to something the property of being intrinsically good.

The view that in making ordinary ethical judgments one is (1) asserting something one takes to be true or false and (2) something that is *distinctively* ethical has been recognized by philosophers who take very different stands on the truth of such judgments. Maurice Mandlebaum, for example, writes:

I believe that if anyone examines his own moral judgments he cannot doubt that at the time at which he makes them he is attempting to say something he regards as true. When one says "that would have been wrong," or "he ought to do that," or "that was a courageous thing to have done," one means that a certain moral quality truly belongs to that of which it is predicated. . . . In other words, that a particular moral predicate really characterizes that of which it is predicated.[1]

John Mackie, who maintains that there are no objective values and that there is no knowledge of them, rejects noncognitivist analyses of ordinary ethical beliefs and language:

The ordinary user of moral language means to say something about whatever it is that he characterizes morally, for example, a possible action, as it is in itself, or would be if it were realized, and not about, or even expressive of his, or anyone else's attitude or relation to it. . . . I conclude then, that ordinary moral judgments include a claim to objectivity, an assumption that there are objective values in just the sense in which I am concerned to deny this.[2]

1. Maurice Mandlebaum, *The Phenomenology of Moral Experience* (Glencoe, Ill.: Free Press, 1955), p. 258.
2. John L. Mackie, *Ethics: Inventing Right and Wrong* (New York: Penguin Books, 1977), pp. 33–5.

Mandelbaum and Mackie tell us that ordinary moral judgments are taken to be true by those who make them and that they are assertions of something distinctively ethical. Any analysis or explication that is not adequate to such facts must be mistaken as an account of our ordinary ethical beliefs.

As Mandlebaum and Mackie point out, the ordinary user of moral language is *asserting* something ethical, that is, making genuine judgments. I suggest that such ethical assertions can be understood along the lines of other sorts of assertions or judgments, namely, in terms of the acceptance of ethical states of affairs and the attribution of ethical properties. In making a moral judgment, the ordinary user of moral language is not merely expressing his attitude the way one expresses disgust by uttering "Ugh!" or joy by exclaiming "Hurray!" Such attitudes may be present and even expressed, but the ordinary ethical judgment asserts something that the judge takes to be true or false. Our ordinary ethical judgments cannot be identified with mere prescriptions, imperatives, or commands if the latter are construed as something that does not involve an *assertion* of something ethical. That the ordinary user of ethical language is *asserting* something he takes to be true is supported by the fact that he expresses his judgments in declarative or assertive form. We say such things as "Cheating on an exam is wrong," "Smith's indifference to the plight of his neighbors is wicked," and "Beneficence requires gratitude." These sentences can function unproblematically in the antecedent of conditionals if we take them to be indicative. For example, we can say, "If cheating is wrong, then one ought not to submit others' work as one's own." But it is far from clear that mere prescriptions or imperatives or expressions of attitudes can meaningfully take the place of such antecedents. What does it mean to say, "If don't cheat, then. . . ," or "If boo to cheating, then . . . ?"[3] Moreover, we do commonly take ourselves to know that some things are right or wrong, good or bad, and in taking ourselves to know such things, we presuppose that what we know is true, that we are accepting some ethical fact. Furthermore, we believe that in some cases people *ought to know* that what they are doing is wrong, that in some cases people should have known better than to act as they did.[4] Similarly, we sometimes excuse a person from moral blame when we believe that he lacked the capacity to know what is right or wrong. The fact that we accept this as an excuse without excusing everyone who does wrong

3. See Ernest Sosa, "Moral Relativism, Cognitivism, and Defeasible Rules," *Social Philosophy and Policy*, forthcoming.
4. See David O. Brink, *Moral Realism and the Foundation of Ethics* (Cambridge: Cambridge University Press, 1989), p. 27.

shows that we commonly assume that people do have the capacity to know what is right or wrong.

Mandlebaum and Mackie claim not only that our ordinary moral judgments are truly judgments or assertions, but also that they are of a distinctive kind. They hold that in making an ordinary ethical judgment one is asserting something *distinctively* ethical, and not, for example, merely describing his own psychological state or society's general attitudes. It is not easy to say precisely what this amounts to, even if the basic idea seems clear enough. At least part of their view is that in making a judgment that something is intrinsically valuable, one is not simply judging that it is liked by some person or some group, and we may take them also to hold that one is not merely judging that it is pleasant or would be desired by someone fully informed and reflective. In making an ordinary moral judgment that something is intrinsically good, one is not simply attributing to it the property of being pleasant or liked.

Of course, it is consistent with this view for some people to use ethical language in ways that are different from its ordinary use. It may be allowed that when some people say, "It is wrong for Smith to do that," these people are merely expressing disgust with Smith's action or they mean merely that Smith's action will be condemned by his peers. But Mandlebaum and Mackie hold, correctly I think, that this is not what the ordinary user of ethical language means, that it is not what he believes when he judges that Smith's action is wrong. Similarly, it may be allowed that when some persons say, "That's good," they mean what is ordinarily expressed by "I like that" or "That's pleasing." But we need not and should not hold that this is what the ordinary user of ethical language means whenever he says that something is good.

If there is ethical knowledge, then there are ethical facts and states of affairs and ethical properties and relations. In this respect, anyone who accepts the existence of ethical knowledge is committed to the existence of ethical facts, states of affairs, or properties, to the existence of ethical objects. By the same token, I have suggested, following Mandlebaum and Mackie, that our ordinary ethical or moral judgments also presuppose the existence of ethical objects such as ethical states of affairs or properties. Consequently, whether or not there are any ethical *facts* of the form "X is intrinsically good," to make an ordinary moral judgment that X is intrinsically good is to be thinking of something that is an ethical state of affairs or an ethical property. Mackie, of course, denies that there are objective values. If we understand ordinary moral judgments about intrinsic value in the way suggested earlier, then there is a property of intrinsic goodness and there are states of affairs of the form "X is intrinsically good." Mackie's position may be interpreted as telling us that no such states of affairs obtain and that nothing has the property of being intrinsically good.

Realism about material objects is often taken to be the view that there are material objects that exist independently of our awareness or consciousness of them and independently of the manner in which we think about them. Let us take "ethical realism" to be the view that there are ethical objects that exist independently of our awareness or consciousness of them and independently of the manner in which we think about them. Is the view presented earlier a form of ethical realism? I think the answer is "yes," for we have said that (1) there are ethical objects, properties, and states of affairs, which are the objects of ethical knowledge and belief and (2), as we assumed in Chapter 2, states of affairs and properties are abstract objects that exist independently of our thinking about them. Whether a state of affairs or property exists does not depend on someone's thinking or conceiving of it. Thus, quite apart from considerations of knowledge, the understanding of our ordinary ethical judgments and beliefs presented earlier presupposes a form of ethical realism.

The view presented earlier is a form of ethical realism insofar as it holds that there are ethical objects, ethical properties or states of affairs, and that these are abstract objects that exist independently of our thinking about them. It is worth noting, however, that if we take ethical realism to be the view that there are ethical objects that exist independently of our awareness of them, then the view presented earlier is not the only form that ethical realism could take. It is possible, perhaps, that one could hold a nominalistic form of ethical realism, a form that denies the existence of any sorts of abstract objects. Such a view would hold that there are ethical objects that exist independently of our thinking of them, but these ethical objects are not abstract properties or states of affairs.

NONNATURALISM AND TRADITIONAL NATURALISM

One of the claims of the traditional view described at the outset of Chapter 1 is roughly that intrinsic goodness is *distinct* from any natural entity. How shall we understand this claim? I suggest that we may take it to mean (1) that states of affairs of the form "X is intrinsically good" are not identical with and unanalyzable by any natural state of affairs and (2) that if there is a property of being intrinsically good, then it is not identical with or analyzable by any natural property. The traditional view may thus be thought of as making a claim about abstract objects, about properties and states of affairs.

In taking this stand, the traditional view is opposed to a certain traditional form of "ethical naturalism," which holds that all ethical states of affairs and properties are either identical with or analyzable by natural states of affairs and properties. Traditional naturalism, as I understand it, does not entail that there is no property of being intrinsically good or that there are no states of affairs of the form "X is intrinsically good." There are, as we shall see, other forms of naturalism, but the sort of ethical naturalism most prominent in this century is the sort that takes the ethical to be identical with or analyzable by the natural. Since the traditional view described at the beginning of Chapter 1 and in the preceding paragraph rejects this view, it may fairly be considered a form of "ethical nonnaturalism." Yet in spite of these differences, both ethical naturalism and nonnaturalism accept the view that there are ethical facts, and both views traditionally hold that there can be knowledge of such facts.

Although traditional nonnaturalism may be thought of as making a claim about abstract objects, about ethical properties and states of affairs, we should note that this is not the only form that nonnaturalism can take. As we noted at the end of the last section, one might hold a nominalistic form of ethical realism, and it seems possible that one might hold a nominalistic form of ethical nonnaturalism. On this view, there are ethical objects that are neither (1) abstract objects nor (2) identical with or analyzable by natural objects. Similarly, it is possible that one might hold a nominalistic version of naturalism that claims that there are ethical objects (1) that are not abstract objects and (2) that are either identical with or analyzable in terms of natural objects. I do not intend to imply that either naturalism or nonnaturalism is committed to an ontology of abstract objects. Still, I focus on those versions of naturalism and nonnaturalism that accept the existence of abstract objects. I do so for several reasons. First, I believe that the most plausible accounts of the bearers of intrinsic value – for example, what is intrinsically good and what is intrinsically worthy of love – require the existence of abstract objects, in particular the existence of states of affairs. Second, I am concerned to defend the plausibility of the traditional nonnaturalistic view, which accepts the existence of abstract objects. Third, though I cannot defend the claim here, I think realism about abstract objects is more plausible than nominalism. Fourth, if one has nominalist sympathies, I suggest that one take my references to abstract objects as a way of describing these various positions and treat the language

108

of properties and abstract objects as a *façon de parler*. I would also suggest that the nominalist try to show how talk about ethical properties and states of affairs could be translated in a way that preserves the distinction between naturalism and nonnaturalism and provides a satisfactory account of the bearers of value while eliminating the commitment to abstract objects.

If we take ethical nonnaturalism and naturalism to accept the existence of ethical properties and states of affairs, and yet to differ on whether these are identical with or analyzable by natural properties or states of affairs, then we may ask, what are natural properties and states of affairs supposed to be? In *Principia Ethica*, Moore sought to explain what he meant by natural and nonnatural characteristics, but his explanation there is not especially clear or helpful. In his reply to his critics in *The Philosophy of G.E. Moore*, Moore called the explanation offered in *Principia* "utterly silly and preposterous" and did not offer any better account.[5] More recently, David Brink, a defender of naturalism, has suggested that "natural facts and properties are presumably something like those facts and properties as picked out and studied by the natural and social sciences (broadly conceived); whereas supernatural facts and properties are studied in other ways (e.g., by religion)."[6] Unfortunately, this is not as clear or helpful as one might wish. The fact that I had eggs for breakfast is not likely to be picked out and studied by any natural or social science. Would it count as a natural fact? Moreover, being picked out and studied by the natural and social sciences would seem to be a contingent property of any sort of fact or property, since it is a contingent fact that there are any natural or social sciences at all. Are we to assume that there are no natural facts or properties as yet unpicked out and unstudied by the natural and social sciences, or that if there had been no natural and social sciences, there would have been no natural facts or properties? Perhaps it would be better to say that a natural fact or property is one that it is possible to know through the kinds of inquiry that are characteristic of the natural and social sciences. At least on this view, the existence of natural facts and properties would not be dependent on the actual existence of the natural and social sciences. But even this formulation is rather vague, for what exactly are we to understand as the kinds of inquiry that are characteristic of the natural and social sciences? Would knowledge of mathematical facts, such as $2 + 2 = 4$, or modal facts, such as that it is impossible for something to be round

5. G. E. Moore, *The Philosophy of G. E. Moore*, Volume Two, edited by Paul Arthur Schilpp (La Salle, Ill.: Open Court Publishing Co., 1942), p. 582.
6. Brink, *Moral Realism and the Foundations of Ethics*, p. 22.

and square at the same time, count as natural facts on this view? The inability to define or explicate a clear sense of "natural property or fact" threatens the intelligibility of traditional naturalism, as well as its staunch rejection by Moore and others.

Given the difficulty of defining what a natural fact or property is supposed to be, we might ask, what turns on the debate between the naturalist and the nonnaturalist? Unfortunately, it is not easy to give a simple answer or an answer that all naturalists or nonnaturalists will find satisfactory. This is due, in part, to the fact that what one thinks important or unimportant about the debate will turn on (1) what one takes a natural or nonnatural property or fact to be and (2) one's other philosophical views. If, for example, one takes a nonnatural property or fact to be one that can be discerned only by a peculair faculty of moral sense, and if one rejects the existence of such a faculty, then it becomes very important to argue that ethical facts and properties are not nonnatural if one thinks we have knowledge of such properties and facts. Of course, this particular view of why the debate is important would not be acceptable to anyone who rejected this particular view of a nonnatural property or thought that there was no knowledge of ethical facts or properties. So, given a variety of ways of construing what a natural or nonnatural property or facts is, and given different background philosophical commitments, it is difficult to give a simple answer to the question at stake in the naturalist/nonnaturalist debate.

However, although it is not easy to give a simple answer, I think we can identify two general concerns that underlie much of the interest in the debate. The first is epistemological and the second is metaphysical. First, it has seemed to many naturalists that there are severe epistemological problems with the view that some ethical properties and facts are nonnatural. If we think we have knowledge of ethical facts and properties, and if we think that nonnaturalism is committed to a false or implausible epistemic account, then it is very important for us to show that ethical facts and properties are natural. The objection that nonnaturalism is committed to an implausible epistemic view has been endorsed by Mackie, Frankena, and Philippa Foot.[7] Many naturalists hold that the only way in which we can give a plausible account of our knowledge of ethical facts and properties is if those facts and properties are either identical with or

---

7. See Mackie, *Ethics,* pp. 38–9; William Frankena, *Ethics,* 2nd edition (Englewood Cliffs, N.J.: Prentice-Hall, 1973), pp. 102–5; Philippa Foot, editor, *Theories of Ethics* (Oxford: Oxford University Press, 1979), pp. 2–3.

analyzable by natural facts and properties to which we have presumably unproblematic access. In the following two chapters, I argue that nonnaturalism is not committed to a false or implausible epistemic view.

The second concern is metaphysical. Some nonnaturalists express qualms about the relations or connections that some nonnaturalists have claimed to find between natural and nonnatural properties or facts. Some nonnaturalists, for example, hold that nonnatural ethical facts and properties are necessitated by or supervene on natural facts and properties. Some naturalists find the notion of necessitation or supervenience problematic. Such an objection is raised by Mackie:

> What is the connection between the natural fact that an action is a piece of deliberate cruelty – say, causing pain just for fun – and the moral fact that it is wrong? It cannot be entailment, a logical or semantic necessity. Yet it is not merely that the two features occur together. The wrongness must somehow be "consequential" or "supervenient"; it is wrong because it is a piece of deliberate cruelty. But just what *in the world* is signified by this "because"?[8]

In Mackie's case, his qualms about supervenience are partly epistemological, for he wonders, just how are we to know that one property supervenes on another? But it is also partly a concern about the notion of supervenience itself, a doubt that there is any such thing. I argue later in this chapter that Mackie's worries about supervenience do not pose a serious problem for nonnaturalism.

Still, for all this, if we cannot say clearly what a natural property is supposed to be, then how are we to assess the truth of naturalism or the claim that it is false? It is very tempting to dismiss the entire debate until some clearer account of natural properties and facts is provided. It is not clear, though, that such a dismissal is required. It may be the case that even if we do not have a general criterion for a natural property, we have an intuitive grasp or a rough appreciation for what should count as a natural property. Indeed, Moore, Brink, and others who take seriously the distinction between natural and nonnatural properties typically assume that we have such a grasp. In order to assess the truth of naturalism, it is not necessary that one have a general criterion of the natural, but only that one can tell in general for certain proposed analyses whether or not the analysans involves only natural properties or facts. One might consider here the claims of those who say that psychological properties can be defined or analyzed in terms of behavioral dispositions or physical properties. It would seem to be a mistake to dismiss the thesis and the accom-

8. Mackie, *Ethics*, p. 41.

panying debate as unintelligible merely because one had no ready criterion of a psychological property or behavioral disposition. A rough grasp and a capacity to distinguish between psychological properties and behavioral dispositions can substitute for a general criterion. Indeed, it seems that such an intuitive apprehension of the difference would be necessary in formulating any satisfactory criterion for either the psychological, behavioral, or natural. Naturalists and their critics assume that such properties as being pleasant and being desired are natural properties.

For the purpose of evaluating naturalism, then, I will assume that we can recognize certain properties and states of affairs as natural. If there are some properties that seem pretty clearly to be natural and that provide a satisfactory analysis of intrinsic goodness, then one has reason to believe that traditional naturalism is true. However, I suggest that if, after considerable reflection, one finds that there are no such properties, then one has some reason to think that it is false. I take this position for the following reasons. First, withholding belief in naturalism and nonnaturalism seems to be the appropriate stance at the outset of investigating of their claims. We need not assume that there is a presumption in favor of either view. Second, the failure of many careful thinkers after prolonged reflection to provide a satisfactory analysis must, I think, weaken the epistemic status of naturalism. If this failure does weaken the epistemic status of naturalism and if the appropriate initial stance toward naturalism is that of withholding belief, then it seems that this failure must be some reason, if only a defeasible one, to think that naturalism is false.

THE IDENTITY THESIS AND INTENTIONAL CRITERIA OF IDENTITY

Let us consider the claims that the property of being intrinsically good and the state of affairs of the form "X is intrinsically good" are *identical* with some natural property or states of affairs. Let us say that anyone who accepts these claims accepts the identity thesis. I argue in this section that given plausible intentional criteria of identity for properties and states of affairs, we have some reason for thinking that the identity thesis is false.

What would be a satisfactory criterion of identity for properties and states of affairs? Let us begin by introducing the following concepts, where p and q stand for states of affairs and F and G for properties:

(D6) p implies q = Df. p is necessarily such that if it obtains, then q obtains.

(D7) F implies G = Df. F is necessarily such that whatever has it has G.

112

The state of affairs *something's being red* implies *something's being colored*. It also implies *something's being red or round*. The property of *being red* implies the property of *being colored*. It also implies the property of *being red or round*.

Shall we say that a state of affairs p is identical with a state of affairs p just in case p implies q and vice versa? This criterion of mutual implication does not seem satisfactory. It would tell us that every state of affairs that obtains necessarily is identical with every other such state of affairs, since every state of affairs that necessarily obtains implies every other necessary state of affairs. It would tell us that *7's being a prime number* is identical with *2 and 2's being equal to 4* and with *all men being men*. It would also imply, implausibly I think, that *something's being an equilateral triangle* is identical with *something's being an equiangular triangle*. Similar considerations can be raised against treating mere mutual implication as an identity criterion of properties. There are certain universal properties that everything has, for example, *being colored if red, being red or nonred, being such that 2 and 2 are 4*. These properties are necessarily such that if something has one, it has the others. The criterion of mutual implication implies incorrectly that these distinct properties are identical.

A more promising approach is offered by Chisholm. He proposes criteria of identity for properties and states of affairs that make use of certain intentional attitudes, such as conceiving, entertaining, and attributing. In formulating an intentional criterion of identity for properties and states of affairs, let us make use of the following definition:

(D8) *p involves q* = df. p is necessarily such that whoever entertains p entertains q.

Entertaining a state of affairs is not the same thing as grasping it or accepting it. There are states of affairs I grasped and accepted a few minutes ago without entertaining. For example, I accepted states of affairs such as my being a man and my being in a room without entertaining them. According to (D8), *something's being red or round* involves *something's being red,* since one cannot entertain the former state of affairs without entertaining the latter. But we should note that the former does not *imply* the latter, since it is possible for the former to obtain without the latter. Properties can also involve one another. Let us say:

(D9) *F involves G* = Df. F is necessarily such that whoever entertains it entertains G.

Grasping or understanding a property is not the same as entertaining it. If a few minutes ago I accepted the proposition that I am a man, I then grasped the property of *being a man*. But I was not then entertaining that property. Moreover, entertaining a property is not the same as attributing it, since I can entertain the property of being a mermaid without attributing that property to anything. The property of *being red or round* involves *being red*, since one cannot entertain the former property without entertaining the latter. However, the former property does not imply the latter. Given these concepts, we can define the concept of "entailment":

(D10)   *p entails q* = *Df. p* implies *q* and *p* involves *q*.
(D11)   *F entails G* = *Df. F* implies *G* and *F* involves *G*.

The state of affairs *something's being red and round* entails *something's being red*, since the former both implies and involves the latter. Similarly, the property of *being red and round* entails *being red*, since the former implies and involves the latter.

What would be satisfactory criteria of identity for states of affairs and properties? Given the concepts set forth earlier, let us say:

(C1)   State of affairs *p* is identical with state of affairs *q* if and only if *p* entails *q* and *q* entails *p*.
(C2)   Property *F* is identical with property *G* if and only if *F* entails *G* and *G* entails *F*.[9]

According to (C1), the states of affairs *something's being colored if red* and *no man's being taller than himself* are not identical, since neither state of affairs entails the other. Similarly, *all triangles having three sides* is not identical with *all squares having four sides,* since neither state of affairs entails the other. Furthermore, (C2) tells us that the property of *being round or nonround* is not identical with *being colored if red* and that the property of *being triangular* is not identical with the property of *being trilateral,* since there is no mutual entailment between these properties.

These intentional criteria are relevant to the identity thesis. For if they are adequate, and I think they are, *something's being pleasant* is not identical with *something's being intrinsically valuable,* since the former does not entail the latter and vice versa. There is no mutual entailment because it is possible to entertain the former and not the latter, and vice versa. Furthermore, if there is a property of being intrinsically good, then according

9. See Roderick Chisholm's discussion of property identity in *On Metaphysics* (Minneapolis: University of Minnesota Press, 1989), pp. 144–5.

to this criterion, it is not identical with the property of being pleasant, since it is possible to entertain the former without entertaining the latter, and vice versa.

If we accept these criteria of identity for properties and states of affairs, then it is reasonable for us to hold that the state of affairs *something's being intrinsically valuable* is not identical with *something's being pleasant or approved or desired*. This is so simply because it is possible that someone can entertain or conceive the latter states of affairs without conceiving the former, and vice versa. Even if it were true that whoever accepts that a thing is intrinsically good also approves or desires that thing, it is possible that he could conceive or entertain that thing's being intrinsically good without conceiving of his approving or desiring that thing. One can entertain something's being good without entertaining something's being desired or approved, and vice versa. Furthermore, if there is a property of being intrinsically good, it is possible that someone can entertain that property without entertaining the properties of being pleasant, desired, or approved, and vice versa.

These psychological facts are reflected in the following passage by Moore:

> But whoever will attentively consider what is actually before his mind, when he asks the question "Is pleasure (or whatever it may be) after all good?" can easily satisfy himself that he is not merely asking whether pleasure is pleasant. And if he will try this experiment with each suggested definition in succession, he may become expert enough to recognize that in every case he has before his mind a unique object, with regard to the connection of which with any other object, a distinct question may be asked. Everyone does in fact understand the question "Is this good?" When he thinks of it, his state of mind is different from what it would be were he asked, "Is this pleasant, desired, or approved?"[10]

Moore sees that considering or entertaining whether something is intrinsically good is not the same psychological state as considering whether something is pleasant or desired. Moore appeals to these psychological facts in formulating his "open question argument." The conclusion Moore draws from that argument is that intrinsic goodness is *simple* and *unanalyzable,* but in appealing to these facts, we are *not* asserting anything about the simplicity or the unanalyzability of intrinsic goodness or intrinsic value. Instead, it is being urged that when taken in conjunction with the

10. G. E. Moore, *Principia Ethica* (Cambridge: Cambridge University Press, 1903), pp. 16–17.

criteria of identity adopted here, these facts imply that intrinsic goodness is not *identical* with these natural properties or states of affairs.

It is important to recognize that it does not strictly follow from the criteria of identity proposed earlier that intrinsic value is not identical with some natural property, relation, or state of affairs. For all that has been said so far, it may yet turn out that there is some natural state of affairs that mutually entails a state of affairs of the form "*X* is intrinsically good" or that there is some natural property that mutually involves the property of being intrinsically good. Still, it is reasonable to doubt that this is so, if only because the historically most prominent identifications of intrinsic value with the pleasant, desired, or approved fail to satisfy the proposed criteria of identity. If there is no mutual entailment between something's being intrinsically good and something's being pleasant, desired, or approved, there is equally no such mutual entailment between the former state of affairs and something's being desired or approved by the vast majority of men or something's being approved or desired by someone who knows and is vividly aware of all nonevaluative facts. Since the historically most prominent attempts to identify intrinsic value with some natural property or state of affairs fail, there is a strong presumption in favor of believing that intrinsic value is not identical with any natural property or state of affairs. The defender of the distinctiveness of intrinsic value need only show that the proposed identifications fail in order to support and to establish a presumption in favor of his view.

It is also important to note that the criteria of identity set forth earlier do not imply that intrinsic value is not necessitated by or dependent on natural facts. The state of affairs *something's being red or round* is not identical with the state of affairs *something's being red*. But the latter may be said to necessitate the former in the sense that it is necessarily such that if it obtains, then so does the former. Similarly, consider the states of affairs *something's being triangular* and *something's being trilateral*. I assume that these states of affairs are not identical, since it is possible that someone can conceive the former without conceiving the latter, and vice versa. But even if these states of affairs are not identical, they are necessarily such that if the one obtains, the other obtains. We may say that these states of affairs necessitate one another, even if they are not identical. Consequently, even if intrinsic value is distinct from any natural property, relation, or state of affairs, nothing claimed so far is incompatible with its being necessitated by the natural.

Let us consider some objections to the intentional criteria presented earlier. Consider the following argument: (1) One can conceive of the

116

property of being lightning without conceiving of the property of being a massive discharge of electrons. (2) If the intentional criterion of property identity is true, then the property of being lightning is not identical with the property of being a massive discharge of electrons. (3) But lightning is a massive discharge of electrons. (4) Therefore, the intentional criterion of property identity is false. In response to this argument, it need only be pointed out that the conclusion does not follow from the premises. The intentional criterion tells us something about property identity, but the third premise, although true, does not tell us anything about property identity. It does not assert a truth about property identity that is incompatible with the intentional criterion of property identity. In order for this argument to be valid, we must replace the third premise with (3') the property of being lightning is identical with the property of being a massive discharge of electrons. Although (3) is true, it is far from clear that we have any reason whatever to think that (3') is true. On the contrary, when the scientifically unsophisticated man attributes to something the property of being lightning, he is not attributing to it the property of being a discharge of electrons. It is important to note that even though (3') is false, it does not follow that there are no significant relations between these two properties. It might be that whatever has the one property has the other, and vice versa. Indeed, this might even be necessarily true. But neither of these claims would imply that these properties are identical.

A second objection could be put this way: (1) You have said that one can entertain the property of being intrinsically good without entertaining the property of being pleasant, and vice versa, and thus, according to the intentional criterion, these are distinct properties. (2) But if the property of being intrinsically good is identical with the property of being pleasant, then one cannot entertain and attribute the one without entertaining and attributing the other. (3) Therefore, the argument that these properties are not identical simply begs the question against this form of naturalism. The simplest response to this argument is that we do in fact know that we can entertain and attribute the property of being pleasant without entertaining and attributing the property of being intrinsically good. We know, for example, that we have attributed to malicious pleasures the property of being pleasant and have not attributed to them the property of being intrinsically good. The proponent of this argument would suggest that we are mistaken in thinking that we have ever done so. Perhaps this is begging the question against a certain form of naturalism, but it does not seem an unreasonable stance. If one were to bother responding to a solipsist that one knows that his solipsism is false because one knows that one exists, this would also be to beg the question against the solipsist. Yet our argument against him would be sound, and we would know that he is mistaken. We do know that we can attribute and entertain the property of being intrinsically good without attributing or entertaining the property of being pleasant. We know that anyone who denies this is mistaken.

CONSTITUTIONAL NATURALISM

The claim that intrinsic value is not identical with or analyzable by natural properties of states of affairs is the central thesis of nonnaturalism. Nonnaturalism per se does not imply that intrinsic value is dependent on, supervenient on, or necessitated by natural properties and states of affairs. Of course, many nonnaturalists have held that nonnatural ethical properties and facts are intimately connected to natural facts and properties. For example, W. D. Ross writes, "Goodness is always a consequential attribute; that which is good is good by virtue of something else in its nature, by being of a certain kind."[11] G. E. Moore says, "*To say that a kind of value is 'intrinsic' means merely that the question of whether a thing possesses it, and in what degree it possesses it, depends solely on the intrinsic nature of the thing in question.*"[12] Nonnaturalism is committed to the existence of sui generis ethical properties and states of affairs only in the sense that there are ethical properties and states of affairs that are not identical with or analyzable by natural properties and states of affairs. Nonnaturalism does not imply and is not committed to the thesis that ethical properties and states of affairs are ontologically independent of natural properties and states of affairs. In this respect, nonnaturalists may be said to distinguish between "ontological distinctiveness" and "ontological independence." Insofar as they hold that intrinsic value is not identical with any natural property, nonnaturalists claim that intrinsic value is ontologically distinct from any natural property. But nonnaturalists are not committed to the view that intrinsic value is independent of the exemplification of natural properties.

It is open to the nonnaturalist to hold (1) that certain natural states of affairs are necessarily such that if they obtain, then so do certain ethical states of affairs, and (2) that if a state of affairs of the form "*X* is intrinsically

11. W. D. Ross, *The Right and the Good* (Oxford: Oxford University Press, 1930), p. 155.
12. G. E. Moore, "The Conception of Intrinsic Value," *Philosophical Studies* (London: Routledge & Kegan Paul, 1922), p. 260.

good" obtains, then there is some natural state of affairs, *p*, such that *p* obtains and *X*'s being intrinsically good obtains in virtue of *p*'s obtaining. These claims about the relationship between natural states of affairs and intrinsic value are at least part of what seems to be involved in the notion that intrinsic value is dependent or supervenient on the natural. With respect to (1), the nonnaturalist might hold, for instance, that the state of affairs *someone's being pleased* is necessarily such that if it obtains, then so does the ethical state of affairs *someone's being pleased is intrinsically good*. Similarly, he may hold that *someone's being wise* is necessarily such that if it obtains, then so does *someone's being wise is intrinsically good*. With respect to (2), he might hold that if the state of affairs that obtains, such as *someone's being pleased is intrinsically good*, then there is some natural state of affairs that obtains, such as *someone's being pleased*, and that the former ethical state of affairs obtains in virtue of the latter's obtaining.

As we noted earlier, one objection to nonnaturalism concerns the relationship between nonnatural and natural properties and facts. Some philosophers object to the claim that nonnatural ethical properties and facts are necessitated by or supervenient on natural properties and facts. Mackie, for example, finds the notion of supervenience queer or mysterious. There are several points to be made in response to this objection. First, if we take nonnaturalism to be the view that there are ethical properties and facts that are not identical with or analyzable by natural properties and facts, then nonnaturalism itself is not committed to the view that the nonnatural supervenes on the natural. Even if there is no such thing as supervenience, it would not follow that nonnaturalism is false. Second, to hold that the nonnatural is necessitated by or supervenient on the natural is not obviously mistaken or implausible. The notion that one fact or property might necessitate others, as being square necessitates being shaped, does not seem grounds for embarrassment. Moreover, the notion of supervenience is not employed solely by nonnaturalists. It is not uncommon to find philosophers claiming that psychological facts supervene on physical facts, that epistemic facts supervene on psychological facts, or that biological facts supervene on chemical and physical facts. If the notion of supervenience is a metaphysically problematic notion, then it is not a problem solely for the nonnaturalist in ehtics. Third, it is not clear that one should reject the notion of supervenience because it is difficult to define or explicate. The concept of causation, for example, is notoriously difficult to define or explicate, yet few philosophers, including many sympathetic to naturalism, would want to deny the existence of casual facts and relations. Even if the notion of supervenience resists a satisfactory analysis, it does not seem that this a good reason to reject claims of supervenience.

Recently, some philosophers have sought to defend a position that we may call "constitutional" naturalism. According to constitutional naturalis, ethical facts are constituted by natural and social scientific facts, that is, those facts that are studied by the natural and social sciences. David Brink, for example, suggests that naturalism in ethics is best construed as the thesis that ethical facts are constituted by such facts. He writes:

> Moral facts and properties, so construed, are constituted, composed, or realized by organized combinations of natural and social scientific facts and properties. The former are, then, in a certain sense nothing over and above the latter. This naturalist claim should be understood on the model of other common constitution claims: for instance, tables are constituted by certain combinations of microphysical particles, large scale social events such as wars and elections are constituted by enormously complex combinations of smaller scale events and processes. . . . [13]

How shall we understand the claim that ethical facts "are nothing over and above" natural social and scientific facts? Does this mean that ethical facts are identical with natural social and scientific facts? No, for Brink denies that the relation between the two is identity.[14] Constitutional naturalism seems to involve the following three claims. First, every ethical property or state of affairs is constituted by natural properties or states of affairs. Second, ethical properties or states of affairs *are* natural properties or states of affairs.[15] Third, ethical properties and states of affairs do not merely supervene on natural properties and states of affairs; rather, ethical properties and states of affairs enter into causal relations and play a role in causal explanations.[16] This third claim is incompatible with what we may call "ethical epiphenomenalism", that is, the view that whereas ethical properties and states of affairs are dependent on natural or nonethical states of affairs, the former are causally inert. Constitutional naturalists reject ethical epiphenomenalism. Constitutional naturalism has moved quite a ways from the traditional naturalistic claims. It does not claim that ethical properties and facts are identical with natural properties, such as being pleasant or desired, and offers nothing that can be construed as a philosophical analysis or definition of something's being intrinsically good.

In spite of its appeal, there are various problems with constitutional naturalism. Let us consider the second claim, that ethical properties and

13. Brink, *Moral Realism and the Foundations of Ethics,* p. 159.
14. Ibid., pp. 158–9.
15. Ibid., p. 157.
16. Ibid., p. 191.

states of affairs just are natural properties and states of affairs. One basic problem with this claim concerns Brink's claim that natural properties and states of affairs are those that are studied by the natural and social sciences. The difficulty is simply that there is no natural or social science that studies intrinsic goodness or moral rightness. Those properties and states of affairs of the form "X is intrinsically good" are not the subject matter of any natural or social science. Thus, even if intrinsic goodness is constituted by natural properties, it seems to follow, given Brink's account of natural properties and facts, and certain facts about the natural and social sciences, that intrinsic goodness is not a natural property.

Leaving aside this basic problem, we might ask, what reason is there to think that ethical properties are natural? Perhaps the answer is that they are natural properties because they are constituted by natural properties. But it is not at all obvious that we should accept this inference. It is not obvious that if one type of property or state of affairs, F, is constituted by another type of property or state of affairs, G, then F-properties and states of affairs are G-properties and states of affairs. Suppose, for example, that the facts and properties studied by economics, such as inflation, recession, and economic growth, are constituted by social and biological facts, and that these, in turn, are constituted ultimately by physical properties and facts, by the facts and properties studied by physics. Even if the facts and properties studied by economics are constituted by the facts and properties studied by physics, it does not follow that the facts and properties studied by economics are the facts and properties studied by physics. On the contrary, physics simply does not study the properties of inflation or recession. Physics does not study such facts and properties even if they are ultimately constituted by those that physics does study. Similarly, even if moral facts and properties were constituted by the facts studied by the natural and social sciences, it does not follow that the former are themselves studied by the natural and social sciences or that they are natural facts and properties. In addition, we should consider the following problem. Suppose that certain generic properties, such as the property of being red, are constituted by absolutely particular shades of red, by various *infima species* or by absolutely determinate species, such as absolutely determinate shades of red. Even if being red is constituted by some determinate shade of red that is an *infima species*, it does not follow that the generic property of redness is an *infima species*. In other words, even if the redness of some object is constituted by its having some determinate shade of red, it does not follow that being a determinate shade of red is a characteristic of redness itself. Thus, from the fact that one property is constituted by

121

another property, it does not follow that whatever is true of the latter is true of the former. In light of these examples, I conclude that one cannot argue that anything follows about the naturalness of ethical properties or states of affairs merely from the claim that they are constituted by natural properties.

In addition to these problems, there is another problem for constitutional naturalism and Brink's characterization of natural properties and states of affairs. Constitutional naturalism tells us that ethical properties and states of affairs are constituted only by natural properties and states of affairs. (If ethical properties could be constituted by something other than natural properties, then there would be no reason whatever to accept constitutional naturalism's claim that ethical properties just are natural properties.) I take this to imply that the only good-making properties are natural properties, that intrinsic value supervenes only on natural properties and natural states of affairs. Now, suppose that there are various "supernatural" states of affairs that are intrinsically worthy of love or intrinsically good. Consider the state of affairs *someone's knowing and loving God's divine perfection*. If this state of affairs obtains, then it would seem to be intrinsically good. But whether or not it obtains, it is a state of affairs that is intrinsically worthy of love or favor, a state of affairs that merits a pro attitude. If this is right, then it seems that the property of knowing and loving God's divine perfection is an intrinsically good-making property. It is an intrinsically good-making property in the sense that if anything has it, then the fact that something has it is intrinsically good. Whether anything actually has this property is thus irrelevant to its being a good-making property. But the property of knowing and loving God's divine perfection is not a natural property, any more than the state of affairs *someone's knowing and loving God's divine perfection* is a natural state of affairs. Neither this property nor the corresponding state of affairs is studied by the natural or social sciences. If the property of knowing and loving God's divine perfection is a good-making property, and if constitutional naturalism implies that the only good-making properties are natural properties, then constitutional naturalism is false.

Rather than hold that the only good-making properties are natural properties, there is a weaker thesis open to constitutional naturalism. This is the view that as a matter of fact, intrinsic goodness supervenes only on natural properties, that although there might be nonnatural or supernatural good-making properties, none of them is in fact exemplified. But there are still two problems with this weaker position. First, it is not clear how such a view could account for the fact that certain nonnatural states of affairs are worthy of love. For whether a state of affairs, such as *someone's knowing and loving God's divine perfection,* is worthy of love is independent of the obtaining of that state of affairs or the actual exemplification of the property of knowing and loving God's perfection. We may ask *what* natural property or state of affairs makes *someone's knowing and loving God's divine perfection* worthy of love? Second, it is simply not obvious that no nonnatural or supernatural good-making properties are exemplified. It is not clear that any of us are now in a position to know that this is true; consequently, none of us would be in position to know that constitutional naturalism is true.

Constitutional naturalism faces some serious problems. Given certain views, such as Brink's, about what natural properties are, there is every reason to think that ethical properties and states of affairs are not natural properties or states of affairs. Moreover, even if ethical properties and states of affairs are constituted by natural properties and states of affairs, it does not follow from this fact that the former are natural. Finally, given Brink's account of natural properties, there is reason to doubt that ethical properties are constituted solely or ultimately by natural properties. This is because there seem to be some good-making properties that are not natural properties. If all this is true, then we have good reasons for rejecting two of the three central theses of constitutional naturalism. There remains, of course, the claim that ethical properties and states of affairs enter into causal relations and play a role in causal explanations. Brink's acceptance of this claim figures prominently in his response to an argument against ethical facts, an argument that we shall consider in the next section. I shall not discuss this claim here beyond simply pointing out that, as far as I can tell, nothing in traditional nonnaturalism rules out this possibility. As far as I can tell, traditional nonnaturalism is simply not committed to this claim or to its negation.

Before leaving the topic of constitutional naturalism, it is worth making one point about Brink's treatment of nonnaturalism. As we have already seen, W. D. Ross and G. E. Moore take intrinsic goodness to be a dependent or consequential attribute. Yet Brink claims that nonnaturalism is committed to the ontological independence of ethical properties and states of affairs from the natural. Brink makes this mistake, I believe, because he takes the nonnaturalist to accept what he calls the "semantic test of properties." The test has two parts: "(a) terms express or designate the same property just in case they are synonymous, and (b) a pair of terms

'F' and 'G' stand for properties F and G such that C necessitates F just in case it is part of the meaning of 'G' that G things are F.''[17] Brink adds, "The motivation for the semantic test of properties lies, I think, in the philosophical tradition that views all necessary truths as analytic truths or truths by virtue of meaning."[18] It is the second part of this test that makes the dependence of the ethical on the nonethical seem implausible. If the nonnaturalist were to accept the second part of this test, then he would have to hold, implausibly, that being pleased or being wise necessitates being good only because it is part of the meaning of "pleased" and "wise" that such things are good, only because "Being pleased is good" and "Being wise is good" are analytic truths. But clearly, the nonnaturalist is not committed to either part of this test and is not committed to the view that the only forms of necessity are analytic. It is clearly and plainly historically inaccurate to attribute this view to nonnaturalists such as Moore, Ross, Prichard, and Broad. Consider the following passage by C. D. Broad:

Suppose that a person regards goodness as a non-natural characteristic, and admits that it is always dependent on the presence of certain natural characteristics which are good-making. Then, if he holds that the connection between a good-making characteristic and the goodness which it confers is *necessary* he will be obliged to hold that there are *synthetically necessary* facts and that he knows some of them. . . . The necessary connection between those natural characteristics of a thing which are good-making and the goodness which their presence necessarily confers on the thing cannot be analytic. For this would involve that the *non-natural* characteristic of goodness is contained as a factor in the analysis of a purely *natural* good-making characteristic, and this would be self-contradictory.

Now people think it is self-evident that all necessary connection must be analytic and that there can be no synthetic *a priori* judgments. I do not find this principle in the least self-evident.[19]

Wise nonnaturalists have rejected, and should continue to reject, the second part of the "semantic test of properties." A defense of the claim that ethical properties and states of affairs are not identical with natural properties and states of affairs need not rest on it. The intentional criteria of identity for properties and states of affairs presented in the last section do not involve or appeal to considerations about language or the synonymy of terms, and clearly they do not presuppose that all necessity is "analytic."

17. Ibid., p. 163.
18. Ibid., p. 162.
19. C. D. Broad, "Is 'Goodness' a Name of a Simple Non-Natural Quality?", *Broad's Critical Essays in Moral Philosophy,* edited by David R. Cheney (London: George Allen & Unwin, 1971) pp. 122–3.

124

According to the traditional view of intrinsic value described at the beginning of Chapter 1, in making ordinary ethical judgments, one is accepting a distinctive ethical state of affairs or attributing such a property. One is accepting a state of affairs or attributing a property that is not identical with or analyzable by any natural property or state of affairs. If this is so, then there must be such properties or states of affairs in order for them to be accepted or attributed. This understanding of the nature of ethical belief presupposes a commitment to the existence of such ethical objects. Such a commitment, however, does not imply that any ethical states of affairs obtain or that ethical properties are exemplified. In other words, it does not imply that there are any distinctively ethical facts. But if this view of our ordinary ethical beliefs is correct and if any of our ordinary ethical beliefs are instances of knowledge, then there are distinctively ethical facts. Furthermore, if any such beliefs are epistemically justified, then we can be justified in believing that there are distinctively ethical facts. At this point, I wish to consider briefly one argument for the view that there are no distinctively ethical facts.

The argument I wish to consider maintains roughly that we have no reason to believe that there are distinctively ethical facts because such facts never play a role in explaining our ethical beliefs or observations. According to this general view, we have reasons or evidence to believe, and can be justified in believing, that there facts of a given sort only if facts of that sort play some part in a casual explanation (or the best casual explanation) of our beliefs or observations. This argument against ethical facts presupposes what we may call the "explanatory requirement." There are different ways of stating this requirement, but one may put it as follows: p is a reason to believe q only if q (or something that entails q) is part of the explanation for p.[20] The explanatory requirement appears to be met in many cases involving perception. For example, the fact that Mary has the visual experience of a table before her is a reason for Mary to believe that there is a table before her, and it seems that the fact that there is a table before her explains or is part of what explains her having this particular visual experience. According to this general view, we have reason to believe, and are justified in believing, that there are tables only because

---

20. Gilbert Harman says, "We can have evidence for hypotheses of a certain sort only if such hypotheses sometimes help explain why we observe what we observe." *The Nature of Morality* (New York: Oxford University Press, 1977), p. 13.

the existence of tables plays some role in the best causal explanation of our sensory experience of tables.

In keeping with this general view, it is argued that we can have no reason for believing that there are ethical facts, since ethical facts never appear to play any causal role in general and, more specifically, any causal role in explaining our observations or beliefs or those states that we count as reasons for belief in ethical facts. Suppose, for example, that Jane rounds the corner to see Albert set a cat afire, and she forms the belief that Albert's lighting the cat is wrong. It is argued that Jane's belief that Albert's action is wrong is no reason for her to believe that a distinctively ethical fact obtains, since we can best explain her having that belief in terms of her moral training, her psychological background, and her "background moral theory." In short, we can explain why she forms that belief without appealing to the existence of distinctive ethical facts. That she believes his action is wrong tells us something about her moral sensibility, but it is no reason to believe that there is a distinctively ethical fact. The objection claims that we have no reason to believe that there are ethical facts, since whatever would seem to count as a reason for believing in them could always best be explained by something that did not include them, such as the agent's other moral beliefs, training, and so on.

There are at least two lines of response to this argument. The first is to argue that moral facts do enter into causal explanations and that they can play a part in a causal explanation, including causal explanations of our ethical beliefs.[21] For example, one might claim that part of the explanation for the occurrence of a revolution in a society is that the distribution of goods in that society was unjust. One might argue that the fact that the society was unjust is part of the best causal explanation for the occurrence of the revolution. But such attempts are more heroic than promising, for one plausible response is that it was not the fact of injustice that caused the revolution, but the belief of the revolutionaries that the society was unjust. Alternatively, it might be said that what caused the revolution was not the fact of injustice but that wealth and income were concentrated in the hands of a few. In this case, one appeals not to a distinctively ethical fact, but to a fact about the distribution of wealth and income, and it is just a confusion to identify this fact about the distribution of wealth and income with the fact that the society is unjust. The fact that wealth and income are concentrated in the hands of a few might be the reason why the society is unjust, but they are distinct facts.

21. See Brink, *Moral Realism and the Foundations of Ethics,* pp. 182–96.

The second line of response is to reject the explanatory requirement itself. The explanatory requirement has been attacked in one form or another by Quinn, Achinstein, and Pollock. Achinstein, for example, notes that the fact that Jones has a certain chest wound and that all who have had that chest wound have died is a reason to believe that Jones will die. But the fact that Jones will die does not explain the fact that he has that chest wound or the deaths of others who have been similarly wounded.[22] Quinn writes, "The presence of a cause might support an inference to its usual effect, but the effect would not explain the cause. And if we rule out the possibility that the cause might be self-explanatory, it could be true that nothing that implies the effect explains the cause."[23] Pollock argues persuasively that the perceptual knowledge of colors cannot be modeled on inference to the best explanation. He argues that being appeared to redly can function as a reason to believe that something is red, even though something's being red is not part of the best explanation one has for one's being appeared to in that way.[24] Moreover, I think we may say that the fact that one has a throbbing headache is a reason to believe that one has a headache, but neither the fact that one has a headache nor the fact that one believes that one has a headache is an explanation for one's having a headache.

I think that the weakness of the explanatory requirement can also be brought out by reflecting on our mathematical and modal knowledge. We know both mathematical facts and modal facts. We know that 2 and 3 are 5 and that it is necessarily true that 2 and 3 are 5. Observation does not seem to play the same sort of role in our access to these facts as it does in physics. I suggest that our justification for believing such things does not depend on our observations, either directly or indirectly, and that our reasons for accepting such facts are not part of the best explanation for what we observe.

Of course, Gilbert Harman points out that we *do* have indirect observational evidence for our mathematical beliefs, and in this respect our mathematical and ethical beliefs differ:

Observation, however, *is* relevant to mathematics. In explaining the observations that support a physical theory, scientists typically appeal to mathematical principles. On the other hand, one never seems to appeal in this way to moral principles. Since an observation is evidence for what best explains it, and since mathematics

22. Peter Achinstein, "Concepts of Evidence," *Mind,* 87 (January 1978), p. 34.
23. Warren Quinn, "Truth and Explanation in Ethics," *Ethics* 96 (1986), p. 541.
24. John Pollock, *Contemporary Theories of Knowledge* (Totowa, N.J.: Rowman and Littlefield, 1986), pp. 42–4.

often figures in the explanation of scientific explanations, there is indirect observational evidence for mathematics. There does not seem to be observational evidence, even indirectly, for basic moral principles. In explaining why certain observations have been made, we never seem to use purely moral assumptions.[25]

Yet even if we do have indirect observational evidence for our mathematical beliefs, it is not plausible to believe that they are justified *only* in virtue of indirect observation. Our mathematical beliefs are not merely well-confirmed generalizations or explanatory hypotheses. Our mathematical beliefs have a level of warrant and certainty that is greater than that which could be afforded by indirect observational evidence. The belief that 2 and 3 are 5 has a certainty greater than that which could be afforded by the fact that it sometimes helps to explain what we observe. It is far more certain than any of the explanatory laws of the natural sciences. Thus, it is reasonable for us to believe that 2 and 3 are 5 quite independently of the role that mathematical fact plays in explaining my observations. Consequently, it seems that we have some evidence or reasons for accepting certain mathematical facts independently of observation and independently of their playing a part in the best explanation of what we observe. In other words, we can be justified in accepting some kinds of facts independently of their playing a causal explanatory role. If this is so, then the explanatory requirement is false.

Furthermore, we have not only mathematical knowledge, but *modal* mathematical knowledge. We know not only that 2 and 3 are 5, but also that 2 and 3 are necessarily 5. Like our mathematical beliefs, some of our modal beliefs have a level of warrant that is far greater than that which could be the product of indirect observational evidence. Just as important, though, is that it is far from clear that we can have even indirect observational evidence for some of the modal facts we know. In fact, it is hard to see how we could have such evidence, according to Harman's view. For consider any observation, O, for which we might think the modal fact that 2 and 3 are necessarily 5 is part of the explanation for our observing O. It seems that we could explain O by appealing simply to the claim that 2 and 3 are 5 or even that 2 and 3 are usually 5. Since we can explain any observation without appealing to the stronger modal claim, and since the best explanation would also seem to be the one that did not invoke the stronger modal claim, we do not have even indirect observational evidence for the modal claim. Modal facts such as that 2 and 3 are necessarily 5 never seem to be relevant to our explaining observations.

25. Harman, *The Nature of Morality*, p. 10.

But this fact hardly suggests that they cannot be known. Similar considerations pertain to our knowledge of the fact that it is impossible for anything to be red and green all over at the same time. One could surely explain the fact that one has never seen anything with both colors all over at the same time without invoking the strong modal fact that it is impossible. But, again, the fact that one can explain one's observations without appealing to that fact does not imply that one ought to be skeptical of it or that one has any reason to deny the existence of such facts.

Since we have knowledge of and justified belief in mathematical facts that do not depend on indirect observational evidence, it might turn out that our knowledge of and justified belief in ethical facts are similar to our knowledge of and justified belief in mathematical facts. In other words, our epistemic access to certain ethical facts about intrinsic value might turn out to be similar to our access to mathematical and modal facts. I say more about this is the next chapter when we consider how we might have knowledge or justified belief about intrinsic value.

NATURALISM AND ANALYSIS

Nonnaturalism about intrinsic value holds that the property of being intrinsically good and states of affairs of the form "X is intrinsically good" are not identical with or analyzable by natural properties or states of affairs. I have argued that, given certain plausible intentional criteria of identity for properties and states of affairs, it is reasonable to think that at least the first of these claims is true. But what of the second claim? I assume that it is possible for one property to be analyzed by a property that is not identical to it and for one state of affairs to be analyzed by a different state of affairs. If this is so, then the mere fact that the property of being intrinsically good is not identical with any natural property does not imply that intrinsic goodness cannot be analyzed naturalistically.

Before considering this question, it is worthwhile, I think, to make a few remarks about the relevant notion of "analysis." It is extremely difficult to say what it is for one state of affairs to be the analysis of another or for one property to be analyzed by another. I know of no completely satisfactory analysis of analysis. Still, we may take certain examples to be paradigmatic cases of analysis. Among these are the following: "A cube is a regular solid with six sides," "A square is an equilateral rectangle," and "A bachelor is an unmarried man." Each of these statements may be expressed in terms that tell us something about states of affairs or properties. For example, we may say that the state of affairs *something's being square* is analyzed by the state of affairs *something's being an equilateral rectangle*. Alternatively, we may think of analysis as involving the property of being a square and the property of being an equilateral rectangle. Thus, we may say that the property of being a square is analyzed by the property of being an equilateral rectangle.

Nonnaturalism holds that ethical states of affairs and properties cannot be analyzed in terms of natural states of affairs and properties in the sense that one cannot provide a satisfactory philosophical or analytical definition of the former in terms of the latter. This is the sense of analysis in which nonnaturalists maintain that ethical objects are unanalyzable. Of course, constitution claims may be thought to represent a form of analysis. If one can identify what parts constitute a particular horse, then one has given a kind of analysis of that horse. But this is a very different kind of analysis from an analytical definition of the property of being a horse or of states of affairs of the form "*X* is a horse."

Even if we cannot say precisely what it is for one thing to be a philosophical definition or an analysis of another, there are certain conditions that have traditionally been taken to be necessary for an analysis. Chisholm and Potter, for example, claim that an adequate philosophical analysis must satisfy three desiderata.[26] First, a satisfactory philosophical analysis should be enlightening or informative. Second, an analysis should not be circular. The analysans should not involve (as defined in D8 and D9) the analysandum. Third, the analysans must convey everything that is conveyed by the analysandum, and they must imply one another. I wish to make some comments about these conditions.

One requirement for an analysis is strict mutual implication. This condition tells us that if a state of affairs, *p*, is analyzed by a state of affairs, *q*, then *p* and *q* are necessarily such that if *p* obtains, then *q* obtains, and vice versa. *Something's being a square* and *something's being an equilateral rectangle* are necessarily such that if the one obtains, then the other obtains. With respect to properties, this condition may be taken to say that if the property *F* is analyzed by the property *G*, then the properties *F* and *G* are necessarily such that if something has *F* it has *G*, and vice versa.

It is hard to say exactly what is involved in the "enlighteningness" requirement, but an analysis tells us something informative about the thing being analyzed; it adds to or extends our knowledge of that thing. If *p* is analyzed by *q*, then *q* conveys more than *p*, is richer in content than *p*.

---

26. Roderick Chisholm and Richard Potter, "The Paradox of Analysis: A Solution," *The Foundations of Knowing* (Minneapolis: University of Minnesota Press, 1982), pp. 100–1.

Some circular "analyses" fail to meet this condition. Surely there is nothing enlightening in the suggestion that being a square is analyzed by being a square. This suggestion is not informative in the sense that it does not extend our knowledge of the property of being a square. Similarly, the following fail to be enlightening: "Being a square is being something with a square shape," "Being a square is a shape that is not anything but a sqaure," and "Being a square is having a squarish shape."

How shall we understand the requirement that the analysans convey everything conveyed by the analysandum? Some philosophers, including Chisholm and Potter, have suggested that there must be some sort of *intentional* connection between the analysans and the analysandum. There are different ways, however, of construing this intentional connection. One might suggest, for instance, that the analysans and the analysandum are necessarily such that whoever entertains the former entertains the latter. Unfortunately, this does not seem very promising, since it seems that one can entertain the state of affairs *something's being a regular solid with six sides* without entertaining *something's being a cube*. Alternatively, one might say that whoever accepts or attributes the analysans accepts or attributes the analysandum. This is somewhat better, yet even here it is not entirely clear that whoever accepts *something's being a regular solid with six sides* accepts *something's being a cube*.

The most reasonable construal of the intentional connection is, I think, that whoever *grasps* the analysans *grasps* the analysandum. One can grasp a state of affairs or property without entertaining or accepting or attributing it. I am now entertaining the state of affairs *something's being a mermaid,* but five minutes ago I grasped that state of affairs without accepting or entertaining it. To understand the intentional connection in terms of grasping is, I think, to take a comparatively weak interpretation of that requirement, since, for example, one can grasp a state of affairs without entertaining or accepting it, but one cannot entertain or accept a state of affairs without grasping it. Therefore, these stronger interpretations in terms of entertaining or accepting apparently presuppose the notion of grasping. Thus, if one does think that there must be an intentional connection between the analysans and the analysandum, it is hard to see what weaker and more likely connection there could be. Finally, there is, I think, a certain intuitive plausibility behind this interpretation of the intentional connection. To say that the analysans must convey everything conveyed by the analysandum is to say that whoever grasps the analysans grasps the analysandum. Thus, whoever grasps, say, the property of being a regular solid with six sides grasps the property of being a cube. It is

131

reasonable to think that once someone has grasped what it is for something to be a regular solid with six sides, they have grasped the property of being a cube. Similarly, to have grasped what it is to be an unmarried man is to grasp the property of being a bachelor.

Let us return to traditional naturalism and intrinsic value. Suppose we assume that an analysans and an analysandum are such that whoever grasps the former grasps the latter. Given this assumption, states of affairs of the form "*X* is intrinsically good" are analyzable by some natural state of affairs only if the latter is necessarily such that whoever grasps it grasps the former. Thus, the state of affairs *something's being intrinsically good* is analyzable by *something's being pleasant* only if it is impossible for anyone to grasp the latter without grasping the former. Now it seems to me that in reflecting on this particular proposal, it *is* possible for someone to grasp *something's being pleasant* without grasping *something's being intrinsically good*. It seems possible that young children can take things to be pleasant without grasping the property of being intrinsically good or any states of affairs to the effect that something is intrinsically good. The same is true of properties such as being desired, being desired by some group, or being desired by someone fully informed. It is possible that someone could grasp these properties without grasping the property of being intrinsically good.

Unfortunately, this line of argument is not as persuasive as the non-naturalist might hope for at least two reasons. First, even if we assume that we have got the intentional connection right, intuitions about whether one can grasp one property or state of affairs without grasping another will often differ. It is not clear how to resolve such conflicting intuitions. Of course, such conflicts cut both ways. For if we have got the intentional connection right, then it is unclear how one could *show* that the unanalyzability thesis is false without showing that one of such conflicting intuitions is false. Second, this line of argument presupposes a particular understanding of analysis, an understanding that is not uncontroversial. Still, the notion of analysis is a philosophically difficult concept, and it is unlikely that any argument that appeals to the requirements of an analysis beyond mutual implication and lack of circularity could be uncontroversial. Even if they are controversial, the requirements for an analysis and the interpretation of the intentional connection presented here are, I think, defensible.

Let us take a more straightforward approach to the unanalyzability thesis. Consider states of affairs of the form "*X* is intrinsically better than *Y*,"(1). Is there some natural state of affairs that mutually implies (1) and that is enlightening enough to be an analysis of it? One way of assessing the unanalyzability thesis is to consider various proposed analyses and ask whether there is a mutual implication between intrinsic value, or states of affairs like (1), and a given natural state of affairs that is enlightening enough to be a plausible analysis. If on reflection we find that it is not reasonable to believe that there is such an implication, then it is reasonable for us to believe that we have not found a satisfactory analysis. And if, after considering a variety of such proposals, we find none that strike us as plausible, then we shall have some reason to believe that the unanalyzability thesis is true. Of course, even if we do find that there is a mutual implication between something's having intrinsic value or between (1) and some nonethical state of affairs, it will not follow that the unanalyzability thesis is false, since mutual implication is not sufficient for an analysis. In this respect, the test of mutual implication is only a negative test that tells when a proposed analysis is not acceptable.

Writers such Moore and Ross have already soundly and thoroughly criticized many naturalistic analyses. Indeed, Moore's *Ethics* and Ross's *The Right and the Good* contain far more thorough discussions of a wider variety of naturalistic analyses than I could present, and many of the criticisms I would make would be familiar to careful readers of Moore and Ross. Unfortunately, such readers seem rare these days. Although it does not hurt to cover old ground, it is often tiresome to linger there too long, so I have relegated a discussion of various naturalistic analyses to Appendix B and have sought to keep my remarks there brief, considering only some of the more common and popular proposals that, like bad pennies, keep turning up.

8

Intrinsic value and modest a priori justification

In the last chapter, it was claimed that in making an ordinary judgment that something is intrinsically good, one is attributing to it the property of being intrinsically good, or accepting a state of affairs of the form "X is intrinsically good." It was argued that it is reasonable for us to believe that this property and such states of affairs are not identical with or analyzable by any natural state of affairs or property. The ontological distinctiveness of intrinsic value is one of the theses of the traditional view set forth in Chapter 1. But a further claim, central to that tradition, is that there is knowledge that some things are intrinsically good, some bad, and some better than others. The claim that we have such knowledge is accepted by philosophers such as Brentano, Moore, and Ross, though it is not clear that they agree about *how* we have it or what is the nature of such knowledge.

PRELIMINARY REMARKS AND ASSUMPTIONS

I begin, however, by stating four general assumptions about the nature of epistemic justification or warrant and two more specific assumptions about justified belief in intrinsic value. Let us begin with the general assumptions. First, I assume that there is a difference between justified belief and true belief. The set of one's justified beliefs need not be identical with the set of one's true beliefs. If a person makes a lucky guess about the outcome of a horse race, forming a belief about the winner on the advice of his tea leaf reader, his belief might be true but unjustified. Similarly, if Jones believes that Brown is a thief simply because Jones dislikes Brown, then Jones's belief might be true even if it is unjustified. On the other hand, a person might have strong evidence that Jones is a thief and be justified in believing that he is a thief even if that belief is false. Thus, I assume that it is possible for a justified belief to be false and for a true belief to be unjustified. Still, there is a positive relation between epistemic justification

134

and truth. Though the precise nature of this relation is difficult to formulate, one may say roughly that if one wants to believe what is true and not to believe what is false, then the most reasonable thing to do is to believe what is justified and not to believe what is unjustified.[1]

Second, some beliefs are more justified for a person at a certain time than others. For example, I am now more justified in believing that I am in a room with a desk than that the pope is in Rome. The fact that it is more reasonable for a person to believe one thing rather than another is not the same as the degree of confidence with which he might hold a belief. Even if I were now more confident that the pope is in Rome, even if I felt more sure of this claim, it would be no more reasonable for me to believe. The degree of conviction in a proposition does not necessarily reflect the reasonableness of believing that proposition.

Third, the sort of justification with which I am concerned is *epistemic* justification. There can be nonepistemic forms of justification and nonepistemic reasons for belief. For example, a sick man might have prudential and moral justification for believing that his condition will improve if adopting such an optimistic attitude will cause his condition to improve. Similarly, the chances of a baseball player getting a hit might improve if he believes that he will succeed. But the fact that one has prudential or moral reasons for believing something does not imply that he has epistemic reasons for believing it. My concern is with epistemic justification and not prudential or moral justification.

Fourth, there is a difference between a belief's being justified and justifying a belief. The latter is an activity in which one engages, usually when the truth of one's belief has been challenged. Being justified, however, is simply to be in a certain sort of state. This is an important distinction, for one can be justified in believing something without having tried to justify it to anyone. Indeed, most of our justified beliefs are such that we have never attempted to justify them. Thus, when we ask what it is that justifies a person in believing that something is intrinsically good, we are not asking how that person would justify that belief to himself or another. We are not asking how one might *prove, show,* or *demonstrate* that something is intrinsically good. We are not asking how one might convince or persuade someone else that it is intrinsically good. And we are not asking how one came to hold the belief that it is intrinsically good.

In addition to these four assumptions about the general nature of epi-

1. Roderick Chisholm, *The Foundations of Knowing* (Minneapolis: University of Minnesota Press, 1982), p. 4.

stemic justification, I shall now make two more specific assumptions regarding justified belief about intrinsic value. I assume (1) that there *is* knowledge and justified belief about intrinsic value and (2) that there *is* knowledge and justified belief that there is knowledge and justified belief about intrinsic value. In other words, I am assuming that some people know, for example, that some things are intrinsically good *and* that they know that they know such things. If we take "radical value skepticism" to be the position that there is no knowledge about intrinsic value and no epistemically justified attributions of intrinsic value, then I am assuming that radical value skepticism is false. The task of this chapter is *not* to show or demonstrate that such value skepticism is false. In asking "What justifies someone in believing, for example, that pleasure is intrinsically better than pain?", we are not asking how one might show or demonstrate than it is better. The task with which I am concerned is perhaps best construed in terms of trying to answer the question "Given that we do know that such things as pleasure are intrinsically better than pain, how do we know them?" Alternatively, we might ask, "Given that it is reasonable for us to believe such a thing, what makes it reasonable for us to believe it?" or "What account can we give of the nature of such knowledge?"

In investigating our knowledge of intrinsic value, it is wise to recall Moore's observation: "We are all, I think, in this strange position that we do *know* many things, with regard to which we *know* further that we must have evidence for them, and yet we do not know *how* we know them."[2] Even if the attempt to discover what justifies beliefs about intrinsic value is unsuccessful, even if we cannot discover what justifies such beliefs, it hardly follows that we have no justified beliefs about intrinsic value. Whether we have justified beliefs about intrinsic value is quite independent of our having a satisfactory, correct epistemic theory about what makes those beliefs justified. In this respect, beliefs about intrinsic value are no different from beliefs about ordinary physical objects. One can have justified beliefs about tables, chairs, and trees without knowing what makes those beliefs justified, without knowing the warrant-making properties of such beliefs or having a correct epistemic theory. Were this not so, then, of two epistemologists with incompatible epistemic theories concerning what justifies such beliefs, at most one of them could have justified beliefs about physical objects. But surely some philosophers who have mistaken epistemic theories know, and are justified in believing, that there are tables

---

2. G. E. Moore, "A Defense of Common Sense," *Philosophical Studies* (London: Routledge & Kegan Paul, 1922), p. 44.

and chairs. Furthermore, young children and some animals know things about the world without having any theory about what justifies their beliefs. Indeed, they may not even have the concepts of justification or knowledge. The task, then, of ascertaining what justifies our beliefs about intrinsic value should not be seen as one that must be completed before one can know or have justified beliefs about it. And it must not be assumed that failure in this task implies that we have no such justified beliefs or that skepticism toward beliefs about intrinsic value is the reasonable epistemic stance.

Not only is our having justified belief about intrinsic value and physical objects independent of our having a satisfactory account of what makes those beliefs justified, the lack of such an account does not preclude our knowing and having justified beliefs to the effect that we do have justified beliefs about intrinsic value and physical objects. Just as one can know that there are tables and chairs without knowing what justifies that belief, one can also know that he knows that there are tables and chairs without knowing what justifies this higher-order epistemic belief. One can have this sort of epistemic knowledge and justified beliefs about one's epistemic states without being an epistemologist. Even an epistemologist, mistaken about what justifies his belief that there are tables and chairs, can be justified in believing that he is justified in believing that there are tables and chairs. Discovering what justifies our beliefs about intrinsic value is not, therefore, something one must do in order to be justified in believing that one is justified in believing that certain things are intrinsically valuable.

Someone might object at this point: "What is the point of this investigation, of asking these questions about justification, if we are already assuming that we have knowledge about intrinsic value?" In response, we may say that one reason for asking what justifies our beliefs about intrinsic value is that finding an answer will satisfy the intellectual interest in what distinguishes justifies belief from blind prejudices and mere lucky guesses. Inquiry into the sources and nature of justification is as reasonable as any other inquiry motivated by common philosophical curiosity. It is reason enough that, as a popular tabloid proclaims, inquiring minds want to know.

But a second reason is that critics of the view that there are ontologically distinctive ethical properties have often maintained that there is no plausible account of how these distinctive ethical objects can be known. John Mackie, for example, maintains that anyone who claims knowledge or justified belief about distinctive ethical properties and states of affairs is ultimately committed to some form of ethical intuitionism, a view that he takes to imply the implausible thesis that we have a "faculty of moral intuition." William Frankena writes that the nonnaturalist in ethics is committed to the view that basic normative and evaluative judgments, particular or general, "are self-evident and can only be known by intuition; this follows, it is maintained, from the fact that the properties involved are simple and non-natural."[3]

If our ordinary ethical beliefs about intrinsic value involve a commitment to the reality of distinctive ethical objects, and if the view that such beliefs are justified involves a commitment to an implausible epistemic picture, then the reality of such distinctive ethical objects would certainly be suspect. But I argue that the cognitivist about such objects is not committed to an implausible account, to a faculty of moral intuition, or to the claim that basic ethical judgments must be self-evident. Some cognitivists about value maintain that some general truths about value are known a priori, and from these, other facts are deduced in conjunction with nonethical premises. But this claim commits one to no faculty of moral intuition any more than the claim that there are *modal* facts commits one to the claim that there is a faculty of modal intuition. The development, then, of a plausible answer to the question of what justifies our beliefs about intrinsic value, where those beliefs are understood to presuppose a commitment to the reality of distinctive ethical properties and states of affairs, will thus serve to forestall one sort of criticism of the view that there are such properties and states of affairs and that we know them.

One way to develop a plausible account of the warrant-making or justification-making properties of beliefs about intrinsic value is to present and defend an account in which the sorts of properties that confer warrant on beliefs about intrinsic value are not radically different from the sorts of properties that confer warrant on other types of justified belief. In other words, it is to present and defend an account of the warrant-conferring properties of beliefs about intrinsic value that reveals that those properties are no more mysterious, queer, or problematic than the sorts of properties that confer warrant on other beliefs.

Still, the following basic argument is faced by anyone who accepts the view that there is knowledge or justified belief about distinctive ethical properties, states of affairs, and facts (*distinctive* in the sense that they are not identical with or analyzable by natural properties, states of affairs, or facts). Beliefs about these objects are justified either a priori or empirically

3. William Frankena, *Ethics,* 2nd edition (Englewood Cliffs, N.J.: Prentice-Hall, 1973), p. 103.

or a posteriori. Beliefs about these objects do not seem to be justified either a priori or empirically. But if these judgments cannot be justified either a priori or empirically, then it seems that they are not really justified at all. Consequently, even if there are distinctive ethical properties, states of affairs, and facts, we can have no justified beliefs about them and no knowledge of them. If this is so, then ethical skepticism is true.

I argue that some basic ethical beliefs, including some beliefs about intrinsic value, can be justified or reasonable for us to believe a priori. Now whether it is reasonable to think that there are moral beliefs justified a priori depends in part on our understanding of a priori justification. In the next section, I consider Roderick Chisholm's account of a priori knowledge and justification and the problems that it poses for a priori moral knowledge. Chisholm's account is a fairly standard and traditional one that takes basic or foundational a priori knowledge to be certain and indefeasible. This is a strong conception of a priori knowledge and justification, and it poses some severe problems for the view that we have ethical beliefs justified a priori. In the sections that follow, I defend the existence of modest a priori justification, that is, beliefs that are justified a priori but that are neither certain nor indefeasible. I argue that the existence of moral beliefs justified a priori is more plausible if we allow ourselves the notion of modest a priori justification.

A STRONG CONCEPTION OF A PRIORI KNOWLEDGE

Let us begin by considering the view of a priori knowledge developed by Roderick Chisholm in the third edition of *Theory of Knowledge*. Chisholm explicates his view of a priori knowledge through a series of definitions.

(D12)   *h* is an *axiom* = *Df.* h is necessarily such that (1) it is true and (2) for every *S*, if *S* accepts *h*, then *h* is certain for *S*.[4]

Given this definition, the following propositions may be said to be axioms: *all men are men; if some Greeks are men, then some men are Greeks;* and *all rounds things have a shape.* Chisholm says that for those who really *do* consider these propositions, they may be said to be *axiomatic* in the following sense:

4. Roderick M. Chisholm, *Theory of Knowledge,* 3rd edition (Englewood Cliffs, N.J.: Prentice-Hall, 1989), p. 28.

(D13) *h* is *axiomatic* for *S* = *Df.* (i) *h* is an axiom and (ii) *S* accepts *h*.[5]

Our a priori knowledge is not limited to what is axiomatic for us, for we know some things a priori because we can see that they follow from what is axiomatic for us. The Pythagorean theorem is not axiomatic for us, but we can know it a priori. Chisholm says that we can capture this broader notion of a priori as follows:

(D14) *h* is *known a priori* by *S* = *Df.* There is an *e* such that (1) *e* is axiomatic for *S*, (2) the proposition, *e* implies *h*, is axiomatic for *S*, and (3) *S* accepts *h*.[6]

If we understand a priori knowledge this way, then everything we know a priori is either axiomatic for us or we know it follows from something we know with certainty and something that is axiomatic for us. This conception of a priori knowledge may be said to have a foundational structure. Those things that are axiomatic for us are at the foundation, and everything else we know a priori rests on what is axiomatic for us.

This is a very strong conception of a priori knowledge. It is strong in two ways: first, in its account of the foundation, and second, in its account of the links between the foundation and the rest of what is known a priori. Let us consider first the description of the foundation. There are two features of the foundation that make it very strong. First, according to this account, foundational or "basic" a priori knowledge is certain. What is axiomatic for us is certain for us, and certainty is the highest level of epistemic warrant. It follows from this view that if any proposition, *h*, is less than certain for us, then our knowledge that *h* is not foundational or basic a priori knowledge. It also follows that if *h* is not certain, yet is known a priori, then our knowledge that *h* must rest on something that is axiomatic and certain for us. Second, foundational a priori knowledge is indefeasible. It is indefeasible in the sense that there is nothing that one could come to know, experience, or be justified in believing that would undercut or defeat one's justification for believing what is axiomatic. This character of indefeasibility follows from the definitions of what it is for something to be an axiom and for something to be axiomatic. Recall that if *h* is an axiom, then *h* is necessarily such that if *S* accepts *h*, then *h* is certain for *S*. If this is so, then as long as *S* accepts *h*, there is nothing that *S* can know, experience, or become justified in believing that will make *S* not justified in believing *h*. Of course, the Chisholmian definitions of an axiom and the axiomatic leave open the possibility that *S* might simply

5. Ibid., p. 28.
6. Ibid., p. 29.

stop believing *h*. Now suppose that there is some information that *S* might come to have that causes *S* to quit believing *h*. Would this be enough to show that *S's* justification in believing *h* is defeasible? No, for not just anything that causes a person to quit believing something he is otherwise justified in believing defeats his justification. A sharp rap on the head can cause a person to quit believing something without being a reason to do so. Moreover, people can sometimes quit believing things they are justified in believing on the basis of things that are *bad* reasons, which do not defeat their original justification. Consequently, even if there are some things that a person might come to know or believe that will cause him to stop believing an axiom, it does not follow that this justification for accepting that proposition is defeasible.

In addition to requiring that foundational a priori knowledge be certain and indefeasible, the supporting links between the foundations and the rest of what we know a priori are quite strong. In order to have some nonfoundational bit of a priori knowledge, *h*, there must be some proposition, *e*, that is axiomatic for *S*, and it must be axiomatic for *S* that *e* implies *h*. The nonfoundational bits of a priori knowledge are thus connected, by logical implication, to the foundation, and this is a very tight connection. We may contrast this view of the supporting links with certain foundational views of empirical knowledge that take propositions about the way one is appeared to as foundational. On these views, the acceptance of various propositions about the way one is appeared to provide evidence for or support beliefs about external, physical objects without logically implying the existence of such objects. For example, one might hold that the belief that one is appeared to in a whitish, roundish way provides some evidence for or supports one's belief that there is a white, round object before one. Such a belief provides support for the belief that there is a white, round object before one even though the propositional object of the former does not imply the object of the latter. The account of a priori knowledge presented earlier forecloses the possibility of such nondeductive support for those bits of a priori knowledge outside the foundation.

Conceiving of a priori knowledge in this way sets a very high standard for a priori knowledge in both epistemology and ethics. Still, it is plausible to think that there might be some ethical and epistemic propositions that are known a priori. Candidates for such status are "If an action is obligatory, then it is permissible," "If *A* is intrinsically better than *B*, then *B* is not intrinsically better than *A*," and "If it is more reasonable for *S* to believe *p* than withhold *p*, then it is more reasonable for *S* to believe *p* than not-*p*." We might call such principles "formal" principles. However, more interesting principles would be "substantive" or "material" principles that tell us under what conditions an action is right, a belief is justified, or what sorts of things are intrinsically good. Consider the various epistemic principles, asserted by various philosophers, that describe the conditions under which a belief is justified. An example of such a principle might be *If S has a vivid experience of blue, and S has no reason to doubt that there is something blue before him, then it is reasonable for him to believe that there is something blue before him.* Such a principle can be thought of as an epistemically evaluative principle, since it tells us that beliefs of a certain sort have the favorable status of being reasonable. Just as ethical principles tell us the right-making or good-making properties of things, these epistemic principles tell us the justification-making or warrant-making properties of a belief. Even philosophers who are sympathetic to the existence of a priori knowledge seem to disagree on whether such principles are known a priori. Robert Audi states: "I believe that it is more reasonable, though by no means obviously correct, to suppose that at least some principles about the conditions for justification are a priori."[7] In contrast to Audi, Chisholm claims: "it would not be plausible to say that they are a priori since many philosophers have understood them without seeing that they are true."[8]

Given the strong conception of a priori knowledge set forth earlier, there is good reason to think that such epistemic principles are not known a priori. This is because they are not axiomatic for us, and thus not foundational bits of a priori knowledge, nor do they seem likely candidates for nonfoundational examples of a priori knowledge. Given the strong conception of a priori knowledge, such principles are not foundational for two reasons. First, if such principles were axiomatic for us, then they would be certain for us. But they are not certain for us and, therefore, they are not axiomatic for us. Very few who have thought about such principles would claim that they are known with certainty, and surely they are not as reasonable for us to accept as such things as *all men are men* or *2 = 2*. Second, even if we accept such principles, we do not typically regard our justification for believing them as indefeasible. Even while accepting them, we remain open to the existence of counterexamples and other forms of argument against them. Our practice is to examine such

7. Robert Audi, *Belief, Justification, and Knowledge* (Belmont, Calif.: Wadsworth Publishing Co., 1988), p. 154.
8. Chisholm, *Theory of Knowledge,* p. 72.

things and look for defeating considerations. In practice, we do not treat them as indefeasible.

Since such principles are neither axiomatic nor certain, and since we do not take them to be indefeasible, the strong account must hold that they are not bits of foundational a priori knowledge. Could they be known a priori yet simply outside the foundation of things that are axiomatic for us? This seems unlikely. In order for them to be known in this way, it would have to be the case that there is some e that is axiomatic for us and such that it is axiomatic for us that e implies the epistemic principles in question. But since there appears to be no axiomatic implication between such principles and anything axiomatic for us, it appears that such principles are not instances of nonfoundational a priori knowledge.

The difficulty in holding that we have a priori knowledge of epistemic principles has, not surprisingly, its analogue for ethical principles and various value claims. Ethical principles, such as the principle of utility or the Kantian principle that we should treat rational beings as ends, can be taken to describe the conditions under which certain kinds of actions are right or obligatory. Such principles can be viewed as the ethical counterparts of those epistemic principles that tell us under what conditions certain beliefs are justified or reasonable. Yet neither the principle of utility, nor the Kantian principle, nor any variation of them is axiomatic. None of these principles enjoys the genuine certainty of *all men are men* or *2 = 2*. Furthermore, most philosophers who take such principles seriously still remain open to the possibility of counterexamples and counterarguments and do not take their acceptance of them to be indefeasible. Consequently, such principles do not seem to be any more foundationally a priori than their epistemic counterparts. Nor do they seem any more plausibly construed as nonfoundationally a priori. It is not clear that there is any proposition that is axiomatic for us and that axiomatically implies any variation of the principle of utility or the "person-as-ends" principle. We simply do not have a "geometrical" demonstration of either.

If, on the strong view of the a priori, there is to be a priori ethical knowledge, it is more likely to be found at the level of prima facie moral principles and in claims about intrinsic value. Principles such as "The keeping of promises is prima facie right" or "It is prima facie wrong to act unjustly" are at least initially plausible candidates for axioms, as are value claims such as "Pleasure, as such, is intrinsically good" and "It is intrinsically better to be wise and happy than foolish and miserable." If, on the strong view, such principles are known a priori, then they are, I suggest, more plausible thought of as foundationally a priori or as axiomatic for those who really do consider them. I think that this is so because it is not clear that there is something that is axiomatic for us and that axiomatically implies any of these propositions. It is not clear that we know these sorts of things because we see that they are implied by things that are axiomatic for us.

In any case, if we assume that such propositions are not nonfoundationally a priori, are they plausibly taken to be axioms? We might say of these claims what Chisholm says of certain epistemic principles, namely, that "it would not be plausible to say that they are a priori since many philosophers have understood them without seeing that they are true." But more precisely, it is simply not clear that such claims enjoy the certainty or the indefeasibility of axioms. It is not obvious that they enjoy the certainty of $2 = 2$ or *all dogs are dogs*. Furthermore, anyone who thinks that there just might be a counterexample or a sound, persuasive argument against these principles believes that they might be defeasible, that one might come to be justified in believing something that would undercut one's justification for believing them. I will not argue that these propositions are not axioms or axiomatic for those who accept them. I do believe that there is reason to doubt that they enjoy this status because there is reason to doubt that they meet demanding requirements for a priori knowledge described above.

MODEST A PRIORI KNOWLEDGE AND JUSTIFICATION

The problems described previously for a priori justification of certain epistemic and ethical propositions arise if we assume that basic or foundational a priori justification must be certain and that our justification for accepting them is indefeasible. But why should we make this assumption? What justifies us in believing such a thing? This claim is not itself something that is axiomatic or certain for us. It does not enjoy the certainty of $2 = 2$ or *all men are men*. Moreover, it does not seem to follow from anything that is axiomatic or certain for us. Consequently, given the notion of a priori knowledge considered previously, the claim that basic a priori knowledge and justification are certain and indefeasible would not itself appear to be something known a priori. If the claim that basic a priori justification is certain and indefeasible is not something that is known a priori, perhaps it is known on the basis of induction. For example, one might claim that every known instance of basic a priori justification is certain and has an indefeasible justification, and therefore it is reasonable for us to assume that all basic a priori justification has the same character. But this sort of argument simply begs the question against those who would claim that there can be basic a priori justification that is not certain and whose warrant is not indefeasible. One might, of course, stipulate that one is going to use the terms "basic a priori knowledge" and "basic a priori justification" so that basic a priori justification refers only to what is certain and indefeasible. But it is not clear why anyone should accept such a stipulation.

In contrast with the strong view of a priori knowledge and justification described earlier, other philosophers have held that a priori justification need not be certain or indefeasible. For example, A. C. Ewing writes, "Many philosophers have preferred to limit the term 'intuition' to cases of certain knowledge, but there are many cases where something presents itself to one intuitively as deserving a certain degree of credence but falling short of certainty or where an intuition has some value but is confused and inextricably blended with erroneous assumptions and inferences."[9] According to Ewing, there are some things that we are immediately and noninferentially justified in believing, independently of experience, that are "deserving of a certain degree of credence less than certainty." Moreover, Ewing holds that the warrant these basic beliefs enjoy is not indefeasible. Concerning these basic a priori beliefs, he writes, "Arguments may well be available which without strictly proving either side to be wrong put a disputant into a position in which he can see better for himself whether he is right or wrong or at least cast doubt on the truth of his view."[10] We can, he says, ask whether these beliefs "fit into a clear and coherent system with the rest or our well-established beliefs."[11] If they do not, then presumably the degree of credence they enjoy would be less than if they did cohere.

Other philosophers have held that a priori justification can be undercut or defeated by the testimony or authority of others. Thomas Reid, for example, asks us to consider the case of a man having completed a mathematical demonstration. "He commits his demonstration to the examination of a mathematical friend, who he esteems a competent judge, and waits with impatience the issue of his judgment. Here I would ask again, Whether the verdict of his friend, according as it has been favorable or

9. A. C. Ewing, *The Fundamental Questions of Philosophy* (London: Routledge & Kegan Paul, 1951), p. 49.
10. Ibid., pp. 50–1.
11. Ibid., p. 50.

unfavorable, will not greatly increase or diminish confidence in his own judgment? Most certain it will, and it ought."[12] On Reid's view, the level of warrant the man's belief enjoys can be affected by the testimony of his friend. Even though he might have a priori grounds for accepting the conclusion, the warrant these grounds confer on the conclusion can be defeated or undercut by the testimony of another. This example of Reid's focuses on the nonbasic a priori justification one has for believing the conclusion of an argument. But he apparently holds that the agreement or disagreement of others who are reasonably believed to be otherwise reliable might also be relevant to the level of warrant one has for a non-inferential a priori warrant. Reid asks, "But is it not possible, that men who really love truth, and are open to conviction, may differ about first principles?"[13] According to Reid, honest disagreement about first principles is possible. He says, "A man of candour and humility will, in such a case, very naturally suspect his own judgment, so far as to be desirous to enter into a serious examination, even of what he has long held as a first principle."[14] When such honest disagreement exists, Reid appears to hold that it is not only natural but appropriate for us to be suspicious of our own judgment. I take him to hold that knowledge of such honest disagreement lowers the credence we ought to place in that judgment.

Recently, Donna Summerfield has defended what she calls "modest" a priori knowledge and justification. Someone has modest a priori justification for believing p if he has an a priori justification for believing p and that justification is defeasible. Summerfield holds that a priori justification must be justification that is "independent of experience," but central to her defense of modest a priori justification is a distinction between two ways in which the justification for a belief can be independent of experience. She writes:

the apriorist's claim that X has some beliefs that are warranted independently of their relations to experience is ambiguous as between (1) At t, X has some warranted beliefs whose warrant does not, at t, depend on, in the sense that it derives from, the warrant of any empirical belief(s) X has at t or the warrant provided by any experiences X has at or before t, and (2) X has some warranted beliefs which would (other things equal) remain warranted no matter what other empirical beliefs X forms and no matter what other experiences X undergoes.[15]

12. Thomas Reid, *Essays on the Intellectual Powers of Man* (Cambridge, Mass.: MIT Press, 1969), Essay VI, Chapter IV, p. 610.
13. Ibid., Essay VI, Chapter IV, p. 603.
14. Ibid., Essay VI, Chapter IV, pp. 603–4.
15. Donna M. Summerfield, "Modest a Priori Knowledge," *Philosophy and Phenomenological Research* 51 (March 1991), p. 42.

As Summerfield points out, "To hold (2) is to hold that there are some beliefs that are indefeasible in the face of experience, but to hold (1) is to hold something much weaker. And yet, (1) articulates a perfectly good sense in which a belief might be warranted independently of experience."[16] According to Summerfield, (1) provides us with a sense in which X's belief that p might have a warrant that is independent of experience *even if* there are possible experiences that X might have that would defeat X's warrant for believing p. In such a case, X's warrant for believing that p depends *negatively* on one's not having the defeating experiences, but it does not depend *positively* on one's experiences or empirical beliefs. Summerfield cites the following analogy by Robert Audi to illustrate the difference between positive and negative dependence:

> when one takes a walk in Washington Square, one's safety depends on one's not being harmed by certain ruffians who are several miles away stalking Central Park, but could have been stalking Washington Square. This is not obviously false, and if one has very high standards for applying the term "safety", one may accept it. But it is perfectly reasonable to say that one's safety on a walk in Washington Square depends simply on what is happening there – or relevantly near there – at the time.[17]

Perhaps we might also illustrate the difference between positive and negative dependence by considering X's justified belief that there is something red before him. X's justification might depend positively on X's experience of something red before him, say, his being appeared to redly, and negatively on his not being justified in believing that he has an eye disease that causes yellow things to appear red to him or his not being justified in believing that there is a red light shining on a white object in his visual field. If X were justified in believing that he has such an eye disease, then his warrant for believing that there is something red before him would be defeated, so the warrant for his belief depends negatively on his not having that defeating belief. But there is intuitively a difference between the way his warrant for believing that there is something red before him depends on his visual experience and his not having this defeating belief. One difference is that his visual experience is a reason for him to believe that there is something red before him, but this is not true of his not being justified in believing that he has an eye disease. Not being justified in believing that one has an eye disease is not a positive reason to believe

16. Ibid., p. 42.
17. Robert Audi, "Foundationalism, Epistemic Dependence, and Defeasibility," *Synthese* 55 (April 1983), p. 131.

that there is something red before him. I shall say more about the notion of reasons and defeaters later.

Can there be a priori justification that is defeasible? Summerfield thinks that some a priori justified beliefs can be defeated by certain sorts of experiences. Among other examples, she considers the following. Suppose that Claudia, an excellent mathematician, undergoes a psychological process of producing a proof of a theorem and comes thereby to believe the theorem. We may suppose that Claudia is justified in believing the theorem. But we can also imagine bizarre counterfactual scenarios in which "leading members of the mathematical community perversely persuade Claudia that her proving abilities are substandard."[18] If Claudia is convinced by these malicious major mathematicians, then the warrant for her believing the theorem is defeated, and she is not justified in believing the theorem. Summerfield's point is that in the actual situation, in the absence of these defeating experiences, Claudia is justified in believing the theorem and her justification is a priori. Claudia's justification for believing the theorem depends positively on her coming to have the belief through a reliable process and negatively on her not having the defeating experiences. Insofar as the warrant for her belief depends on the particular process in question, it is warranted independently of experience in the sense of (1) earlier and so counts as a priori justification.

In considering whether a priori justification is defeasible we might also consider belief in various propositions that lead to Russell's paradoxes. Consider, for example, the proposition: For every property, P, there exists a set, S, such that X is a member of S if and only if X has P. Once we recognize that this proposition leads to paradoxes, we have reasons not to accept it, but could one be justified in believing it *before* discovering the paradoxes? It seems that there is no reason to deny that one could have reason to believe it and be justified in accepting it prior to discovering its paradoxical implications. Indeed, it is because the proposition has an intuitive plausibility, a "ring of truth to it," that the discovery of the paradoxes is so very startling. If, prior to the discovery of the paradoxes, one is justified in believing this proposition, then it seems plausible that one's reason for believing the proposition and one's justification for believing it are a priori (assuming, for example, that one did not accept it merely on the basis of another's testimony). If this is so, then some a priori reasons and justifications are defeasible. One difference between this sort of case and that described earlier by Summerfield is that the defeating consider-

18. Summerfield, "Modest a Priori Knowledge," p. 50.

148

ations are not empirical and do not involve doubts about the reliability of one's rational faculties. If this sort of case is plausible, then it shows that a priori justification can be defeated by other things one is justified in believing a priori, and not simply by empirically justified beliefs or doubts about the reliability of one's rational powers. In short, a priori justification can be defeated by beliefs justified either a priori or empirically.

If the preceding considerations are sound, then the strong view of a priori knowledge and justification presented in the last section is too strong. It sets too high a standard for a priori knowledge and justification in requiring that such knowledge and justification be indefeasible. In addition, it seems to set too high a standard in requiring that foundationally justified a priori beliefs be certain. There are several reasons to question such a stringent standard. First, there is simply no obvious reason why we should think that every foundationally justified or basic a priori belief must be certain, that it must enjoy the highest possible level of epistemic warrant. It is worth noting that the view that basic or foundational *empirical* beliefs must be certain has been challenged by other philosophers.[19] Second, if one could have basic or foundational a priori justification in believing one of the propositions that leads to Russell's paradoxes, there is no reason to think that one must also be certain that it is true. Prior to the discovery of the paradox, one might be justified a priori in believing the proposition, but all that this entails is that the proposition has some positive epistemic status, not that it be as reasonable to believe as *all men are men* or $2 + 2 = 4$. Third, if some beliefs can be justified a priori and be defeasible, this seems to be incompatible with their being certain. To see this, consider the following argument. If some proposition, p, is certain for X, then there is no other belief that it is more reasonable for X to have. But if p is certain for X at t, then X's holding p at t will be at least as reasonable for X to hold as any alleged defeating proposition, d, and at least as reasonable as the epistemic proposition that d is a defeater for p. But if it is as reasonable for X to hold p at t as it is for X to hold d and d is a defeater for p, then it seems that there is no compelling reason for X to give up X's belief in p. In such a case, there would be nothing unreasonable about X's continuing to believe p even when confronted with d and with the fact that d is a defeater for p. But if there is nothing unreasonable about X's continuing to believe p when confronted with d, then

19. See Mark Pastin, "Modest Foundationalism and Self-Warrant," *Essays on Knowledge and Justification*, edited by George S. Pappas and Marshall Swain (Ithaca, N.Y.: Cornell University Press, 1978), p. 280.

d cannot be a defeater, since a defeater would make it unreasonable for *X* to believe *p*. Consequently, it seems that if some proposition is defeasible, then it cannot be certain. Thus, if *X* has an a priori, yet defeasible, justification for believing that *p*, then *p* is not certain for *X*.

If the arguments of this section are sound, then the concept of modest a priori knowledge and justification ought to be taken seriously. Beliefs that enjoy modest a priori justification need be neither certain nor indefeasible. Consequently, one cannot argue that a particular ethical belief is not a piece of basic a priori knowledge or a basic belief justified a priori simply because it is does not enjoy the certainty of *all men are men* or *2 + 2 = 4* or because one thinks that it is possible for there to be defeating reasons for it. Our attitude toward those propositions that enjoy modest a priori justification should be like the attitude that Reid recommends toward anything set forth as a "first principle": "Let us deal with them, as an upright judge does with a witness who has a fair character. He pays a regard to the testimony of such a witness, while his character is unimpeached. But if it can be shewn that he was suborned, or that he is influenced by malice or partial favor, his testimony loses all its credit, and is justly rejected."[20]

The concept of modest a priori justification allows us to handle certain other sorts of objections about basic beliefs justified a priori. As we have seen, Chisholm says that it is not plausible to think that certain epistemic principles are known a priori because "many philosophers have understood them without seeing that they are true." A similar criticism might made of the claim that certain ethical principles are known a priori. But if we accept the notion of modest a priori justification, such a criticism is misguided. At most, it would show that those epistemic or ethical principles are not axioms. It is perfectly compatible with the concept of modest a priori justification that some philosophers have an a priori justification for believing a proposition, *p,* and for others who consider *p* not to believe it. This is so simply because those who do not believe *p* might have (or merely think they have) defeating reasons that are not had by those who accept *p*. If some philosophers do not believe that *p* because they have or think they have defeating reasons for *p,* it is still perfectly possible for others who lack those (alleged) defeating considerations to be justified in believing *p*. Moreover, nothing in the account presented in this section implies that those propositions that are foundational and justified a priori

20. Reid, *Essays on the Intellectual Powers of Man,* Essay I, Chapter 2, pp. 40–1.

must be "doxastically compelling" in the sense that they must be believed by anyone who grasps and considers them.

Finally, the concept of modest a priori justification allows us to recognize the importance of certain kinds of "coherence" in the justification of moral beliefs. There are at least two ways in which various notions of coherence can play important roles. First, if X's belief that p is not defeated by anything else that X believes, then we may say that X's belief that p enjoys a form of coherence with X's other beliefs. This sort of coherence is essential for modest a priori justification.[21] We may say that modest a priori justification depends negatively on lack of the kind of incoherence that consists in the having of defeaters.

A second, perhaps more interesting role for coherence would be the enhancing of X's level of justification for believing p. If X has an a priori justification for believing p, the level of X's justification for believing p need not be very high. For example, the a priori warrant for X's believing p might result in p's being merely probable for X. But the fact that X's belief that p coheres with certain other things that X believes, insofar as it bears certain explanatory and supporting relations to them, might raise X's justification for p to some higher level, such as being beyond a reasonable doubt or being evident. Nothing in the notion of modest a priori justification rules out the important role for this sort of coherence. Of course, if X's level of warrant for believing p is enhanced by the fact that X's belief that p coheres with a set of propositions some of which are empirical, then the level of warrant or justification X's belief enjoys will not depend entirely on a priori grounds. But this is still compatible with our holding that X has some a priori grounds for believing p and that X's belief that p is to some extent justified a priori. How could the level of warrant for X's believing p be enhanced by its cohering with certain empirical propositions? One possibility is that X might know that X's belief that p concurs with the judgment of other people X has reason to believe are reliable and trustworthy judges about p and related subject matters. If p is a mathematical proposition and X has some a priori warrant for believing that p, the level of justification of X's belief might be enhanced by learning that other competent, trustworthy mathematicians also accept it. The situation here is the reverse of Summerfield's Claudia, whose war-

---

21. For the sake of simplicity, I'm ignoring the real possibility that a defeating belief might itself be defeated and that a defeated justification can be restored by the defeat of a defeater.

151

rant for believing a mathematical theorem is defeated by the perverse testimony of competent mathematicians.

THE CONCEPT OF AN INTRINSICALLY ACCEPTABLE PROPOSITION

Summerfield argues persuasively in favor of modest a priori justification and knowledge. Yet her defense of modest a priori justification is set in the context of a reliabilist theory of knowledge and justification. Reliabilist theories of justification face several serious objections.[22] But the concept of modest a priori justification and knowledge need not be tied to a reliabilist framework. In this section, I briefly sketch a view of a priori justification that does not presuppose the truth of reliabilism.

Let us begin by trying to make more precise the notion of a reason and a defeater. Let us introduce John Pollock's definition of a "reason" and a "defeater":

(D15) A state M of a person S is a reason for S to believe Q if and only if it is logically possible for S to become justified in believing Q on the basis of being in state M.[23]

It is plausible to think that perceptual and mnemonic experiences are reasons, that, for example, one's being appeared to redly is a reason to believe that there is something red before one, and that one's seeming to remember that one had eggs for breakfast is a reason to believe that one did indeed have eggs for breakfast. Concerning defeaters, let us say:

(D16) If M is a reason for S to believe Q, a state $M\star$ is a defeater for this reason if and only if it is logically possible for S to be in the combined state consisting of being in both state M and the state $M\star$ at the same time, and this combined state is not a reason for S to believe Q.[24]

If something's looking red to me is a reason to believe that something red is before me, this reason can be defeated by my coming to learn that there is a red light shining on that thing or by my coming to learn that I have an eye disorder that makes white objects look red to me. Given what we have said in the last section, being justified in believing certain things about the unreliability of one's rational faculties can be a defeater for some

22. See Richard Feldman, "Reliability and Justification," *The Monist,* 68 (April 1985), pp. 159–74; John L. Pollock, *Contemporary Theories of Knowledge* (Totowa, N.J.: Rowman and Littlefield, 1986), pp. 93–122.
23. Pollock, *Contemporary Theories of Knowledge,* p. 175.
24. Ibid., p. 176.

beliefs. Becoming justified in believing that certain false propositions are implied by a proposition one believes is also a defeater.

What kind of reason can one have for believing a basic a priori proposition? If the proposition is truly basic, then one must have a reason for that proposition that does not consist in one's being justified in believing some *other* proposition. What might such a reason be?

One unacceptable proposal is the view that one's reason for believing a basic a priori proposition is that it is "doxastically compelling." According to this view, the fact that one grasps and considers a proposition *p* and cannot help but believe *p* is reason to believe it. Thus, if one considers the proposition that pleasure in the good is intrinsically good and one cannot help but believe that proposition, then one has a reason to believe it. This view is unacceptable, since it does not seem that one's being so constituted psychologically that one cannot help believing some proposition tends to make it at all reasonable for one to believe it. It is not a reason or a ground for believing a proposition even though it might be an *excuse*. We must be careful not to confuse reasons with excuses. Certain forms of insanity might excuse a man for committing murder without being a reason to commit murder. Similarly, if a woman fails to keep her promise to return a book, her forgetting might be an excuse for failing to return the book, but it is hardly a justifying reason. We'd hardly be sympathetic to someone who said indignantly, "I had a perfectly good reason for not returning your book – I forgot to do so."

A somewhat different, yet still unacceptable, account of our reasons for believing certain propositions is proposed by Panayot Butchvarov:

A self-evident proposition is one that is evident but not in virtue of being inferred from another proposition. Its being evident consists in its appearing to us to be true, and this more precisely, consists in our being unable to think that we are mistaken. . . . The foundation of knowledge is self-evidence understood as our finding mistake unthinkable.[25]

According to Butchvarov, what justifies us in believing that all men are men is that we find it unthinkable or inconceivable that we are mistaken in believing it. This view differs from the previous account insofar as finding a mistake in believing a proposition, *p,* unthinkable is not the same as finding oneself compelled to believe to believe *p*. A religious fanatic might, for example, find that he cannot help believing certain things and yet concede that it is possible that he is mistaken. Similarly,

25. Panayot Butchvarov, *Skepticism in Ethics* (Indianapolis: Indiana University Press, 1989), p. 143.

someone compelled to believe something under the influence of drugs might still find it conceivable that he is mistaken.

Butchvarov's view presupposes the following principle:

(P1)   If S finds it inconceivable or unthinkable that he is mistaken in believing that p, then S is justified in believing that p.

But what exactly is it for S to find it inconceivable that he is mistaken in believing that p? There are at least two different ways that this can be understood, and so there are at least two different ways of taking (P1).

(P1')   If S cannot conceive or think of the proposition that S is mistaken in believing that p, then S is justified in believing that p.

(P1")   If S cannot believe that he is mistaken in that p, then S is justified in believing that p.

I doubt that Butchvarov would find either of these principles satisfactory interpretations of his view, but I am simply unsure how we might understand the inconceivability of a mistake in a way that generates a plausible principle of justification. In any case, what's wrong with (P1') and (P1")? One problem with (P1') is that it cannot account for what justifies me in believing that all men are men, since I *can* conceive of the proposition that I am mistaken in believing that all men are men. In fact, I am conceiving of that proposition now. In general, if I can conceive p, then I can also conceive the proposition that I am mistaken in believing p. If so, then any proposition I am justified in believing is also such that I can conceive the proposition that I am mistaken in believing it. Thus, (P1') could not be a satisfactory account of what justifies us in believing anything. (P1"), on the other hand, seems to be one more version of a compulsion account, and if we are right in rejecting compulsion accounts, then we should also reject this version. If being unable to disbelieve something does not justify one in believing it, it does not seem any more likely that being unable to believe that one is mistaken in believing it would tend to make one's belief justified.

What, then, is the nature of our reasons for believing those propositions for which we have basic a priori justification? Let us begin by noting that some philosophers have suggested that there is an analogy between what is "directly evident" or certain for us and what is intrinsically good or valuable. Such a view was proposed by Franz Brentano.[26] But let us recall

26. Franz Brentano, *The Origin of Our Knowledge of Right and Wrong,* translated by Roderick Chisholm and Elizabeth Schneewind (London: Routledge & Kegan Paul, 1969), esp. pp. 19–20, 146–7.

what Chisholm has said about the notion of intrinsic value. Chisholm says that a state of affairs, p, is intrinsically preferable to a state of affairs, q, just in case "p and q are necessarily such that, for any x, the contemplation of just p and q by x requires that x prefer p to q."[27] According to Chisholm, the contemplation of certain states of affairs *ethically* requires that one have a certain emotional, nondoxastic attitude toward those states of affairs. Analogously, we might say that there are certain propositions that are necessarily such that, for any x, the contemplation or the comprehending consideration of those propositions *epistemically* requires that x accept or believe them. The analogy between the intrinsically valuable and certain propositions may be said to consist in this: Just as the comprehending consideration of certain states of affairs is an *ethical* reason to favor or prefer them, so also the comprehending consideration of certain propositions is an *epistemic* reason to believe or accept them. The view I wish to defend takes the comprehending considering of certain propositions as an epistemic reason to believe those propositions.

In keeping with this analogy to the intrinsically valuable, we should say that the comprehending consideration of some propositions, such as *all men are men,* is an epistemic reason to believe them. This is simply to say that it is logically possible for one to become justified in believing, say, that all men are men on the basis of one's comprehending consideration of the proposition that all men are men. Given this concept of a reason, we can define the concept of an "intrinsically acceptable proposition." Let us say:

(D17) h is an *intrinsically acceptable proposition* = Df. h is necessarily such that, for any S, S's grasping and considering h is a reason for S to believe h.

If grasping and considering some proposition is a reason for believing it, then we may say that it is an a priori reason for believing it. Such a reason might properly be called a priori because it is a reason that one has independently of one's sense experience, independently of being appeared to in a certain way or of one's mnemonic experience. According to the present view, what justifies one in believing that all men are men is the fact that one comprehendingly considers *that* proposition. One's warrant for believing that proposition does not rest merely on one's considering something, but specifically on one's considering the proposition that all men are men. We may say roughly that one's warrant depends on the specific nature or content of the proposition, as well as on the fact that

---

27. Roderick Chisholm, "Defining Intrinsic Value," *Analysis,* 41 (March 1981), p. 100.

one is comprehendingly considering it. In this respect, an intrinsically acceptable proposition is like those states of affairs that are intrinsically good, for it is not the mere fact that one considers something that requires that one have a pro attitude toward a state of affairs: It is that one considers a state of affairs having a specific content or nature.

What would be examples of intrinsically acceptable propositions? Examples would include those things that Chisholm and others have taken to be axioms, such things as all *men are men, all round things have a shape,* and *if some Greeks are men, then some men are Greeks.* One's comprehending consideration of these propositions is a reason to believe them insofar as it is possible for one to become justified in believing them on the basis of one's comprehending consideration of them. Yet if all axioms are intrinsically acceptable propositions, it does not follow that all intrinsically acceptable propositions are axioms. For nothing in the concept of an intrinsically acceptable proposition implies that they are certain or indefeasible. If there is such a thing as modest a priori justification, a priori justification that is defeasible, then we should distinguish between those propositions that are axioms, those that are merely intrinsically acceptable, and those that are neither. Just as there are many states of affairs that are not intrinsically good, there are many propositions that are not intrinsically acceptable. Propositions such as *the pope is in Rome, it is raining,* and *there are stones* are not such that grasping and considering them is a reason to believe them. I can now, for example, grasp and consider the proposition *the pope is in Rome* without having any reason to believe it.

Believing an intrinsically acceptable proposition on the basis of one's comprehending consideration of it *can* be a source of a priori justification. If one accepts a proposition on the basis of an a priori reason that is undefeated, then one is justified in accepting that proposition a priori. Let us say:

(P2)   If (1) *h* is an intrinsically acceptable proposition, and (2) *S* believes *h* on the basis of *S's* grasping and considering *h,* and (3) this reason is not defeated by anything that *S* is justified in believing, then *S* is justified in accepting *h* a priori.

(P2) leaves open the degree or level of warrant of *S*'s justification. It does not imply that if *S* is justified in accepting *h* a priori, then *h* is certain for *S.* It also does not imply that *S's* a priori reason for accepting *h* is an indefeasible reason. For these reasons, (P2) describes a way in which beliefs can be justified a priori that avoids the chief problems faced by the alternative view described in the second section. What about a priori knowledge? It seems that if h is true and the level of $S's$ justification is high enough, say, h is evident for S, then S would also know that h. Moreover, if someone knows or is justified in accepting a proposition, h, in the manner described in (P1), then that knowledge and justification is basic insofar as one's reason for accepting h does not consist in one's having inferred h from some other proposition and one's reason for accepting h does not consist in one's being justified in believing some other proposition.

Given the concept of an intrinsically acceptable proposition and (P2), we can say how certain substantive ethical propositions can be the objects of a priori justified belief and knowledge without implying that those propositions are certain for us or that our reasons for holding them are indefeasible. It is not my concern in this chapter to defend any particular ethical proposition as an instance of a priori knowledge or justified belief, but merely to defend an account of that sort of knowledge and justification that does not rule out certain claims on the ground that they lack certainty and might be defeasible. *If* propositions such as *Pleasure is, as such, intrinsically good* and *It is prima facie wrong to act unjustly* are intrinsically acceptable, then one is justified in believing them a priori if one believes them on the basis of one's comprehending consideration of them and one has no defeating ground or reason for believing them.

According to the present view, some propositions, but not all, are such that one's comprehending consideration of them is a reason to believe them. Let us consider briefly some possible objections to this view. First, someone might object that grasping and considering an intrinsically acceptable proposition is not sufficient for one's being justified in believing it. "Suppose that Jones grasps and considers the proposition *everything flat is extended* while he is preoccupied in attempting to figure out what Smith just said. It seems possible that Jones does so without being justified in believing it." The response to this is that if Jones is really preoccupied in attempting to figure out what Smith said, then it isn't clear that he has really considered whether *everything flat is extended* is true. If he is attempting to figure out what Smith said, he is not considering the truth of the proposition in question, though he might be considering something else.

A second objection may be put this way: "This account really does not tell us what we want to know about what justifies us in believing an intrinsically acceptable proposition. It says that some propositions are such that one's comprehending consideration of them is a reason to believe them and that other propositions are not like this. Yet it does not tell us *why* some propositions are like this and others aren't." In response to this objection, it must be admitted that no explanation has been offered for why some propositions have this status and others don't. Frankly, it is not clear why some propositions have this character, or even that there must be some deeper explanation of why some have it and other don't. In any case, it would be a mistake to conclude that this account is empty or that it tells us nothing significant. For if we are asking what our reason is for believing propositions such as *all men are men,* then we *do* have an answer: It is the fact that we comprehendingly consider that proposition. For every intrinsically acceptable proposition, *p,* we can identify our reason for believing it, namely, the fact that we comprehendingly consider *p.* If there is some deeper explanation of the fact that some propositions have this status, it would surely be desirable to have it, but it is not obvious that there is any such explanation, and it is not necessary that we have it before us in order to have answered the original question.

A third objection, related to the second, is that this view leaves us with a "scattered" plurality of warrant-making properties, a plurality having no common, unifying feature.[28] It is not clear, though, how damaging an objection this is. After all, why should we presume or presuppose that there must be some deep, comprehensible unity among warrant-making properties? It is not obvious that we should presume that the sources of epistemic warrant are any less diverse than the sources of intrinsic value or beauty. Why should we presuppose that the warrant-making properties of belief are any less diverse than intrinsically good-making properties or beauty-making properties? If the view advanced earlier is right, then a correct epistemic theory about what makes beliefs justified resembles the pluralism of certain theories of intrinsic value rather than a normative theory that identifies one fundamental right-making property such as maximizing utility or acting in accord with Kant's categorical imperative. A plurality of such warrant-making properties is objectionable only if a more unified account is compatible with and explains what we recognize or reasonably take to be instances of justified belief.

It is appropriate to note that a similar problem appears to confront any theory that appeals to the concept of defeasible reasons. Take any theory that claims that a belief is justified only if it is undefeated by the set of a

---

28. See Ernest Sosa's objection to foundationalist views about justification in "The Raft and the Pyramid: Coherence versus Foundations in the Theory of Knowledge," *Midwest Studies in Philosophy V* edited by Peter French, Theodore E. Uehling, and Howard Wettstein (Minneapolis, Minnesota: University of Minnesota Press, 1980), esp. pp. 20–3.

subject's other beliefs or experiences. It is fair to ask whether it offers any systematic account or criterion by which we can pick out defeaters. Consider my belief that there is a table before me. Although we recognize that there are beliefs and experiences that would defeat my justification for believing that there is a table before me, it is not clear that there is any criterion by which we can identify all and only the things that would be defeaters. Furthermore, such things as memory beliefs are also subject to defeat. If I seem to remember certain things happening to me as a child, but my parents assure me that those things never happened, then I have a defeater for what I seem to remember. No epistemic theory, to my knowledge, offers us a criterion by which we can identify all and only perceptual and mnemonic defeaters. In this respect, then, any epistemic theory that makes use of the concept of defeat seems open to a version of the "scatter" objection.

Even if there is no general criterion or method by which we can pick out those propositions, including ethical propositions, that are intrinsically acceptable, it hardly follows that we cannot be justified in believing that certain particular propositions have that status. Take the proposition *the comprehending consideration of the proposition that someone's being pleased is intrinsically good is a reason to believe it*. This is an *epistemic* proposition because it is a claim about what constitutes an epistemic reason. Shall we say that this epistemic proposition is an axiom? That it is certain and indefeasible for anyone who believes it? No. Instead, we may say that this epistemic proposition is one that is intrinsically acceptable. We may say that our grasping and considering this proposition is itself a (defeasible) reason to believe it, and that we are justified in believing it if we believe it on that basis and we have no defeating reason. In short, some epistemic propositions to the effect that certain other propositions are intrinsically acceptable might be intrinsically acceptable themselves.

The account defended here does not, then, offer anything that I should care to call a test or method for ascertaining what has intrinsic value. It does not offer a method for resolving disputes about what has intrinsic value or prove that anything has intrinsic value. But none of these things were among the aims of this chapter, and none of these things are necessary in order to know that something is intrinsically good. I assume that we do have some knowledge of intrinsic value, and the account presented here is an attempt to explain how we can be justified in believing that some things are intrinsically good.

Whether one favors a reliabilist account of a priori justification, the account presented in this section, or some alternative, the chief concern of this chapter has been to defend the importance of recognizing modest a priori justification. The existence of substantive moral beliefs justified a priori is more plausible given the notion of modest a priori justification. For those who are not reliabilists, it seems especially fitting that we take as our model for a priori justification what Chisholm and others have said about the concept of intrinsic value. Though Chisholm's own account of a priori justification poses problems for moral beliefs justified a priori, what he says about the concept of intrinsic value suggests a way around these problems and a more promising approach. It seems especially fitting that the key to understanding our knowledge of intrinsic value might lie in our thinking about epistemic reasons in a manner analogous to the way we ought to think about intrinsic value itself.

9

Coherence and experience

In the last chapter, I argued that it is more reasonable to think that we have a priori knowledge and justification of certain value claims if we accept the notion of modest a priori justification instead of restricting ourselves to a strong view that takes basic a priori justification to be certain and indefeasible. In this chapter, I examine two alternative approaches, two alternative answers to the question "What justifies us in believing that something is intrinsically valuable?" These are coherence theories and broadly empirical theories that take emotional experiences to be evidence or reasons for value beliefs. I will argue that neither alternative is adequate.

COHERENCE THEORIES

I take a coherence theory of justification to hold roughly that the only thing that confers justification or warrant on S's believing p is the fact that S's believing p coheres with the rest of S's beliefs. Coherence theories, so construed, tell us that a belief is warranted because and only because it coheres with a subject's other beliefs. They tell us that there is one basic or ultimate warrant-conferring characteristic of a belief, namely, belonging to a coherent set of beliefs. There are two fundamentally important features of coherence theories. First, coherence theories deny that there are any basic or foundational beliefs. A "basic" or "foundational" belief is one that has some level of epistemic warrant that does not derive from or depend positively on one's other beliefs or justified beliefs. A basic or foundational belief has at least some level of warrant that is independent of the warrant, if any, that it might derive from its logical relations to, or its cohering with, one's other beliefs. Second, coherence theories are doxastic theories of warrant and justification insofar as they maintain that one's warrant is a function of one's beliefs or doxastic states. Though some noncoherentists hold that basic beliefs are justified in virtue of being the product of a reliable belief-forming process and others hold that basic beliefs can be justified in virtue of certain sensory or perceptual states, coherence theories deny that such things are sources of justification or warrant-making properties of beliefs. Nondoxastic states such as sensations or the sensibly "given" play no justificatory role in a coherence theory. Of course, this does not prevent the coherentist from holding that beliefs about one's sensations or perceptual experiences can play an important warrant-conferring role.

Coherence theories have enjoyed considerable support among moral philosophers. Their proponents claim that one is justified in accepting any ethical proposition just in case it coheres with one's other beliefs. These other beliefs might include beliefs about particular cases and general principles, as well as beliefs about human nature, social institutions and principles, and the general aims of an ethical theory. There are at least three possible reasons to favor a coherence account of the justification of moral beliefs. First, its appeal to moral philosophers is natural and understandable if the alternatives are weak or especially problematic. Suppose that we think the alternatives are either a strong conception of a priori justification or a theory that takes some form of emotional experience as a source of justification. The weakness of a strong conception of a priori justification in accounting for substantive moral justification was noted in the last chapter, and the notion that one's emotional attitudes might justify value beliefs seems, at first glance, positively bizarre. How could an emotional experience provide evidence for thinking that a moral or value judgment is true? Is there any reason to think that one's feeling favorably toward something is any reason to think that it is good or right? A coherence approach offers an appealing alternative.

Second, it might seem that a coherence theory is the best, most plausible account of nonmoral knowledge and justification, that it is the best account of our scientific knowledge or our ordinary empirical knowledge of things like tables and chairs. If it is the mere fact of coherence that justifies those beliefs, then it is plausible to think that moral beliefs would also be justified by mere coherence. Furthermore, although some philosophers think that a belief in distinctive moral facts and properties is committed to an implausible or mysterious epistemic picture, if a coherence theory is the best account of our ordinary empirical beliefs, then appealing to the same fact of coherence to justify moral beliefs should not strike anyone as mysterious or eerie. It seems that one can appeal to a coherence theory to justify moral beliefs without having to invoke a mysterious faculty of moral perception or intuition or any of the embarrassments that moral skeptics try to foist on the cognitivist.

162

A third possible reason would be the existence of compelling arguments in favor of a coherence theory as the only adequate account of epistemic justification in general. Such arguments would purport to show that all justification is ultimately a matter of the coherence of beliefs and that any other approach to justification must be mistaken. Chief among these arguments is the doxastic ascent argument.

If these three possible reasons for preferring a coherence account of the warrant of our moral beliefs can be reasonably rejected, this would undermine the main reasons for favoring such an approach. The first reason, that the coherence theory is stronger than any alternative account, has already been partially addressed. Our alternatives are not limited to a strong conception of a priori justification or the broadly empirical view that takes emotional experience as evidence. The possibility of modest a priori justification is a plausible alternative and, I have argued, a better account of moral justification than the strong conception. Given the objections to coherence theories advanced later, it is reasonable to think that it is better than any purely coherentist account. In short, we should not embrace a coherence account simply because it is better than the alternatives. With respect to the other possible reasons for adopting a coherence theory for moral beliefs, I consider in the next section two arguments in favor of coherence theories of justification. These are the doxastic ascent argument and the related argument that nondoxastic states cannot be sources of epistemic warrant. I argue that neither argument is successful, that neither argument presents a compelling case for a coherence account of either empirical or moral beliefs. In the following section, I consider some objections to coherence theories in general.

THE REGRESS ARGUMENT AND THE DOXASTIC ASCENT ARGUMENT

Opponents of coherence theories often take as their starting point the "regress argument." This argument begins with the assumption that some beliefs are inferentially justified, that some beliefs are justified in virtue of our being justified in believing certain other things. According to the regress argument, if S is inferentially justified in believing p, then there must be some other proposition, q, such that S is justified in believing p on the basis of believing q. Now either q is a terminating belief in a chain of justifying propositions or S is inferentially justified in believing q on the basis of believing some other proposition, r, that is either a terminating belief or an intermediate link in a chain of justification. In asking what justifies S in believing p, we seem to have the following four possibilities.

(1) The chain of justification does not terminate but goes on ad infinitum.
(2) The chain of justification terminates in a belief that is not justified.
(3) The chain does not terminate but eventually circles back on itself.
(4) There is a chain of justification terminating in a belief that is basically justified, that is, a belief that is justified and does not depend for its justification on any other belief.

Of these four possibilities, (1) does not seem very plausible mainly because we simply do not have an infinite number of beliefs. Possibility (1) relies on an implausible psychological assumption. Possibility (2) is also unsatisfactory, since it is unreasonable to think that one could be epistemically justified in believing a proposition on the basis of believing something that one is not justified in believing. If one is not justified in believing q, then believing p on the basis of q does not justify one in believing p. Defenders of basic beliefs claim that (3) is also implausible, arguing that a circular chain justifies nothing. It is unreasonable to claim that one is justified in believing p on the basis of q and q on the basis of r and r on the basis of p. Proponents of basic beliefs hold that such circles are vicious and justify nothing, even when they are very large. If the proponents of basic beliefs are right in rejecting (3), then, according to the regress argument, we have some reason to believe that there are basic beliefs. Since coherence theories deny the existence of basic beliefs, we have some reason to think that coherence theories are false.

Despite its apparent plausibility, the regress argument is not a conclusive refutation of coherence theories. Perhaps the best response coherentists can make to this line of argument is to deny that inferential justification is *linear,* insisting instead that justification is a matter of one's belief that p cohering with one's entire system of beliefs. Coherentists may claim the justification of the belief that p is a matter of mutual dependence of all the beliefs in the system.[1] Coherence theories would thus not be committed to the vicious circles that the proponents of basic beliefs attribute to them. In making this response, coherentists might emphasize the distinction between *justifying a belief* and *a belief's being justified.* Justifying a belief is an activity that one engages in typically, though not always, when the truth of a belief has been called into question by oneself or by others. Being justified in believing something is a state that one is in. Clearly, we

1. See Laurence BonJour's response to the regress argument in *The Structure of Empirical Knowledge* (Cambridge, Mass.: Harvard University Press, 1985), pp. 24–5.

all have particular justified beliefs, even though we have made no attempt to justify them. Even if the activity of justifying a belief proceeds in a linear fashion, it does not follow that the inferential support that actually justifies a belief is linear or viciously circular. The notion that all inferential justification is linear seems plausible if we confuse these two and less plausible if we see the difference between them. This response is sufficiently plausible for us to hold that the regress argument has not shown that we must accept the existence of basic beliefs or reject a coherence theory of justification.

Coherentists take the offensive by attacking the existence of basic beliefs. One of the most influential forms of attack is the "doxastic ascent argument." A form of this argument, which challenges the existence of basic empirical beliefs, is stated clearly in the following passage from Laurence BonJour's *The Structure of Empirical Knowledge:*

(1) Suppose that there are *basic empirical beliefs,* that is empirical beliefs (a) which are epistemically justified, and (b) whose justification does not depend on that of any further empirical beliefs.
(2) For a belief to be epistemically justified requires that there is a reason why it is likely to be true.
(3) For a belief to be epistemically justified for a particular person requires that this person be himself in cognitive possession of such a reason.
(4) The only way to be in cognitive possession of such a reason is to believe *with justification* the premises from which it follows that the belief is likely to be true.
(5) The premises of such a justifying argument for an empirical belief cannot be entirely *a priori;* at least one such premise must be empirical.
Therefore, the justification of a supposed empirical belief must depend on the justification of at least one other empirical belief, contradicting (1); it follows that there can be no basic empirical beliefs.[2]

BonJour argues that in order for a belief, *B,* to be epistemically justified, one must have a reason why it is likely to be true. According to BonJour, this reason can only consists in one's being justified in believing two other things, namely, (1) that *B* has some property, *F,* and (2) that beliefs that have *F* are likely to be true. On this view, one's justification for any empirical belief depends essentially on one's having certain other justified beliefs. Recalling the distinctions made by Summerfield and Audi in the last chapter, BonJour argues that every empirical belief depends *positively* on one's having some other justified belief.

The targets of BonJour's attack are basic *empirical* beliefs. Other philoso-

2. Ibid., p. 32.

phers have used versions of the doxastic ascent argument to attack the existence of basic or foundational *moral* beliefs. For example, Brink writes:

There are no foundational beliefs, because justification in holding a belief p requires that one base p on second-order beliefs about what kind of belief p is (e.g., under what conditions p was formed) and why p-type beliefs should be true. A fortiori, there are no foundational moral beliefs as intuitionism claims. Justification in holding a moral belief p requires that one base p on second order beliefs about what kind of belief p is and why p-type beliefs should be true.[3]

According to Brink, these second-order beliefs must themselves be justified beliefs. He says, "if these second-order beliefs are to help in the justification of p, then they must not merely be held but reasonably or justifiably held."[4] Brink thus employs against basic moral beliefs the same line of argument that BonJour uses against basic empirical beliefs. On this view, every epistemically justified moral belief depends essentially for its warrant on one's being justified in believing that it is of a certain kind and that beliefs of that kind are likely to be true. The target of Brink's version of the doxastic ascent argument is broader than BonJour's, since BonJour argues that there are no basic empirical beliefs and Brink that there are no basic beliefs of any kind. Whether or not it is ultimately consistent with his general stand on epistemic justification, BonJour allows that there are some kinds of basic beliefs, for example, basic a priori beliefs.[5] Brink's argument excludes this possibility.

The doxastic ascent argument is an important step in establishing the truth of coherentism. It argues that there are no basic or foundational beliefs, since every warranted belief, B, depends for its justification on one's being justified in believing that B has a property, F, and that beliefs having F are very likely to be true. Yet from these claims, it does not strictly follow that coherentism is true. There is still the possibility that what makes some belief, B, warranted is some combination of a nondoxastic, noninferential element *along with* one's having the justified beliefs that B has F and that beliefs having F are likely to be true. This possibility

3. David O. Brink, *Moral Realism and the Foundations of Ethics* (Cambridge: Cambridge University Press, 1989), p. 122.
4. Ibid., p. 124.
5. See BonJour's discussion of a priori justification in *The Structure of Empirical Knowledge*, pp. 207–11. BonJour's view of a priori justification resembles in some ways the one presented in the last section of Chapter 8. Bonjour holds that there are some a priori propositions that one can become justified in believing by understanding them. But BonJour does not recognize the existence of modest a priori justification.

represents a "mixed" theory that seeks to combine some nondoxastic component in the source of warrant while admitting the central conclusions of the doxastic ascent argument. The mixed view might tell us, for example, that what justifies S in believing that he has a headache is *both* (1) S's having the nondoxastic, phenomenological awareness of a headache and (2) S's being justified in believing that his belief that he has a headache is an introspective belief of a certain sort and that introspective beliefs of that sort are likely to be true. A mixed theory of this kind could deny one central claim of the coherence theory, namely, that the warrant of a belief is ultimately a matter solely of the coherence of beliefs. Such a mixed theory would not be a purely doxastic theory.

Yet, as a compromise position, this mixed theory is not terribly persuasive, chiefly because there seems to be no real justificatory role for the nondoxastic element. Suppose we concede that being justified in believing B requires that one be justified in believing that B has some property F and that beliefs having that property are likely to be true. In other words, suppose we concede that these metabeliefs are necessary for being justified in believing B. If these metabeliefs are necessary for justification, they also seem to be sufficient for it, since if I am justified in believing that some belief of mine has a property F and that every belief having F is likely to be true, then it seems that this would be sufficient to justify my belief. There is really no point in appealing to any additional factor as a source of warrant such as nondoxastic phenomenological states. The mixed theory introduces factors that contribute nothing important in the explanation of justified beliefs. Thus, if we accept the conclusions of the doxastic ascent argument and reject such mixed theories, we have a powerful case in favor of a coherence theory of justification.

The doxastic ascent argument, at least the general version of the argument employed by Brink, is a direct and serious challenge to any noncoherentist theory of the justification of moral beliefs. This includes the account of modest a priori justification developed in the last chapter, for there we defended the view that there is such a thing as basic, yet modest, a priori justification. The doxastic ascent argument is a serious challenge to Summerfield's reliabilist account, as well as to the nonreliabilist account that treats some propositions as intrinsically acceptable. This is because neither account requires of justification the presence of those metabeliefs that the doxastic ascent argument takes as necessary. Instead, these accounts require roughly that one have no defeating reasons for holding a belief. One's warrant depends negatively on the absence of these defeaters, but it does not depend positively on one's having the metabeliefs. Consequently, a full defense of the approach adopted in the last chapter requires that we address the doxastic ascent argument.

Furthermore, whereas Brink's challenge to foundational moral beliefs is direct, BonJour's attack on foundational empirical beliefs is indirectly relevant to moral epistemology. If one could show that the best, indeed the only plausible, account of ordinary empirical beliefs is a coherentist account, then this would strengthen the case for a coherentist moral epistemology, since if mere coherence can justify empirical beliefs, it is plausible to think that it can justify moral beliefs. Thus, it is important to take a close, hard look at the doxastic ascent argument.

There are several problems with the doxastic ascent argument. The first concerns BonJour's treatment of the justification of an ordinary perceptual belief, say, that there is a red book on the desk. Such beliefs are justified inferentially, and BonJour tells us that the justificatory argument looks like this:

(6) I have a cognitively spontaneous belief of kind K that there is a red book on the desk.
(7) Conditions C obtain.
(8) Cognitively spontaneous beliefs of kind K in conditions C are very likely to be true.
(9) Therefore, my belief that there is a red book on the desk is very likely to be true.
(10) Therefore, (probably) there is a red book on the desk.

BonJour says, "if my belief is to be justified by appeal to this argument, the premises of the argument must themselves be justified; and if the resulting account is to be genuinely coherentist, these further justifications must make no appeal to basic beliefs."[6] It is important to note that BonJour tells us that each of the premises of this argument must be justified. I wish to focus on the justification of the first premise. What justifies me in believing (6)? Given the requirements on justification presupposed by the doxastic ascent argument, the warrant of (6) would appear to depend essentially on one's being justified in believing that this belief has a property F and that beliefs having that property are likely to be true. This view of what justification requires naturally suggests that (6) is justified in virtue of the following sort of argument:

(11) I have an introspective belief that I have a spontaneous visual belief that there is a red book on the desk.

6. Ibid., p. 118.

(12) Introspective beliefs (of certain sorts) are very likely to be true.
(13) The conditions specified in (12) obtain.
(14) Therefore, my belief that I have a spontaneous belief that there is a red book on the desk is likely to be true.

Now given the assumed requirements on justification, we are justified in believing the first premise of this argument, (11), only if we are justified in believing that *this* belief has some property F and that beliefs having that property are likely to be true. In other words, we are justified in believing (11) only if we have yet another introspective belief about our introspective belief about our visual belief. The first premise in the justifying argument for 11 would be:

(15) I have an introspective belief that I have an introspective belief that I have a spontaneous visual belief that there is a red book on the desk.

If we are justified in believing (15), then we must be justified in believing an even more complicated proposition about it, and so on and so on. The upshot is that the requirements on justification presupposed by the doxastic ascent argument apparently involve the implausible view that the justification of any introspective belief depends on our having an infinite number of increasingly complex introspective beliefs.

This is a serious problem for the doxastic ascent argument, yet one BonJour recognizes. In order to circumvent the problem of an implausible infinite regress, he holds that the justification of (6) involves an appeal to what he calls the "doxastic presumption." Unfortunately, BonJour is not very clear about the what the doxastic presumption is or how it functions in the justification of (6). The doxastic presumption does not by itself entail that (6) is true, and BonJour says that it does not function as a premise in an argument for (6). As BonJour points out, if it were to function as a premise in an argument for (6), "I would need further premises to the effect that I do in fact believe myself to have such and such specific beliefs, and the justification of these further premises would obviously be as problematic as before."[7] But if the doxastic presumption does not justify (6) by functioning as a premise in an argument, then how does it do its justificatory work? BonJour tells us that if someone questions whether I am justified in believing that there is a red book on the desk, then he must be assuming or taking it for granted that I *do* believe that there is a red book on the desk. In other words, the truth of (6) is pre-

7. Ibid., p. 104.

supposed by raising the question of justification in the first place. He writes:

the essential starting point for epistemological investigation is the *presumption* that the believer has a certain specific belief, the issue being whether or not the belief thus presumed to exist is justified, but the very existence of the belief being taken for granted in the context of the epistemological inquiry. And the further suggestion is that this presumption–that the believer in question does indeed accept the belief in question–though clearly empirical in content, is for these reasons available as a premise, or at least can function as a premise, in this context without itself requiring justification.[8]

BonJour's point seems to be that if I or someone else raises the question of whether my cognitively spontaneous visual belief is justified, then the questioner must presuppose that I have that belief. Thus, if someone raises the question of whether (6) is a justified belief, he must be presupposing that (6) is true. This is not a persuasive response, for we may still ask, what justifies us in believing (6)? Premise (6) functions as a premise in an argument for an ordinary perceptual belief. Indeed, BonJour tells that "a justificatory argument for positive observational knowledge involves in effect three distinct subpremises: first, that I have the belief whose justification is at issue; second, that it is a belief of a specified kind; and third, that it is cognitively spontaneous."[9] If (6) is a premise in an argument for positive observational knowledge, then it must be justified if the conclusion based on it is justified. Indeed, we have seen that BonJour concedes this point. Now to say that (6) is presupposed in a justificatory argument does not, as BonJour now seems to suggest, obviate the need for justification. Presuppositions can themselves be justified or unjustified. As far as I can tell, the doxastic presumption does not explain what justifies us in believing (6). Furthermore, to talk about what one is presupposing in raising a question of justification seems to confuse what is presupposed in justifying a belief with the conditions that are necessary for a belief's being justified. In raising a question about the justification of a belief, one might presuppose that one has the belief in question, but it does not follow that this presupposition is itself a justified belief.

I conclude that BonJour's account of what justifies our ordinary perceptual beliefs is unsatisfactory. The requirements for justification specified in the doxastic ascent argument, if applied consistently, lead to a

8. Ibid., p. 81. Later he says, "it is plausible to hold that the existence of the justificandum belief is presupposed, in something like the Strawsonian sense, by the very raising of the issue of justification, so that it does not need to be even included as a premise" (p. 128).
9. Ibid., p. 128.

vicious infinite regress of increasingly complex beliefs. BonJour tries unsuccessfully to avoid this result by invoking the doxastic presumption. We can either abandon the view that we have justified observational beliefs or the requirements for justified belief laid out in the doxastic ascent argument and, consequently, that argument against basic beliefs. Surely the latter is the more plausible course.[10]

Ernest Sosa points to a second problem with the doxastic ascent argument. Sosa says that we can think of epistemic justification or warrant as an evaluative feature or characteristic of a person's belief. When we say that a person's belief is warranted or justified, we are evaluating it favorably, and when we say that a person's belief is unwarranted or unjustified, we are evaluating it unfavorably. Furthermore, Sosa says, we can think of epistemic justification as being akin to other evaluative characteristics insofar as it supervenes on or is dependent on certain nonevaluative characteristics. For example, we might think of the goodness of an apple as supervening on its being ripe, sweet, juicy, and so on; the rightness of an action as supervening on its producing a greater balance of pleasure over pain than any alternative; or the beauty of a painting supervening on its colors and their arrangement. Sosa argues that the doxastic ascent argument leads to a denial of the highly plausible view that epistemic justification is an evaluative characteristic and that, like other evaluative characteristics, it depends ultimately on the nonevaluative. According to Sosa, if every justified belief depends for its warrant on one's being justified in holding two other beliefs, then there is no possibility of there being a wholly nonevaluative source of justification for any belief. If every belief has as its source of justification other justified beliefs, then there will never be a nonevaluative source or basis of justification; there will be no nonevaluative fact in virtue of which a belief is justified. Sosa argues that the doxastic ascent argument "would preclude the possibility of supervenience, since it would entail that the source of justification *always* includes an *epistemic* component."[11]

A third objection to the doxastic ascent argument is simply to deny that the only epistemic reasons for belief or the only reasons for holding beliefs

10. I have made these criticisms of the doxastic ascent argument in "Coherence and Epistemic Priority," *Philosophical Studies* (May 41 1982), pp. 299–315; and "Epistemic Priority and Coherence," *The Current State of the Coherence Theory* edited by John W. Bender (Dordrecht: Kluwer Academic Publishers, 1989), pp. 178–87.
11. Ernest Sosa, "The Raft and the Pyramid: Coherence versus Foundations in the Theory of Knowledge," *Midwest Studies in Philosophy V,* edited by Peter French, Theodore E. Uchling, and Howard Wettstein (Minneapolis: University of Minnesota Press, 1980), p. 18.

consist in other justified beliefs. Take the view that one's having a head-ache is a (defeasible) reason for one to believe that one has a headache. On this view, one's belief that one has a headache is justified not in virtue of one's having certain other beliefs, but in virtue of one's having a certain sort of sense experience and not having any experiences or beliefs that defeat that reason. To the question "What reason to do you have for believing that you have a headache?", the proponent of this view finds it perfectly acceptable to answer that it is because he does have a headache. Advocates of this view hold that some reasons need not be beliefs or doxastic states. BonJour, and indeed any coherence theorist, rejects the view that nondoxastic experiences or the sensibly given can be reasons for belief or sources of justification. BonJour writes:

the proponent of the given is caught in a fundamental and inescapable dilemma; if his intuitions or direct awarenesses or immediate apprehensions are construed as cognitive, at least quasi-judgmental (as seems clearly the more natural interpreta-tion), then they will be both capable or providing justification for other cognitive states and in need of it themselves; but if they are construed as noncognitive, nonjudgmental, then while they will not themselves need justification they will also be incapable of giving it.[12]

Yet it is far from obvious that the second horn of this dilemma is true. Of course, a headache is not a belief or a doxastic state, but why should we think that only beliefs can confer warrant on other beliefs? Perhaps BonJour believes that if something is incapable of having justification, then it cannot confer it on anything else. But it is not obvious that this principle is true. Consider the apparently analogous case of right or wrong actions and decisions. Right and wrong are characteristics of decisions and actions, and not properties of states of pleasure and pain or happiness and unhappiness. Now in some cases, it seems that what makes a decision or an action right are not further actions and decisions and actions, but rather the consequences of those actions and decisions in terms of pleasure and pain or happiness and unhappiness. The rightness of an action or decision is conferred on it not by a further right decision or action, but by its having certain other kinds of things such as its consequences, which are not themselves right or wrong. Similarly, it is, strictly speaking, only per-sons who are deserving of punishment and not actions. Only persons can be punished and deserving of punishment; actions can be neither. But persons can be deserving of punishment in virtue of their actions. They are punished for their actions. The fact that a person has performed a

12. BonJour, *The Structure of Empirical Knowledge*, p. 69.

certain sort of action can make the person deserving of punishment even though that fact is not, strictly speaking, something that can be punished or deserving of punishment. Actions are reasons or grounds for punishment, making persons deserving of punishment, even though actions cannot be punished or deserving of it. Thus, even if nondoxastic states, such as headaches and other phenomenological states, are not the sorts of things that have epistemic justification, it is not obvious that they cannot be the ground or reason of other things, that is, beliefs, having it.[13]

One final criticism of the doxastic ascent argument is that it simply sets the standards of justification too high in requiring that one have beliefs about one's justified beliefs. According to the doxastic ascent argument, a belief, *B,* is justified only if one is justified in believing that *B* has some property, *F,* and that beliefs having *F* are very likely to be true. But how often do we in fact have these beliefs about our beliefs? When a person walks into a room, forming the justified belief that there is a table in the room, it is typically false that he has the accompanying belief that he has a visual belief that there is a table in the room. In our everyday lives, we do not usually form such beliefs about our beliefs. Furthermore, young children, animals, and the deeply unreflective may not even have the general belief that visual beliefs are likely to be true. Since the doxastic ascent argument requires that we actually have these beliefs, then it seems that very few, if any, of our everyday beliefs about the world would be justified. But since it is reasonable for us to think that many of these beliefs are justified, we may reject these requirements on justification and the doxastic ascent argument.

SOME OBJECTIONS TO COHERENCE THEORIES

If the regress argument has failed to show that there must be basic or foundational beliefs, the doxastic ascent argument has failed to show that there are none. Furthermore, though BonJour claims that the proponent of the given is caught in a fundamental dilemma, there is no reason to think that the second horn of that dilemma is true. There is no reason to think that some nondoxastic states cannot be reasons for belief or sources of justification. The failure of the doxastic ascent argument and the alleged dilemma for defenders of nondoxastic sources of justification are important. They are important because one major motivation for accepting a

---

13. See Sosa, "The Raft and the Pyramid," pp. 7–8; James Van Cleve, "Epistemic Supervenience and The Circle of Belief," *The Monist* 68 (1985), pp. 97–99.

coherence account of the warrant of moral beliefs is the view that there are powerful arguments in favor of coherence theories. Neither the doxastic ascent argument nor the alleged dilemma constitutes such an argument. To accept a coherence account of the warrant of empirical beliefs on their basis, as BonJour does, or to accept a coherence account of moral beliefs on the basis of the doxastic ascent argument, as Brink does, is a mistake.

Still, the failure of the doxastic ascent argument does not imply that all coherence theories are false. Indeed, some coherence theories are not committed to the strong requirements for epistemic justification that this argument presupposes. All that coherence theories really require is that the ultimate source of justification consists in the fact that one's belief coheres with one's other beliefs. The coherentist need only maintain, for example, that a belief is warranted in virtue of the fact that it is a member of a coherent body of beliefs or in virtue of the fact that it bears certain inferential relations to such a set of beliefs. This body of beliefs need not contain the metabeliefs or the second-order beliefs on which the proponents of the doxastic ascent argument insist. There are thus versions of coherentism that would reject the doxastic ascent argument. For this reason, we must find other arguments against coherence theories, arguments that do not simply attack the doxastic ascent argument.

Let us consider one objection to coherence theories raised by Ernest Sosa.[14] Imagine a man with a splitting headache whose belief that he has a headache coheres with the rest of his beliefs. Let us assume that this man's belief that he has a headache is justified for him. Now suppose that this man's belief is altered so that he believes that he does *not* have a headache, and let his other beliefs be changed where necessary to cohere with this belief. Thus, he now believes that he has no pain, that he has not recently desired aspirin, and so on. In this case, the belief that he has no headache would not be a justified belief even though it coheres with the rest of his beliefs. Perhaps this point can be made more clear by considering two men in "mirror" worlds who have all the same beliefs. Suppose that A is suffering a painful headache, believes he has a headache, and let this belief cohere with the rest of his beliefs. Imagine that our other man, B, has no headache, but let him have the same body of beliefs: that he has a headache, that he is in pain, that he has recently desired aspirin, and so on. In each case, we can assume that the set of beliefs is equally coherent, but it does not seem that each man is justified in believing that

14. Sosa, "The Raft and the Pyramid," pp. 20–3.

he has a headache. *B* does not seem justified in believing that he has a headache. His belief is an unjustified bit of hypochondria. Even if we adopt the weaker stance that *A* is *more* justified in his belief than *B*, then he is justified in virtue of something other than the mere coherence of his belief, since their beliefs are *ex hypothesi* equally coherent. If *A*'s belief is more justified than *B*'s, then something other than mere coherence is relevant to the warrant of a belief. If *B*'s belief is not justified, then the mere fact that one's beliefs coheres with the rest of one's beliefs is not sufficient for justification.

It is often charged that coherence theories "cut justification off from the world," that they "do not allow justification to be tied to down to the world." Sosa's example illustrates one sense in which this is true. Coherence theories do not allow anything outside the circle of one's beliefs to count as a reason or a source of epistemic justification. Coherence theories treat nondoxastic states, such as sensory and perceptual experiences, as irrelevant to the warrant of a subject's beliefs. In the last section, we saw that BonJour argues that nondoxastic states cannot be sources of justification, that they cannot confer justification on belief. But, as we have argued, there is no reason for us to accept the view that only states that are themselves epistemically justified can be sources of justification.

John Pollock also raises a serious objection to coherence theories. Pollock points out that a person can hold a belief on the basis of a bad reason such as wishful thinking. But a belief based solely on wishful thinking is not a justified belief even if it happens to cohere with the rest of one's beliefs. If this is so, then the mere fact of coherence is not sufficient to justify a belief. Pollock offers the following illustration of his point.[15] Suppose, for example, that John's daughter has gone to a football game, the evening has suddenly turned cold, and John is worried about whether his daughter took her coat. John believes, on the basis of wishful thinking, "Oh, I'm sure she took her coat." John does not believe at the moment he forms this belief that it is the product of mere wishful thinking, and the belief that she took her coat might cohere with the rest of John's beliefs. But surely John is not justified in holding it, since he believes it merely on the basis of wishful thinking. John might later realize that he held the belief on the basis of mere wishful thinking and abandon it. Yet even before he comes to believe that his belief was simply the product of

---

15. Pollock, *Contemporary Theories of Knowledge* (Totowa: N.J.: Rowman and Littlefield, 1986) p. 128. Pollock's entire discussion of coherence theories is excellent.

wishful thinking, the belief is one that he is not justified in holding. Pollock also illustrates this point with the case of the exasperated mathematician:

> recall the example . . . of the person who is constructing a mathematical proof, who wants to draw a particular conclusion at a certain point, who has earlier lines in his proof from which that conclusion follows immediately, but who overlooks that conclusion and in despair simply writes down the desired conclusion, thinking to himself, "Oh, that's got to be true." That person is not justified in believing the conclusion, and the reason that he is not justified is that he does not believe it on the basis of the earlier lines from which it follows.[16]

The mathematician's belief in the conclusion is not justified, even though the conclusion coheres with the rest of his beliefs. A belief is not justified if it is held on the basis of a bad reason or no reason, even if it should happen to cohere with the rest of one's beliefs. If this is so, then the mere fact of coherence cannot be sufficient to justify one's belief.

If these objections are sound, then coherence theories are mistaken in holding that the coherence of one's beliefs is the sole warrant-making property of beliefs. Indeed, these arguments show us that the mere fact that a belief coheres with the rest of one's beliefs is not sufficient to justify that belief. Consequently, coherence theories must be false. Coherence theories as general accounts of the nature of epistemic justification are mistaken. This has important consequences for moral epistemology and for our views on what justifies moral beliefs. First, we cannot appeal to such general accounts of epistemic justification to support accepting a coherence account of the justification of moral beliefs. In other words, we cannot argue that *moral* beliefs are justified in solely in virtue of coherence because *all* warranted beliefs are justified solely in virtue of coherence. Second, at the beginning of this chapter, we noted that one motivation for favoring a coherence account of the warrant of moral beliefs is that coherence accounts of ordinary empirical beliefs seemed promising. But since coherence accounts of the warrant of empirical beliefs are not adequate, this is a poor motivation for favoring a coherence account of moral beliefs. The promise of accounting for moral beliefs in the same way that one explains the warrant of ordinary empirical beliefs is unfulfilled by the coherence theory.

If we reject the view that all warranted beliefs are justified solely in virtue of coherence, there remains a more modest form of coherentism that holds roughly that *moral* beliefs are warranted solely in virtue of their

16. Ibid., p. 86.

coherence with other moral and nonmoral beliefs. This more modest view concedes that some beliefs, such as empirical and observational beliefs, are not warranted solely in virtue of coherence, but it claims that the situation with moral beliefs is significantly different. According to this view, the warrant of a moral belief depends solely on its cohering with one's other moral beliefs and with one's justified empirical beliefs. The warrant of these empirical and observational beliefs need not be dependent solely on coherence. Let us call this view "limited coherentism." At least one motivation for limited coherentism is the seemingly plausible view that although sensory and perceptual states seem to be reasons for empirical and observational beliefs, they do not seem to be, at least not by themselves, reasons for moral beliefs. Thus, one's having a headache might be a reason for believing that one does in fact have a headache, but the having of a headache is not in itself, according to this view, a reason to believe that one's headache is bad.

Not surprisingly, limited coherentism faces some of the same problems of more general coherence theories. Recall, for example, Pollock's criticism that a belief based on a bad reason is not justified, even if it happens to cohere with rest of one's beliefs. The same criticism applies to limited coherentism because moral beliefs, like other beliefs, can be held on the basis of bad reasons. Suppose, for example, that Malcomb has had a run of bad dealings with strangers lately and feels especially pessimistic and resentful. Suppose that he believes, on the basis of exaggerated pessimism, that any world containing pain is, on the whole, intrinsically bad, no matter what else it may contain. According to limited coherentism, Malcomb's belief is justified as long as it coheres with the rest of his moral and nonmoral beliefs. Now exaggerated pessimism is in some ways the opposite of wishful thinking. If beliefs formed on the basis of wishful thinking are not justified even when they cohere with the rest of one's beliefs, then it seems just as plausible to hold that beliefs formed on the basis of exaggerated pessimism and resentment are no more justified, even if they happen to cohere with the rest of one's beliefs. In contrast to Malcomb, suppose that Bonnie believes, on the basis of wishful thinking, that any world containing any instance of moral goodness is, on the whole, intrinsically good, no matter what else it may contain. Bonnie wants desperately to believe that the world is good. But as Pollock claims, a belief that is formed on the basis of wishful thinking does not seem to be a warranted belief, even if it happens to cohere with the rest of the subject's beliefs. Of course, both Malcomb and Bonnie might come to realize that they have formed their beliefs on the basis of bad reasons. They might also come to realize that their beliefs are not accepted by others whom they take to be otherwise reliable moral thinkers. If they do come to have these beliefs, then at that point, their respective value judgments might no longer cohere with their other beliefs. But before they realize these things, their beliefs are still unjustified, for they are held for bad reasons, which is to say, for no reasons at all.

In addition to the preceding objection, limited coherence theories are open to the objection that they are too generous in ascribing warrant to fanatical or unreasonable moral beliefs. Let us take hedonistic egoism to be the view that S has a moral obligation to do an act, A, just in case there is no alternative to A for S that would produce a greater balance of pleasure over pain for S. This was apparently the view of Epicurus and his followers, and occasionally one encounters its staunch defenders in undergraduate ethics courses. However rare the view is, it does seem that one could have a coherent body of beliefs that included the principle of hedonistic egoism, along with particular egoistic judgments about actual and hypothetical cases. In other words, the proponent of hedonistic egoism might have a coherent body of beliefs. Of course, some philosophers, such as G. E. Moore, have argued that ethical egoism is incoherent. Other philosophers have argued that egoism is not a moral theory, that it is not a theory of moral obligation. But neither of these claims is persuasive.[17] Yet, in their own ways, they agree that the principle of hedonistic egoism, along with some of its implications, are not reasonable or justified moral beliefs.

Hedonistic egoism is not a widely held view among either moral philosophers or nonphilosophers. It is not widely held because it seems pretty obviously false. It implies that if one could produce the same amount of pleasure for oneself by doing either A or B, where B would result in tremendous misery for others and A in tremendous happiness for others, then there is no moral obligation or moral reason to do A rather than B. Let us call this proposition p. Proposition p is false, but it could be part of someone's coherent body of beliefs. In making a case against limited coherentism, we do not need to claim that it is impossible for anyone to be justified in believing that p. (Of course, if this were impossible, then the coherence theory would, of course, be false, since p could cohere with the rest of one's beliefs. We would then have a belief that cohered with

17. For an excellent discussion of these claims see the chapter on "Egoism" in Ramon M. Lemos, *Rights, Goods, and Democracy* (Cranbury, N.J.: Associated University Presses, 1986), pp. 15–29.

other beliefs but could not possibly be justified.) For the sake of argument, we may allow that someone, under some possible set of conditions, such as moral brainwashing or delusional religious experience, could be justified in believing that p is true. To make a case against limited coherentism, we need only claim that some proponents of egoistic hedonism, such as the ordinary, garden-variety egoist, are not justified in believing it, that it is not reasonable for them to accept it even if it coheres with the rest of their beliefs. Indeed, it appears that they ought to know better than to believe it; either they have some reason to think that p is false or they have no reason to believe it, even if it coheres with the rest of their beliefs. Suppose that an ordinary egoist were to act on p, choosing an act that brought tremendous unhappiness to others, knowing that there was an alternative that would produce just as much pleasure for himself and great happiness for others. Only someone already in the grip of egoism or coherentism would be sympathetic to the view that he was acting on a reasonable moral position or take toward him the same tolerant, even charitable, attitude that we take toward those holding what we think are mistaken, yet reasonable, moral positions. If the ordinary egoist is not justified in believing p even when p coheres with the rest of one's beliefs, then mere coherence is not a sufficient condition for justification, and even a limited coherence theory is false. Similarly, if we think that it is more reasonable for us to reject p than for the ordinary egoist to accept p, that we are more reasonable in rejecting p than he is in accepting it when our rejection and his acceptance cohere equally well with our respective beliefs, then there must be something other than the mere coherence of belief that accounts for the difference in our respective epistemic positions. As in Sosa's headache example, there must be something other than mere coherence that is relevant to justification.

Coherence theories seem excessively generous in according warrant to the egoistic beliefs of ordinary egoists. The same point could be made with respect to ordinary "group" egoists who think that their sole fundamental moral obligation is to promote the pleasure, happiness, or welfare of their family, race, or religion. If it is possible for someone to be unjustified in holding these beliefs even when they cohere with the rest of his beliefs, then coherence is not a sufficient condition for the justification of moral beliefs and limited coherentism is false. I conclude that we have reason to think that a coherence account of the warrant of our moral beliefs is not satisfactory. We have reason to think that the mere fact that a moral belief coheres with the rest of a subject's beliefs is not sufficient to justify him in holding that belief.

179

At this point, I wish to consider a family of approaches that are fundamentally opposed to coherence theories. Unlike coherence theories, these theories take certain forms of nondoxastic experience, in particular various forms of emotional experience, as reasons or grounds for moral and value beliefs. Several philosophers have recently suggested that things other than beliefs can function as grounds or reasons for ethical beliefs. For example, in "Moral Facts and Moral Knowledge," William Lycan writes, "Let me now make a third and novel suggestion about the nature of moral data: that *desires* can serve as data just as beliefs can."[18] John Pollock has also suggested that approving or disapproving of certain abstract "situation-types" constitutes a reason for believing that certain types of actions are right or wrong.[19] William Tolhurst defends the view that "moral experience can play a role in the formation and justification of our moral beliefs analogous to the role which perception plays in the formation and justification of our beliefs about the world around us."[20] Lycan, Pollock, and Tolhurst take certain nondoxastic states as grounds or reasons for holding moral beliefs. Lycan and Pollock are concerned with beliefs about right and wrong, and Tolhurst with beliefs about both right and wrong and good and bad. Furthermore, there are differences among them regarding what nondoxastic states play this role, but insofar as they accept this possibility, their views are incompatible with coherence accounts of justification, for the latter hold that no nondoxastic state can ever play this role.

There is a strong tradition of objective theories of value that take emotional experience as a source of warrant for beliefs about value. Let us say that an objective theory of value holds that certain things are good in themselves independently of the attitudes that people have toward them or are disposed to have toward them. Such theories maintain that there are things that are good in themselves independently of their being sought, loved, or desired and independently of anyone's being disposed to love or seek them. Objective theories of value have been held by Brentano, Scheler, Meinong, Moore, and Ross. Some proponents of objective theories have held that our warrant for value claims arises out of certain types

18. William Lycan, "Moral Facts and Moral Knowledge," *The Southern Journal of Philosophy* 24 Supplement (1986), p. 89.
19. John L. Pollock, "A Theory of Moral Reasoning," *Ethics* 96 (1986), pp. 512–15.
20. William Tolhurst, "On the Epistemic Value of Moral Experience," *The Southern Journal of Philosophy* 29 Supplement 1990, p. 67.

of experiences involving our emotional attitudes. This is the position taken by Brentano, Scheler, and Meinong. For these philosophers, our emotional experiences do not confer goodness or badness on things; rather, they make value known to us. Such experiences confer justification on our belief about value. For example, Meinong writes, "When I say, 'The sky is blue,' and then say 'The sky is beautiful' a property is being attributed to the sky in either case. In the second case a feeling participates in the apprehension of the property, as, in the first case, an idea does."[21] Scheler says, "The actual seat of the entire value-a priori (including the moral a priori) is the *value-cognition* or *value-intuition* that comes to the fore in feeling, basically in love and hate. . . . A spirit limited to perception and thinking would be absolutely *blind* to values, no matter how much it might have the faculty 'of inner perception,' i.e. of psychic perception."[22]

An objective theory that accepts the warrant-conferring role of certain emotional experiences is in a strong position to meet the charge that objective theories do not attend to the connections between value and psychological attitudes. There are, of course, many kinds of connections one might claim between value and the emotions, and though objective theories do in principle reject some of these connections, they need not reject others. Objective theories can hold that there are *normative* connections between value and the emotions – for example, that if something is good in itself, then loving it in and for itself is fitting to it. But objective theories might also hold that there are *epistemic* connections between value and certain forms of emotional experience, that value is known through our having such experiences.

Theories that take emotional experience as grounds or reasons for value judgments can have many forms, but I shall begin by considering the view advanced by Franz Brentano. In his 1889 lecture "The Origin of Our Knowledge of Right and Wrong," Brentano writes, "Our knowledge of what is truly and indubitably good arises from the type of experience we have been discussing, where a love is experienced as being correct."[23] In another place he writes, "when someone who loves with a love experienced as being correct perceives himself as loving correctly we say that

21. Alexius Meinong, *On Emotional Presentation*, translated by Marie-Luise Schubert Kalsi (Evanston, Ill.: Northwestern University Press, 1972), p. 28.
22. Max Scheler, *Formalism in Ethics and Non-Formal Ethics of Values*, translated by Manfred S. Frings and Roger L. Funk (Evanston, Ill.: Northwestern University Press, 1973), p. 68.
23. Brentano, *The Origin of Our Knowledge of Right and Wrong*, translated by Roderick Chisholm and Elizabeth Schneewind (London: Routledge & Kegan Paul, 1969), p. 24.

he recognizes something as good."[24] Brentano's remarks suggest that his is a nondoxastic theory of warranted value judgments insofar as it is the *experience* of correct love that justifies us in believing that something is good, that our knowledge is based on this sort of experience. One might suggest that Brentano does not hold a nondoxastic theory by construing the experience of correct love as a doxastic state, as merely a matter of believing or judging that one's attitude is correct. But such an interpretation would do violence to Brentano's view that the correctness of one's attitude is experienced and not merely something about which one has formed a belief. Furthermore, such an interpretation would merely lead us to question what justifies this belief in the correctness of one's attitude. Such an interpretation would leave the question of value knowledge unanswered.

Bearing in mind that Brentano is concerned with what is intrinsically good or good for its own sake, we might take Brentano's remarks to suggest the following epistemic principle:

(1) If S experiences his love of p as correct, then S knows that p is good.

In addition to experiences of correct love, Brentano maintains that we can experience the correctness of other attitudes such as hate and preference simpliciter. When we experience ourselves as hating something correctly, we know that the thing is bad and we derive our insights about what is better from acts of preference that are experienced as being correct. What does Brentano mean by "correct love"? He says, "One loves or hates correctly provided that one's feelings are adequate to their object-adequate in the sense of being appropriate, suitable, or fitting."[25] If we take the correctness of love or hate as a matter of fittingness, then perhaps we may take Brentano as holding that it is the experience of love as fitting that confers warrant on the belief or judgment that something is good. Thus, we might take (1) to mean that if a person experiences his love of p as fitting to p, then S knows that p is good.

The notion of experienced fittingness and the related notion of an experienced demand or "calling for" as a source or basis for the warrant of value judgments is seen by many as fundamental to our understanding of moral experience. For example, Tolhurst writes that "moral experience always involves the experience of fittingness, i.e., it always involves con-

24. Brentano, *The Foundation and Construction of Ethics,* translated by Elizabeth Schneewind (New York: Humanities Press, 1973), pp. 133–4.
25. Brentano, *The Origin of Our Knowledge of Right and Wrong,* p. 74.

struing one thing as being fitting, appropriate to, or required by another."[26] Of course, there are beliefs about fittingness, but is there such a
thing as an experience of fittingness and, in particular, of emotions as being
fitting to an object? Brentano suggests that attention to certain of out
attitudes reveals the distinction between emotions that are experienced as
fitting or correct and those that are not. He writes:

Imagine now another species quite different from ourselves; not only do its members have preferences with respect to sense qualities which are different from ours;
unlike us they also despise insight and love error for its own sake. So far as the
feelings about sense qualities are concerned, we might say that these things are
matters of taste. . . . But this is not what we would say of the love of error and
the hatred of insight. . . . In the former case the feeling of compulsion is merely
instinctive. But in the latter case the natural feeling of pleasure is a higher love
which is experienced as being correct.[27]

Other writers have been open to the possibility of experienced fittingness.
For example, John Findlay says:

we can *experience* succession as well as project it and perceive it, and we can
experience such features of succession as smooth continuity, sharp change, frag-
mentation into brief phases, etc. In the same way we can live through passivity
and live through activity: our experiences *qua* experiences have passivity or activity
as internal characters. . . . If all these cases of experiencing are possible, then there
seems to be no good reason why we should not experience correctness, and there
is certainly a sense of inner authority in many of our more considered valuations.[28]

A much stronger endorsement of experienced fittingness can be found in
Mandlebaum's *The Phenomenology of Moral Experience:*

It is a basic fact of perceptual experience that some things belong or fit together,
and that others do not. A curve may demand a certain completion and seem to
reject all others; this completion appears appropriate to the nature of the curve.
Whatever be our explanatory hypothesis, the facts are incontrovertible. In perceptual experience we find things belonging together, demanding and rejecting
certain completions, appropriately and inappropriately organized.[29]

Mandlebaum claims that there is an experience of fittingness and unfit-
tingness in many aesthetic and quasi-aesthetic experiences. When we see
colors as complementary or clashing, or hear notes and chords as har-
monious, or find something "wrong" with the way a picture hangs crook-

26. Tolhurst, "On the Epistemic Value of Moral Experience," p. 78.
27. Brentano, *The Origin of Our Knowledge of Right and Wrong*, p. 22.
28. John Findlay, *Axiological Ethics* (London: Macmillan and Co., 1970), p. 22.
29. Maurice Mandlebaum, *The Phenomenology of Moral Experience* (Glencoe, Ill.: Free Press, 1955), pp. 95–6.

edly on a wall, we experience things as fitting or unfitting. In some of these cases we also experience a demand that things be otherwise, but this experience of a demand, according to Mandlebaum, presupposes the perception or experience of things as being unfitting or unsuitable in some way. Mandlebaum is not claiming merely that we have beliefs or judgments about the fittingness of things, but rather that we experience things in this way. We see or hear things *as* fitting or unfitting. Finally, Tolhurst tells us, "To experience something as being good is to experience it as demanding some sort of positive response from us."[30]

It is important to note two features of Brentano's position. First, he insists that emotions play an essential role in our recognition of value, that without a positive attitude or a love of *p,* we could not recognize *p* as good in itself. Second, Brentano rejects the view that "blind" emotions, those not experienced as fitting or unfitting, are a source of value knowledge. With respect to the first point, Brentano rejects the view that we are capable of recognizing something as good in itself in the absence of emotional experience. He rejects the notion of a purely rational insight into a thing's intrinsic value. Even if we had the concept of wisdom or knowledge and that of something's being worthy of love, we could not know that wisdom is worthy of love simply by a consideration of the concepts. For Brentano, when we consider something that is intrinsically worthy of love, the contemplation of that thing causes us to love it, and we experience that love as fitting or appropriate to that thing. Although he insists that emotional experience is thus essential for the recognition of value, he also maintains that "the fact that a thing is loved is no indication that it is worthy of being loved–just as we may say that the fact that something is accepted or affirmed is no indication that it is true."[31] Brentano observes that a miser might come to love money for its own sake, but the miser's love of money does not result in the miser's knowing that money is good in itself. In claiming that the mere fact that a thing is loved for its own sake is no indication that it is worthy of love, Brentano appears to hold that loving something for its own sake does not justify one in believing that it is intrinsically good and that it is not a reason to believe that it is good in itself. He says that blind emotions are akin to judgments based on sense perception and memory, and of these judgments he says, "What is affirmed in this way may often be true, but it is just as likely to be false."[32] Insofar as he treats blind emotions as similar to blind judgments

30. Tolhurst, "The Epistemic Value of Moral Experience," p. 78.
31. Brentano, *The Origin of Our Knowledge of Right and Wrong,* p. 19.
32. Ibid., 19.

184

based on external perception and memory, we may take Brentano to hold that such emotions are no more a source of justification or evidence than is external perception.

Let us leave aside for the moment Brentano's rejection of the justificatory role of blind emotions. Let us assume that there are experiences of correct emotion and consider the merits of (1) as an epistemic principle. Brentano treats the experience of correct emotion as a guarantee of the truth of the corresponding value judgment, as an infallible indicator of intrinsic value. Thus, if I have the experience of a love that is fitting to p and I believe that p is good, then this belief is true. Noting this feature of Brentano's view, Findlay writes, "if correctness can thus be experienced, we cannot be wrong about it: an act of love or hate, experienced as correct, simply is, as an experience, correct."[33] Findlay's remark reflects Brentano's views of these experiences as guarantors of truth, but it is not clear that it provides any compelling reason for this view. Surely in one sense of "experience" it is false that "if correctness can be experienced we cannot be wrong about it." For in one sense of "experience," experiences need not be veridical. Macbeth might have seen a dagger before him had the visual experience of a dagger before him, but that experience was not veridical. Perhaps we can say that if one experiences an emotion as correct, then one cannot be mistaken in believing that one experiences the emotion as correct. But it hardly follows that one's emotion is correct.

Brentano's insistence that emotions experienced as correct *are* correct is part of the analogy he sees between the correctness of emotions and judgments. Certain judgments, he held, are experienced as correct, and these evident judgments cannot be mistaken. These evident judgments are of two types: a priori insights and judgments about our current mental states. Thus, if it is evident to me that I am in pain, then I am in pain. Although Brentano held that the denial of this claim about evident judgments would lead to skepticism and relativism with respect to truth, it is far from clear that rejecting the infallibility of the evident has such consequences. Yet insofar as we are concerned with the notion of experienced correctness as a source of justified belief, perhaps we may avoid these issues and consider a principle that is weaker than (1):

(2) If S experiences his love of p as fitting to p, then S is justified in believing that p is good.

---

33. Findlay, *Axiological Ethics*, p. 22.

This principle is weaker than (1) insofar as it does not imply that the experience of fitting emotion is an infallible indicator of goodness. Its antecedent does not imply that one's love of p is fitting to p.

Although (2) is weaker than (1), it may still be too strong. There are two sorts of considerations supporting this view. Suppose that S experiences his love of p as fitting to p. But also suppose that there are other persons with whom S is in very close general agreement about what is good, and they tell S that they have no experience of correct emotion toward p and that they do not love p for its own sake. In a situation like this, it might be unreasonable for S to believe that p is good in itself. The situation here is like that in which a person might discover that he is color blind with respect to certain colors. In such cases, someone in very close agreement with others about certain colors might acquire reasons, based on the testimony of others, to doubt that objects have the colors he takes them to have. Given their testimony, it is possible that his having an experience of a certain color would not justify him in believing that he was seeing something of that color. Second, many sorts of experience can fail to warrant belief when certain other conditions obtain, and it seems reasonable to expect a similar situation with respect to the experience of correct or fitting emotion. One might, for example, have the visual experience of a thing as red, but at the same time know that the thing one is looking at is illuminated by red lights and that things that are not red often look red under these conditions. Given this additional information, the fact that one experienced the object as red would not justify one in believing that the thing one was looking at was red. Principle (2) seems too strong because it rules out the possibility of defeaters for one's experience of correctness.

Given these objections to (2), we may opt for a yet weaker principle:

(3) S's experiencing his love of p as fitting to p is a prima facie reason for S to believe that p is good.

Principle (3) treats the experience of fitting emotion as a defeasible reason for S to believe that p is good, a reason that can be defeated by other considerations. If we accept (3), then we may say that the experience of fitting emotion functions in a manner analogous to other cases of experience, such as perceptual and mnemonic experience. We may think of (3) as analogous to the principle that x's looking red to S is a prima facie reason for S to believe that x is red. Similarly, we may think of (3) as analogous to the principle that one's seeming to remember that p is a prima facie reason for or tends to support the belief that p.

186

Let us consider critically the view that experiencing one's emotional attitude toward an object as fitting can be a prima facie reason for a judgment of intrinsic value. This is a view for which I have had some sympathy.[34] But I now think that there are some serious problems with it. It is important to note, however, that what we have said about modest a priori justification is compatible with the truth of a principle like (3). It is possible that we could have both a priori and empirical reasons for believing that certain things are intrinsically worthy of love or hate. The fact that one has a priori reasons for believing something is compatible with one's also having empirical reasons. One might have a priori reasons for believing that 2 and 3 are 5, and one might also have reasons to believe it on the basis of experience and the testimony of others. Thus, if we accept a principle like (3), it does not follow that we must reject the account of modest a priori justification defended in the last chapter or the view that we have modest a priori justification for some propositions about what is intrinsically valuable. Both the position of the last chapter and (3) could be true.

Let us grant for the moment that there really is such a thing as the experience of the fittingness of one's emotion. Even if there are such experiences, they cannot be the only source of warrant for value beliefs. This is because there are some propositions about intrinsic value that I am now justified in believing whose warrant for me is not dependent on a nondoxastic experience of fittingness. I assume, for example, that I am now justified in believing the proposition that someone's being happy is intrinsically valuable. Although I *believe* that my love for the state of affairs *someone's being happy* is fitting, I cannot find in my own case anything like a nondoxastic *experience* of fittingness. Now if I am not now having such an experience, then obviously my value belief is not justified for me in virtue of my now having that experience. Moreover, I cannot say that I remember having had an experience of fittingly loving that state of affairs. My value belief does not seem to be the product of memory. It is not the case that my value belief is based on my seeming to remember that someone's being happy is intrinsically good or seeming to remember an experience of fitting love toward that state of affairs. If this is so, then what justifies me in believing now that someone's being happy is intrinsically good is not the immediate experience of the fittingness of my pro attitude toward someone's being happy or my having a memory of it.

34. See my "Warrant, Emotion, and Value," *Philosophical Studies* (October 57 1989), pp. 175–92.

If the preceding points are correct, then it follows that some propositions about value are not warranted in virtue of an experience of fitting emotion. This, of course, does not show that (3) is false, since (3) does not claim that the experience of fittingness is the only source of justification one can have for a value belief. But it does have other important consequences. First, it shows us that Brentano's own view is false, for he held that original insights into value (those not accepted merely on the basis of testimony) *essentially* involve an experience of the fittingness of one's emotional attitude. For Brentano, the origin or source of our warranted value beliefs must lie in experienced fittingness. But it seems clear that we have a great many warranted value beliefs whose warrant does not depend on our presently having those experiences or on memory. Second, it shows us that there is something other than an experience of fittingness that justifies value beliefs. A satisfactory moral epistemology must recognize some source of warrant other than experienced fittingness. If an experience of fittingness does not justify my belief that someone's being happy is intrinsically good, then what does? In keeping with the view defended in the last chapter, I suggest that we can have modest a priori justification for believing it. More specifically, what justifies me in believing that someone's being happy is intrinsically good is that I believe it on the basis of my comprehending consideration of it, and nothing defeats this reason for me.

The fact that I am justified in some value beliefs in the absence of any experience of fittingness does not itself imply that (3) is false. Yet it does point to a serious problem with the view that our warranted value beliefs are based on experiences of fitting emotion. The failure to experience things as being a certain way is, under some conditions, a reason to believe that things are not that way. If I am looking at an object held at arm's length in broad daylight with healthy eyes and fail to have any sensation of redness, then it seems that I have some reason to believe that the thing is not red. My reason for believing that it is not red is that it just doesn't look red. Just as the failure to experience redness, to have a sensation of red, is under some conditions a reason to believe that something is not red, so the failure to have experiences of fitting love or hate toward an object would seem to be, under some conditions, a reason to believe that love or hate was not fitting toward that object. Now, sitting here in my office, I am not presently experiencing the correctness of my emotional attitudes toward a great many states of affairs that I do care about and that I am justified in believing to be intrinsically good. If I *imagine* as vividly as I can the suffering of a little child, I find that although I hate the suffering

188

of the imagined child, I do not experience the fittingness of that hatred. Indeed, even if I *recall* as vividly as I can the suffering of my own child, I do not find that I experience the fittingness of hatred of his suffering. There are, therefore, some states of affairs which I can contemplate, vividly imagine, or vividly recall without having anything like an experience of the fittingness of my emotions. This is not to say that I experience no emotional attitudes toward those states of affairs; of course, I do. I simply do not seem to experience the fittingness of any attitude toward them.

But if we take seriously the view that the experience of fittingness is a reason for value beliefs, then it seems we should also take seriously the view that the failure to experience fittingness under certain conditions also tells us something about value or lack of value. The failure to have experiences of fittingness under conditions where we might reasonably expect to have them would seem to be a reason to think that a thing lacks intrinsic value. Proponents of the view that experienced fittingness is a source of warrant must hold either (1) that, given my failure to have the experience of fitting hatred, I really do have reason to think that the suffering of a little child is not bad or (2) that I am not in the conditions where the failure to have that experience is a reason to think it is not bad, that I am not in the conditions in which it is reasonable to expect that I would have the experience of fittingness. Both options are problematic.

Concerning the first option, it simply seems implausible that to think that my failure to have the experience of the fittingness of my hatred in these conditions is a reason for me to think that the suffering of a little child is not intrinsically bad. I do not have any reason to think that. But even if the absence of that experience were a reason, then the proponents of this view would have to admit that something other than the experience of fitting emotion is the source of our warrant for justified beliefs about value, that what does the real justificatory work in this case is something else entirely. Since the absence of an experience of fitting emotion seems rather common when we contemplate, imagine, or recall states of affairs that we are justified in believing to be good or bad, the real justificatory ground in this wide range of cases must be something other than experienced fittingness. Indeed, the common absence of the experience would seem to be, more than anything, a reason to deny the intrinsic value of things that we are justified in believing have intrinsic value. In other words, the absence of the experience would be, more often than not, a misleading reason, pointing away from what we are, all things considered, justified in believing about value.

The second option concedes that my failure to have the experience of fittingness when I contemplate or vividly imagine or recall various states of affairs is not a reason for me to reject any value claims about them. But it claims that this is because I am not in the right conditions where the failure to have that experience would be such a reason. Just as the failure to have an experience of redness in a darkened room or when one's eyes are closed is not a reason to deny that there is something red before one, so we must concede that there could be conditions in which failure to experience the fittingness of an emotion is not a reason to deny a value claim. The problem with the second option is that if we don't have the relevant sort of experience when we contemplate or vividly imagine or recall states of affairs that we are justified in believing to be good or bad, then under what conditions would failure to have the relevant experiences count as a reason? If the failure to have the experience in *these* conditions is not a reason to deny a value belief, then what could they be? Perhaps one might suggest that failure to experience one's emotion toward *p* as fitting when one is experiencing *p* would be a reason to doubt that *p* has a certain value. But even this doesn't seem very promising. When I experience the pleasures of a warm bath, I do not also experience the fittingness of my liking the pleasures of a warm bath. When I see someone suffering, I do not find that I experience the fittingness of my dislike for that fact, though if I were to reflect, I would believe that disliking it is fitting to it. Experiencing a valuable state of affairs does not seem to produce, at least in me, an experience of the fittingness of an emotional attitude any more than contemplation, imagination, or recollection.

In sum, there are a great many states of affairs, good and bad, that we can contemplate, imagine, recall, and experience without experiencing the fittingness of our emotional attitudes toward them. I am justified in believing that many of these states of affairs are intrinsically valuable. If we take seriously the notion that the experience of fittingness can be a reason for value beliefs, then we ought also to take seriously the absence of that experience toward what we contemplate, recall, and so on as a reason for rejecting various value claims. Thus, this view would appear to imply that I have reasons for rejecting many of the value beliefs I am actually justified in holding. This, in turn, implies either that I am not justified in believing these value claims or that I am justified in believing them on the basis of something other than the experience of fitting emotion. Neither alternative should be welcomed by those who see the experience of fitting emotion as the key to understanding our knowledge of value. Now if one says that the failure to have the relevant sorts of experiences when one contemplates, imagines, recalls, or experiences certain states of affairs is not a reason, then at the very least, we are owed some explanation of why it is not and, better still, some positive account of when the failure to have these experiences would be a reason to reject a value claim. Such an account would also be one that, by implication, told us under what conditions we could expect to have those experiences, what were the "standard" conditions of those experiences.

Finally, none of the preceding objections presuppose that there is no such thing as a nondoxastic experience of the fittingness of one's emotions. Ultimately, the question of whether there is such an experience is not, of course, a matter of philosophical argument. Ultimately, the appeal must be to reflection on the nature of one's own experience and the testimony of others. But when we repeatedly fail to find it in contemplating, imagining, recalling, and even experiencing various good and bad states of affairs, then we may fairly question whether there really is any such thing. I have tried to indicate some of the problems with taking such experiences as reasons for value beliefs. Of course, it there are no such experiences, then these problems can be avoided.

MERE EMOTIONS AS A REASON FOR VALUE BELIEFS

We have seen that Brentano denies that blind emotions, those that are not experienced as fitting, are epistemic grounds for value beliefs. At this point, I wish to consider the case for blind emotions as epistemic grounds. Let us consider the following principle:

(4) *S*'s loving *p* in and for itself is a prima facie reason for *S* to believe that *p* is good.

This principle treats the intrinsic pro attitude of loving something as a reason for value belief. Similar principles would treat hating something per se or intrinsic preferences as defeasible reasons for believing that something is intrinsically bad or that one thing is intrinsically better than another. I take it that Brentano would reject such a latitudinarian conception of the justificatory role of such attitudes, for he says that blind emotions are akin to judgments based on sense perception and memory and that these latter sorts of judgments are "just as likely to be false." Yet, other philosophers have taken a more sympathetic stance on the justificatory role of emotional experience. Everett Hall, for example, writes, "Just as the occurrence of perceptions may be taken as verification of the truth of relevant declarative thing-sentences, so the occurrence of emotions may be taken as justification of the legitimacy of relevant value sentences about

191

their objects. And analogously the occurrence of different emotions under different conditions may offer different degrees of justification."[35]

One obvious advantage that this view enjoys over Brentano's is that it does not appeal to the problematic notion of experienced fittingness. But because it does not involve the notion of experienced fittingness, this view faces a different problem. One might allow that the experience of the fittingness or appropriateness of an attitude toward some state of affairs is a defeasible reason to believe that such an attitude is appropriate or fitting to it. One might allow roughly that experiencing things in a certain way is a reason to believe that things really are that way. But one might urge that what distinguishes (4) from the other principles considered earlier is that it lacks the crucial element involved in these other principles, namely, an experience of the fittingness of one's attitude. And though one might be willing to grant that there is some analogy between experiencing something as square and experiencing one's attitude as fitting in that the former is a reason to believe that something is square and the latter is a reason to believe that one's attitude is fitting, it is far from clear how merely loving something can be a reason to believe that it is *worthy* of love or good for its own sake. "How," one might ask, "can we take the fact that something is loved for its own sake as a reason to believe anything more than that the thing is loved?"

This objection to (4) is important but not conclusive. One way to defend a principle like (4) is to look for analogies with other plausible epistemic principles. One promising set of epistemic principles is suggested by Chisholm's treatment of "higher order" knowledge and justification, that is, our knowing that we know and our being justified in believing that we are justified in believing. Chisholm suggests that what justifies a person in believing a proposition, *p, also* justifies him in believing that he is justified in believing *p.* Chisholm distinguishes between normative states, their objectives, and their substrates. An example of a normative state is *its being beyond reasonable doubt for me that there are sheep.* "The objective of this normative state is the proposition that there are sheep. And the substrate of this normative state is the nonnormative state (say, the perceptual takings) on which the normative state supervenes. The substrate, in other words, is a nonnormative state that is necessarily such that if it obtains, then the normative state obtains."[36] Chisholm adds, "I

35. Everett Hall, "The Empirical Justifiability of Valuative Sentences," *Categorial Analysis,* edited by E. M. Adams (Chapel Hill: University of North Carolina Press, 1964), p. 210.
36. Roderick Chisholm, *The Foundations of Knowing* (Minneapolis: University of Minnesota Press, 1982). p. 52.

suggest that the substrate for this higher order epistemic state is the *same* as that for the lower order epistemic state which is its objective. In other words, those nonnormative states (the perceptual takings) which justify me in believing that sheep exist *also* justify me in believing that it is beyond reasonable doubt that sheep exist."[37] Chisholm's views concerning our higher order justification imply that one's having certain sorts of experiences, such as perceptual takings of sheep, can justify one in believing certain normative, epistemic propositions about what one is justified in believing. The important point here is that the perceptual takings justify those epistemic beliefs, even though the perceptual takings are not experiences of being justified or experiences of the epistemic fittingness of one's believing something. When a person takes there to be a sheep, he does not perceptually take himself to be justified in believing something. There need be no experience of being justified in order for the perceptual taking to serve as the justifier for the higher order epistemic belief. If having certain perceptual takings can justify certain normative epistemic beliefs about what one is justified in believing, then it seems no more problematic to hold that one's having certain emotional attitudes or experiences can justify certain believes about what is intrinsically valuable. Emotional attitudes could be reasons for value claims, even thought they are not experiences of the fittingness of things or experiences of values or requirements.

A more serious problem for (4), however, is the case suggested by Brentano, in which a miser comes to love in and for itself his having a lot of money. Brentano would say, I think, that even though the miser loves that state of affairs in and for itself, he has no reason to think that it is intrinsically valuable. Similarly, one might say that the mere fact that someone loves as such the suffering of another is no reason for him to think that the suffering of another is intrinsically valuable. And the fact that A prefers as such A's being happy and B's being sad to B's being happy and A's being sad is no reason for A to think that the former state of affairs is intrinsically better than the latter. Following Brentano, we may say that there are a great many states of affairs that one can love, hate, prefer, or be indifferent to without having any reason to think that one's emotional attitude is fitting to them. More generally, it seem entirely possible to have no reason to believe that p is intrinsically better than q, and yet at the same time to prefer p to q. The view that intrinsic preferences are epistemic reasons for value claims would imply that this is false.

37. Ibid., p. 55.

Still, someone, I for example, might prefer as such a world that contained huge forests of flourishing oak trees and no works of art to a world that contained every work of Michelangelo and Rembrandt and no forests at all. But this preference does not seem to be any reason for me to think that the one state of affairs is intrinsically better than the other. Such a preference is blind in the sense that it provides no insight into the value of things; it is no reason to think that one thing is better than another. Similarly, it seems possible that someone can love something for its own sake without having any reason to think that it is intrinsically good. Someone might love for its own sake the fact that he is a Texan or that the Red Sox beat the Yankees without having any reason to think that these things are intrinsically good. Finally, it seems possible that someone might know that two states of affairs are of equal intrinsic value and prefer one as such to the other without having any reason to think that either is better. James might know that his being happy is as intrinsically good as John's being happy, and yet James might prefer his being happy to John's being happy. On the view under consideration, this would imply that James has some reason to think that his own happiness is intrinsically better than John's. Such a preference is not a reason, but even if it were, it would have to be a misleading reason, a reason for believing something that is contrary to what James knows to be true. In such a case, the real source of James's value knowledge, the reason for his believing that John's happiness is equal in intrinsic value to his own, would have to consist in something other than his own preference for these states of affairs. In such cases, there would need to be something other than his preference as a ground for his value belief. In short, the view that our emotional attitudes are reasons for value beliefs implies that one can never love, hate, or prefer as such various states of affairs without having some reason to think that they are good, bad, or better. But this seems false. We can and do have emotional attitudes toward things without having reasons to think that those attitudes are appropriate or fitting.

If the conclusions of this chapter are sound, then neither a pure coherence theory nor a broadly empirical theory that treats emotional experience as evidence are adequate accounts of the epistemic warrant of our beliefs about intrinsic value. If the conclusions of the last chapter are sound, then it is more reasonable to accept the existence of some value beliefs justified a priori if we accept the notion of modest a priori justification than if we restrict ourselves to a strong conception of the a priori. Of these four alternatives – a pure coherence theory, the broadly empirical theory, the strong conception of the a priori, and the modest conception

– the last appears to represent the most promising approach to our understanding the justification for value claims. To accept the notion of modest a priori justification for value claims is to allow that they can be defeasible and less than certain. To say that some proposition enjoys modest a priori justification is decidedly *not* to foreclose the possibility of defeating considerations or to bring reflection or discussion to a full stop. Furthermore, the notion of value beliefs justified a priori does not imply that we have any mysterious, spooky faculty of moral intuition any more than the existence of mathematical or metaphysical beliefs justified a priori implies mysterious cognitive faculties. Though a priori justification is perfectly familiar to us and is no real cause of philosophical embarrassment, there are some hard questions about it that merit answers. Chiefly, we may wonder what it is that justifies us in holding those beliefs that we are justified in holding a priori. I have suggested that we may take the comprehending consideration of some propositions as reasons for believing them. If it is plausible to think that there are some states of affairs that are such that our contemplation or comprehending consideration of them is a reason to to love or hate them, then it seems no less plausible to hold that there are states of affairs or propositions whose comprehending consideration is a reason to believe them. Depending on one's point of view, this approach leaves us with either a wonderfully robust variety or a hopelessly scattered plurality of reasons and warrant-conferring states. But there is, I think, no a priori reason to reject a rich variety of warrant-conferring states any more than there is reason to reject a wide variety of states of affairs that are intrinsically worthy of love or hate. In understanding the nature of a priori justification, others will find different approaches appealing, such as, perhaps, a generally reliabilist approach. But this problem in understanding a priori moral and value beliefs is no different from that in understanding any sort of a priori belief and is no reason to reject the approach defended here.

Appendix A: Chisholm's definition of organic unity

I wish to consider briefly Chisholm's attempt to define an organic unity. One merit of his approach is that it does not make use of the notion of a "sum" of values. In *Brentano and Intrinsic Value*, he offers the following definitions:[1]

(D1)   *P* is a part of *Q* = *Df.* *Q* is necessarily such that (a) if it obtains then *P* obtains, and (b) whoever conceives *Q* conceives *P*.

(D2)   Some of the goodness of *G* is defeated by *W* = *Df.* *G* is a good part of *W* and better than *W*; and if *W* has a bad part that is worse than *W*, then that bad part is part of *G*.

(D3)   Some of the badness of *B* is defeated by *W* = *Df.* *B* is a bad part of *W* and worse than *W*; and if *W* has a good part that is better than *W*, then that good part is a part of *B*.

Given the definition of a part in (D1), every state of affairs is a part of itself. Thus, in (D2) and (D3) we should take the definition of "part" to refer to "proper parts." *P* is a proper part of *Q* if and only if *P* is a part of *Q* and *Q* is not a part of *P*.

The defeat of goodness can be illustrated by pleasure in the bad. Consider the state of affairs, Smith's being pleased that Jones is suffering. Let us assume that this state of affairs is bad. This state of affairs has no bad parts, for Jones is suffering is *not* a part of it. (Smith's being pleased that Jones is suffering does not imply that Jones is suffering.) Still, it has a good part which is better than it, namely, Smith's being pleased. The defeat of badness can be illustrated by displeasure in the bad. Consider the state of affairs, Smith's being displeased that Jones is suffering. Let us assume that this state of affairs is good or neutral. It has a bad part which is worse than it, namely, Smith's being displeased. It has no good part.

1. Roderick Chisholm, *Brentano and Intrinsic Value* (Cambridge: Cambridge University Press, 1986), p. 88. Chisholm's statements of (D1) and (D2) contain some misprints that I have corrected here. The correct version of (D1) is given on pp. 77–8, and the correct version of (D2) is given on p. 82.

Given these definitions Chisholm distinguishes the following ten types of organic unities:[2]

OU1   The goodness of G is partially defeated by W = Df. Some of the goodness of G is defeated by W and W is good.

OU2   The goodness of G is totally defeated by W = Df. Some of the goodness of G is defeated by W, and W is not good.

OU3   The goodness of G is transvalued by W = Df. Some of the goodness of G is defeated by W, and W is bad.

OU4   The badness of B is partially defeated by W = Df. Some of the badness of B is defeated by W, and W is bad.

OU5   The badness of B is totally defeated by W = Df. Some of the badness of B is defeated by W, and W is not bad.

OU6   The badness of B is transvalued by W = Df. Some of the badness of B is defeated by W, and W is good.

OU7   W positively defeats its neutrality = Df. W is good, and every proper part of W is neutral.

OU8   W negatively defeats its neutrality = Df. W is bad, and every proper part of W is neutral.

OU9   W enhances the goodness of G = Df. G is part of W; G is good but not as good as W; and every proper part of W that is good has a part in common with G.

OU10   W aggravates the value of B = Df. B is part of W; B is bad but not as bad as W; and every proper part of W that is bad has a part in common with B.

Finally, Chisholm offers the following definitions:[3]

(D4)   W is a mixed whole = Df. Either (a) W has both good and bad parts or (b) W is neutral and has either a good or a bad part.

(D5)   W is an organic unity = Df. Either (a) W is mixed and has no unmixed parts such that it falls in value between them or (b) W is unmixed and has a good part that is better than it or a bad part that is worse than it.

What would be examples of a mixed whole? The following is a mixed whole: A's experiencing pleasure and B's experiencing pain. This is a mixed whole because it has both good and bad parts. A second example of a mixed whole would be any neutral state of affairs in which the goodness of A's experiencing pleasure was precisely balanced by the badness of B's experiencing pain. (If we were to pretend that quantitative hedonism is true and that we could measure quantitatively the intensity of pleasures and pains, an example of this latter state of affairs would be A's having

2. Ibid., pp. 88–9. I believe that the final definition of "aggravation" is a misprint. I have substituted what I take to be the correct definition found on p. 86.
3. Ibid., p. 75.

six units of pleasure and B's having six units of pain.) Such a neutral state of affairs would have a good part and a bad part.

If we assume that the state of affairs *Smith's being pleased that Jones is suffering* is intrinsically bad, then it is also an unmixed whole, since it has no bad parts. According to (D5), it is also an organic unity because it is an unmixed whole that has a good part, namely, Smith's being pleased, which is better than it is. Similarly, if we assume that the state of affairs *Smith's being displeased that Jones is suffering* is intrinsically good, then it is also an unmixed whole, since it has no good parts. According to (D2), it is an organic unity because it is an unmixed whole and has a bad part that is worse than it is. Chisholm's definition of an organic unity is at least adequate to these examples. Unfortunately, Chisholm's definition of an organic unity is not adequate to certain forms of organic unity that he has distinguished. It is not adequate to (OU7), (OU8), (OU9), or (OU10).

What is an example of the "negative defeat of the neutral"? Chisholm suggests one's being aware of what one takes to be one's evil deed and not being ashamed.[4] This whole, he suggests, is intrinsically bad but has no parts that are bad. The "positive defeat of the neutral" is illustrated by one's being aware of what he takes to be someone wronging him and not being resentful. Chisholm says that the concept of "enhancement" may be illustrated by pleasure in the good if we suppose that A's being pleased that someone is happy (W) is better than its simpler part, A's being pleased, (G). Similarly, we might say that an example of "aggravation" is A's being displeased that someone is pleased if we assume that this whole is worse than its simpler part, A's being displeased.

To see that those organic unities that "positively defeat their neutrality" (OU7) are not captured by Chisholm's definition of an organic unity, we need only note that every whole of this sort is unmixed. They are unmixed because they have only neutral parts. The fact that these are unmixed wholes having only neutral parts is the reason they cannot be captured by (D5). According to (D5), an unmixed whole is an organic unity only if it has a good part that is better than it or a bad part that is worse than it. Obviously if a whole has only neutral parts, it can't have a good part or a bad part. The same problem pertains to those organic unities that "negatively defeat their neutrality" (OU8). These wholes are also unmixed, since they have only neutral parts. But again, (D5) tells us that an unmixed

---

4. Chisholm cites Aristotle's remark in the *Nicomachean Ethics*: "shamelessness – not to be ashamed of doing bad actions – is bad." Book IV, Chapter 9, 1128b. Shamelessness is an example of indifference toward the bad.

whole is an organic unity only if it has a good part better than it or a bad part worse than it. So Chisholm's definition isn't adequate to these wholes either.

Definition (D5) is also not adequate to those wholes that are examples of enhancement. Suppose that the whole that is A's being pleased that someone is happy, W, is a case of enhancement, that W enhances the goodness of A's being pleased, G. In this case, W is an instance of enhancement, since it is better than its only good part, namely, G. Now W is an unmixed whole because it is a good whole with no bad parts. But according to (D5), W is an organic unity only if it has a good part that is better than it or a bad part that is worse than it. Yet W does not have a good part that is better than it or a bad part that is worse than it. So Chisholm's definition of an organic unity is not adequate to this case of enhancement.

Furthermore, (D5) is not adequate to certain examples of aggravation. Let's assume that the whole *A's being displeased that someone is happy W,* is an instance of aggravation, that W aggravates the badness of A's being displeased, B. Let's assume that W is worse than its only bad part, B. W is an unmixed whole, since it is bad with no good parts. But again, (D5) claims that an unmixed whole is an organic unity only if it has a good part that is better than it or a bad part that is worse than it. Yet W has no good part that is better than it and no bad part that is worse than it.

If Chisholm's definition of an organic unity is not adequate to these four types of organic unity, it is also not clear that it is adequate to those forms of organic unity that are represented by the *bonum variationis* and the *bonum progressionis*. Let us recall Chisholm's illustration of the *bonum variationis*. Suppose that A is a beautiful painting, that B is a painting exactly like A, and that C is a beautiful piece of music. Assume that the aesthetic contemplation of A has the same value as that of B and the same as that of C. The whole that is the aesthetic contemplation of A followed by the aesthetic contemplation of C is intrinsically better than that whole that is the aesthetic contemplation of A followed by the aesthetic contemplation of B. Chisholm writes, "Hence one could say that the value of a *bonum variationis* is greater than the sum of the values of its constituent parts."[5] If this varied whole is an organic unity, then it does not seem that (D5) captures it. For it would seem to be an unmixed whole that lacks a good part that is better than it.

I believe (D5) faces similar problems from the *bonum progressionis,* but

5. Chisholm, *Brentano and Intrinsic Value,* p. 71.

I shall not pursue them here. Instead, I wish to point out that certain instances of the *bonum variationis* represent forms of organic unity that are not among Chisholm's ten types. Suppose, as before, that the aesthetic contemplation of *A* has the same intrinsic value as the aesthetic contemplation of *B* and the same intrinsic value as having a certain intellectual insight. Now suppose that *S*'s aesthetic contemplation of *A* and *S*'s having that intellectual insight is intrinsically better than *S*'s aesthetic contemplation of *A* and *S*'s aesthetic contemplation of *B*. If the former whole is an organic unity, a kind of *bonum variationis,* then it does not seem to be among Chisholm's ten types. Consider the state of affairs *S's having an aesthetic contemplation of something and S's having an insight.* If this is an organic unity, it is not a case of defeated good, since none of the good parts are better than the whole. It is not a case of enhancement, since it is false that there is a good part of that whole such that every other good part of that whole has a part in common with it. If this is right, then there are more types of organic unity than the ten Chisholm distinguishes. A similar example might involve *S*'s having an aesthetic contemplation of something and someone else, *T,* having an insight. Presumably this is better than if both *S* and *T* have the same aesthetic experience or both have the same insight. Reflection on the *bonum progressionis* will, I believe, reveal similar examples.

Appendix B: Some naturalistic analyses

I wish to consider briefly some familiar attempts to provide a naturalistic analysis of the concept of intrinsic preferability. The following attempts either have implications it is reasonable for us to reject or are not really analyses of intrinsic preferability. Let us consider states of affairs of the following form:

(1) X is intrinsically better than Y.

Can (1) be given a hedonistic analysis such as the following?

(2) X implies a greater balance of pleasure over pain than Y.

If (1) can be analyzed in terms of (2), there must be a mutual implication between them. Unfortunately, it is far from clear that hedonism is true or that there is a mutual implication between (1) and (2). One familiar objection to hedonism concerns *Schadenfreude,* taking pleasure or joy in the suffering or sorrow of another, and *Mitleid,* sorrow in another person's sorrow. Suppose that Jones is pleased that Smith is suffering, *X,* and that Brown is sad that Smith is suffering, *Y.* Even if *X* implies a greater balance of pleasure over pain than *Y,* it is not obvious that *X* is intrinsically better than *Y.* Concerning joy in the suffering of another, Schopenhauer writes, "In a certain sense the opposite of envy is the habit of gloating over the misfortunes of others. At any rate, whereas the former is human, the latter is diabolical. There is no sign more infallible of an entirely bad heart, and of profound moral worthlessness than open and candid enjoyment of seeing other people suffer."[1]

In contemplating the value of *X* and *Y,* we should note that neither state of affairs implies that Smith *is* suffering. Jones's pleasure might be the result of his hearing a story of Smith's misfortune, a story that is, unknown

1. Arthur Schopenhauer, *The Basis of Morality,* translated by A. Broderick Bullocks (London: Swan Sonneschein, 1903), pp. 156–7.

to Jones, entirely false. Jones's pleasure might be based on his false belief that Smith is suffering. Of course, Brown's sorrow might be based on having overheard the same false tale. Pleasure and displeasure, joy and sorrow, can thus be construed as intentional attitudes directed to states of affairs that might or might not obtain. These attitudes are in this respect akin to belief, for the fact that one believes that someone is suffering does not imply that someone is suffering. Bearing this fact in mind, we may also compare Jones's taking pleasure in Smith's suffering, X, with Gray's taking pleasure in Green's joy, Z. The latter state of affairs is an instance of *Mitfreude*, taking joy in another person's joy. If we construe pleasure as an intentional attitude, then we may say that both X and Z imply pleasure but no pain. But is X as intrinsically good as Z? It doesn't seem so.

In addition to the problems raised by *Schadenfreude, Mitleid,* and *Mitfreude,* we may consider the value of pleasures based on false beliefs. Suppose Smith believes that p is true and Smith is pleased that p. Suppose Smith believes that he is seeing an original painting by Reubens, and he is pleased that he is seeing an original Reubens. But imagine that the painting he is looking at is merely an imitation of a Reubens. Consider the states of affairs *Smith is pleased that he is seeing a painting by Reubens and is seeing a painting by Reubens, A,* and *Smith is pleased that he is seeing a painting by Reubens and is seeing an imitation of a Reubens, B.* We may suppose that B implies as much pleasure as A, but it is not obvious that B is as intrinsically valuable as A. The following example suggested by Robert Nozick is also relevant:

Suppose there were an experience machine that would give you any experience you desired. Superduper neuropsychologists could stimulate your brain so that you would think and feel that you were writing a great novel, or making a friend, or reading an interesting book. All the time you would be floating in a tank, with electrodes attached to your brain. Should you plug into the machine for life, preprograming your life experiences?[2]

Nozick's example suggests that taking pleasure in writing a great novel or reading an interesting book, when in fact one is doing neither, is less valuable than taking pleasure in those things when one is actually doing them. If this is right, then the intrinsic value of a state of affairs cannot be simply a function of the pleasure–pain balance they imply. If the preceding

2. Robert Nozick, *Anarchy, State, and Utopia* (New York: Basic Books, 1974), p. 42.

remarks are correct, if there is no mutual implication between (1) and (2), then (1) cannot be analyzed by (2).

Let us consider the possibility that (1) is analyzed by the following:

(3) Someone prefers X as such to Y.

In order to recognize that (3) is unsatisfactory, we need only ask whether the fact that someone prefers one state of affairs as such to another implies that the former is intrinsically better than the latter. Would the fact that someone preferred as such Jones's taking pleasure in Smith's suffering to Gray's taking pleasure in Green's joy imply that the former state of affairs is intrinsically better than the latter? If the preceding criticisms of (2) were correct, then surely the answer is "no." We may also ask whether our own suffering would be intrinsically better than our own joy if someone were to prefer our suffering as such to our joy. Would anyone really think the answer to this "yes"? The mere fact that someone prefers one state of affairs to another does not imply that it is fitting or appropriate to do so.

A further difficulty with the contention that (3) is an analysis of (1) is that it implies that it is impossible for one state of affairs to be intrinsically better than another unless someone prefers the former to the latter. One strange consequence of this view is that certain states of affairs involving the pleasure or pain enjoyed or suffered by brute animals would be without intrinsic value. Consider the world before the evolution of human beings. We can imagine that the brute animals living then suffered pain and enjoyed pleasure, at least the pain of broken limbs and being something's dinner or the pleasures of scratching an itch and basking on a warm rock on a sunny day. Let us suppose that at some time there are 1,248 animals experiencing pleasure and 1,112 animals experiencing pain. It is plausible to suppose that the former state of affairs is intrinsically better than the latter. Such a view is surely plausible by the lights of the hedonistic theory discussed earlier. At least one merit of hedonism is that it supports the view that the former is a better state of affairs than the latter. But in that prehistoric world, we may also assume that none of its animal inhabitants had the conceptual machinery or the cognitive sophistication to conceive of the states of affairs *there being 1,248 animals experiencing pleasure* and *there being 1,112 animals experiencing pain*. But if we suppose that they could not *conceive* of those states of affairs, we may also suppose that they could not *prefer* the former to the latter. Yet in spite of the fact that there is no one at that time who prefers the former to the latter, it is still plausible to believe that the former is better than the latter. If this is correct, then the fact that the former is intrinsically better than the latter does not imply that someone prefers the former to the latter.

To this argument someone might object that the one state of affairs is better than the other only because someone now prefers the former to the latter. But it is surely strange to think that the former is better than the latter only because it is now preferred. According to this view, if no one had ever preferred the former to the latter, then the former would not have been better than the latter; had no beings evolved that could prefer the one state of affairs to the other, the one would not have been intrinsically better than the other. How strange to think that the intrinsic value of these aggregates of animal pleasure and pain depends on someone's being able to conceive and form some preference toward them, that had such a being never come into being, the greater sum of animal pleasure would never be greater in intrinsic value than the lesser sum of animal pain, and that in the absence of such a being, the whole sum of animal pleasure and pain would be without any intrinsic value at all.

Finally, we may note that it is possible for someone to prefer X as such to Y and for someone else to prefer Y as such to X. If two persons had such different preferences, and if preferring one thing as such to another implied that the former was intrinsically better, then it would follow that X is intrinsically better than Y and Y is intrinsically better than X. This result is simply unacceptable if we are attempting to provide an analysis of the traditional concept of intrinsic value, for according to the traditional view, if X is intrinsically better than Y, it is false that Y is intrinsically better than X. Of course, one might urge that he is concerned with providing an analysis of something's being intrinsically better *for* someone and that something can be intrinsically better for one person but not for another. One might urge that he is interested in providing an analysis of a relational concept of intrinsic preferability. But if so, he is not interested in the same concept with which the traditional view is concerned, for that concept is not relational. Even if one were to succeed in providing a nonethical analysis of some relational notion of value, it would hardly follow that there is such an analysis of the traditional concept.

Some of the objections raised against the view that (1) is analyzed by (3) may also be raised against the view that (1) is analyzed by the following:

(4) The majority of human beings prefer X as such to Y.

Against (3) it was urged that the mere fact that someone prefers one state of affairs to another does not imply that the former is intrinsically better than the latter. The mere fact that someone might prefer an instance of *Schadenfreude* to an instance of *Mitleid* or *Mitfreude* does not imply that the former is intrinsically better than the latter. Were someone to prefer Jones's taking pleasure in Smith's suffering to Gray's taking pleasure in Green's joy, his preference would be perverse and ethically inappropriate or unfitting. But if the fact that one person prefers X as such to Y does not imply that X is intrinsically better than Y, it is not clear why we should think that there being a majority of persons having that same preference implies that X is intrinsically better than Y. Why should an instance of *Schadenfreude* be intrinsically better than an instance of *Mitleid* if the majority were to prefer it? The number and percentage of persons are irrelevant. Were the vast majority of persons to have such a preference, their preference would be as perverse and ethically inappropriate as that of a single person. This inappropriate preference would simply be more widespread and common. Furthermore, we may also ask, as before, whether our own suffering would be intrinsically better than our own joy were it true that the majority preferred the former to the latter. It is hard to believe that anyone could seriously think so.

It should also be noted that (4) has the same awkward implications as (3) with respect to the value of certain states of affairs involving the pleasure or pain of brute animals. For (4), like (3), implies that one state of affairs is intrinsically better than another only if the former is preferred to the latter. One may argue that the problem is even more acute with respect to (4), since it is surely true that the majority of human beings have never considered the states of affairs *there being 1,248 animals experiencing pleasure and there being 1,112 animals experiencing pain,* and it is not clear that the majority of human beings actually do prefer the former to the latter, even if it is true that they would do so were they to consider them both. Still, this view implies that the former state of affairs would not be intrinsically better had there not been creatures capable of conceiving them both and forming some preference toward them. Indeed, this view implies something even stronger than (3), namely, that the former would not be intrinsically better had there not been a *majority* of human beings who preferred the former to the latter. According to (4), had the majority of humans been indifferent to animal pleasure and pain or preferred, as grotesque children sometimes do, animal pain to pleasure, the greater aggregate of animal pleasure would not be intrinsically better than the lesser sum of animal pain.

Both (3) and (4) are attempts to provide an analysis of intrinsic preferability in terms of the actual intrinsic preferences of some persons or group of persons. Let us consider the view that (1) can be analyzed by the following:

(5) X would be preferred simpliciter to Y by someone who was fully informed and vividly aware of all (or all available) nonethical facts.

Given the counterfactual nature of (5), it is possible that X is intrinsically better than Y even if no one actually prefers X to Y. This is one respect in which (5) differs from (3). A second difference is that (5) involves the concept of preference in an ideal or highly improved epistemic state. But does (5) ultimately fare any better than (3) as an analysis of (1)? I don't think so. In fact, (5) seems open to many of the same objections raised against (3). We may grant that it is possible that exposure to additional information can change a person's preferences and attitudes. It seems possible that someone has an unfavorable attitude toward a certain class of people or toward people in a certain occupation that is based on false beliefs or partial information and that his attitude would change if he were in a more favorable epistemic state. Perhaps he hates Jews because he was raised hearing lies about them, or perhaps he hates philosophers because he believes they are all too lazy to find productive work. His exposure to additional information might produce a change in his attitude. But even if this is conceded, we have no reason to think that everything that strikes us as an ethically inappropriate preference would be eliminated or "cured" in this way. It seems possible that someone might be indifferent to some other person's pleasure or pain, that he might not prefer as such the other's being pleased to the other's being in pain. But even if this lack of compassion were to survive exposure to the relevant facts, it is still reasonable for us to believe that the other person's being pleased is intrinsically better than his being in pain. Similarly, if someone in the enhanced epistemic state would prefer an instance of *Schadenfreude* to an instance of *Mitleid* or *Mitfreude,* it would not follow that the former was intrinsically better than the latter or that this preference was ethically fitting or appropriate. Nothing in (5) excludes the possibility that such perverse preferences survive the "cognitive psychotherapy" of exposure to full information.

Furthermore, it seems possible that different persons have different intrinsic preferences given full or all available information, that one person in the enhanced epistemic state might prefer X to Y and that another person might prefer Y to X. If this is true and if (5) were an analysis of (1), it would follow that X is intrinsically better than Y and that Y is intrinsically better than X. But it has already been pointed out in the discussion of (3) that this result is simply unacceptable if we are attempting to provide an analysis of the traditional concept of intrinsic value, for the traditional notion is such that if X is intrinsically better than $Y,$ then Y is not intrinsically better than W. At best, (5), like (3), can be taken as an attempt to capture the notion of something's being intrinsically better *for* someone, as an attempt to say what it is appropriate for a particular person to prefer. Yet we may note that if the preceding objection is correct, then (5) does not even succeed in telling us what it is for a particular person's preferences to be ethically fitting or unreasonable.

In light of the arguments given in this appendix, it is prima facie reasonable to hold that intrinsic value is not analyzable by any natural property or state of affairs. Although it has not been demonstrated, proved, or shown that traditional naturalism is false, it is reasonable for us to reject it, if only because of the failure of some of the historically most prominent candidate analyses. Until some candidate emerges that is clearly satisfactory, it is reasonable for us to reject traditional naturalism.

Selected Bibliography

Achinstein, Peter. "Concepts of Evidence." *Mind* 87 (January 1978): 22–45.
Aristotle. *The Basic Works of Aristotle.* Ed. Richard McKeon. New York: Random House, 1941.
  Nicomachean Ethics. Translated by Martin Ostwald. Indianapolis: Bobbs–Merrill Co., 1962.
Audi, Robert. "Foundationalism, Epistemic Dependence, and Defeasibility." *Synthese* 55 (April 1983): 119–39.
  Belief, Justification, and Knowledge. Belmont, Calif. Wadsworth Publishing Co., 1988.
Bender, John W., ed. *The Current State of the Coherence Theory.* Dordrecht: Kluwer Academic Publishers, 1989.
Blanshard, Brand. *Reason and Goodness.* New York: Humanities Press, 1978.
BonJour, Laurence. *The Structure of Empirical Knowledge.* Cambridge, Mass.: Harvard University Press, 1985.
Brentano, Franz. *The Origin of Our Knowledge of Right and Wrong.* Translated by Roderick Chisholm and Elizabeth Schneewind. London: Routledge & Kegan Paul, 1969.
  The Foundation and Construction of Ethics. Translated by Elizabeth Schneewind. New York: Humanities Press, 1973.
Brink, David O., *Moral Realism and the Foundations of Ethics.* Cambridge: Cambridge University Press, 1989.
Broad, C. D. *Five Types of Ethical Theory.* New York: Harcourt, Brace and Co., 1930.
  Broad's Critical Essays in Moral Philosophy. Edited by David R. Cheney. London: George Allen & Unwin, 1971.
Butchvarov, Panayot. *Skepticism in Ethics.* Indianapolis: Indiana University Press, 1989.
Carson, Tom. "Happiness, Contentment, and the Good Life." *Pacific Philosophical Quarterly* 62 (October 1981): 378–92.
Chisholm, Roderick. "Practical Reason and the Logic of Requirement." In *Practical Reason,* ed. Stephan Korner, pp. 2–13. Oxford: Basil Blackwell, 1974.
  Person and Object. LaSalle, Ill.: Open Court Publishing Co., 1976.
  Theory of Knowledge. 2nd ed. Englewood Cliffs, N.J.: Prentice-Hall, 1978.
  "Defining Intrinsic Value." *Analysis* 41 (March 1981): 99–100.
  The Foundations of Knowing. Minneapolis: University of Minnesota Press, 1982.
  Brentano and Intrinsic Value. Cambridge: Cambridge University Press, 1986.

On Metaphysics. Minneapolis: University of Minnesota Press, 1989.

Theory of Knowledge. 3rd. ed. Englewood Cliffs, N.J.: Prentice-Hall, 1989.

Chisholm, Roderick, and Ernest Sosa. "On the Logic of 'Intrinsically Better'." *American Philosophical Quarterly* 3 (July 1966): 244–9.

Dostoevsky, Fyodor. *The Brothers Karamazov*. Translated by Constance Garnett. New York: Macmillan and Co., 1923.

Edwards, Rem. *Pleasures and Pains: A Theory of Qualitative Hedonism*. Ithaca, N.Y.: Cornell University Press, 1979.

Epictetus. *The Encheiridion*. In *Ethics,* 6th edition, ed. Oliver Johnson. Fort Worth Tex.: Holt, Rhinehart, and Winston, 1989; reprint *The Discourses,* Volume II. Translated by W. A. Oldfather. Cambridge, Mass.: Harvard University Press.

Ewing, A. C. *The Definition of Good*. New York: Macmillan and Co., 1947.

Second Thoughts in Moral Philosophy. New York: Macmillan and Co., 1959.

The Fundamental Questions of Philosophy. London: Routledge & Kegan Paul, 1951.

Ethics. New York: Free Press, 1953.

Value and Reality. London: George Allen & Unwin, 1973.

Feldman, Fred. *Introductory Ethics*. Englewood Cliffs, N.J.: Prentice-Hall, 1978.

Doing the Best We Can. Dordrecht: D. Reidel Publishing Co., 1986.

"Two Questions About Pleasure." In *Philosophical Analysis: A Defense by Example,* ed. David F. Austin, pp. 59–81. Dordrecht: Kluwer Academic Publishers, 1987.

Feldman, Richard. "Reliability and Justification." *The Monist* 68 (April 1985): 159–74.

Findlay, John. *Values and Intentions*. London: George Allen & Unwin, 1961.

Axiological Ethics. London: Macmillan and Co., 1970.

Foot, Philippa, ed. *Theories of Ethics*. Oxford: Oxford University Press, 1979.

Frankena, William. *Ethics*. 2nd edition. Englewood Cliffs, N.J.: Prentice-Hall, 1973.

Hall, Everett. *What Is Value?* New York: Humanities Press, 1952.

Our Knowledge of Fact and Value. Chapel Hill: University of North Carolina Press, 1961.

"The Empirical Justifiability of Valuative Sentences." In *Categorial Analysis,* ed. E. M. Adams. Chapel Hill: University of North Carolina Press, 1964.

Harman, Gilbert. "Toward a Theory of Intrinsic Value." *The Journal of Philosophy,* 64 (December 1967): 792–804.

The Nature of Morality. New York: Oxford University Press, 1977.

Hick, John. "Evil and the Infinite Future Good." In *A Modern Introduction to Philosophy*. 3rd edition, ed. Paul Edwards and Arthur Pap, pp. 470–2. New York: Free Press, 1973.

Kant, Immanuel. *Groundwork of the Metaphysic of Morals*. Translated and analyzed by H. J. Paton. New York: Harper & Row, 1964.

Korsgaard, Christine. "Two Distinctions in Goodness." *The Philosophical Review* 42 (April 1983): 169–96.

Lemos, Noah M. "Coherence and Epistemic Priority." *Philosophical Studies* 41 (May 1982): 299–315.

"Warrant, Emotion, and Value." *Philosophical Studies* 57 (October 1989): 175–92.

"Higher Goods and the Myth of Tithonus." *The Journal of Philosophy,* 90 (September 1993): 482–96.

Lemos, Ramon M. *Rights, Goods, and Democracy.* Cranbury, N.J.: Associated University Presses, 1986.

Lewis, C. I. *An Analysis of Knowledge and Valuation.* LaSalle, Ill.: Open Court Publishing Co., 1946.

Lycan, William. "Moral Facts and Moral Knowledge." *The Southern Journal of Philosophy* 24, Supplement (1986): 79–94.

Mackie, J. L. *Ethics: Inventing Right and Wrong.* New York: Penguin Books, 1977.

Mandlebaum, Maurice. *The Phenomenology of Moral Experience.* Glencoe, Ill.: Free Press, 1955.

Meinong, Alexius. *On Emotional Presentation.* Translated by Marie-Luise Schubert Kalsi. Evanston, Ill.: Northwestern University Press, 1972.

Mill, John Stuart. *Utilitarianism.* Edited with an introduction by George Sher. Indianapolis: Hackett Publishing Co., 1977.

Moore, G. E. *Principia Ethica.* Cambridge: Cambridge University Press, 1903.

Review of *The Origin of the Knowledge of Right and Wrong,* by Franz Brentano. In *The International Journal of Ethics* 14 (October 1903): 115–23.

Ethics. Oxford: Oxford University Press, 1912.

Philosophical Studies. London: Routledge & Kegan Paul, 1922.

Philosophical Papers. London: George Allen & Unwin, 1959.

Newman, J. H. *Certain Difficulties Felt by Anglicans in Catholic Teaching.* London: Longmans, Green and Co., 1885.

Nozick, Robert. *Anarchy, State, and Utopia.* New York: Basic Books, 1974.

Parfit, Derek. *Reasons and Persons.* New York: Oxford University Press, 1984.

"Overpopulation and the Quality of Life." In *Applied Ethics,* ed. Peter Singer, pp. 143–64. New York: Oxford University Press, 1986.

Pastin, Mark. "Modest Foundationalism and Self-Warrant." In *Essays on Knowledge and Justification* ed. George S. Pappas and Marshall Swain, pp. 279–88. Ithaca, N.Y.: Cornell University Press, 1978.

Plato. *Philebus.* Translated and with a commentary by R. Hackforth. Cambridge: Cambridge University Press, 1972.

Pollock, John L. *Contemporary Theories of Knowledge.* Totowa, N.J.: Rowman and Littlefield, 1986.

"A Theory of Moral Reasoning." *Ethics* 96 (April 1986): 506–23.

Quinn, Warren. "Theories of Intrinsic Value." *American Philosophical Quarterly* 11 (1974): 123–32.

"Truth and Explanation in Ethics." *Ethics* 96 (1986): 524–44.

Raz, Joseph, ed. *Practical Reasoning.* Oxford: Oxford University Press, 1978.

Reid, Thomas. *Essays on the Intellectual Powers of Man.* Cambridge, Mass.: MIT Press, 1969; reproduced from *The Works of Thomas Reid,* Volumes II and III. Charlestown, Mass.: Samuel Etheridge, Jr., Volume II, 1814; Volume III, 1815.

Thomas Reid's Inquiry and Essays. Edited by Keith Lehrer and Ronald Beanblossom, introduction by Ronald Beanblossom. Indianapolis: Bobbs-Merrill

Co., 1975; selections reproduced from *The Works of Thomas Reid,* 6th edition, ed. W. Hamilton. Edinburgh: Maclachlen and Stewart, 1863.

Ross, W. D. *The Right and the Good.* Indianapolis: Hackett Publishing Co., 1988; reprint Oxford: Oxford University Press, 1930.

Foundations of Ethics. Oxford: Oxford University Press, 1939.

Scheler, Max. *Formalism in Ethics and Non-Formal Ethics of Value.* Translated by Manfred S. Frings and Roger L. Funk. Evanston, Ill.: Northwestern University Press, 1973.

Schilpp, Paul Arthur, ed. *The Philosophy of G. E. Moore,* 3rd edition. La Salle, Ill.: Open Court Publishing Co., 1968.

Schopenhauer, Arthur. *The Basis of Morality.* Translated by A. Broderick Bullock. London: Swan Sonneschein, 1903.

Sosa, Ernest. "The Raft and the Pyramid: Coherence versus Foundations in the Theory of Knowledge," In *Midwest Studies in Philosophy V,* ed. Peter French, Theodore E. Uehling, and Howard Wettstein, pp. 3–25. Minneapolis: University of Minnesota Press, 1980.

"Moral Relativism, Cognitivism, and Defeasible Rules." *Social Philosophy and Policy,* forthcoming.

Summerfield, Donna M. "Modest a Priori Knowledge." *Philosophy and Phenomenological Research* 51 (March 1991): 39–66.

Tolhurst, William. "On the Epistemic Value of Moral Experience." *The Southern Journal of Philosophy* 29, Supplement (1986): 67–88.

Van Cleve, James. "Epistemic Supervenience and the Circle of Belief." *The Monist* 68 (January 1985): 90–104.

Zimmerman, Michael J. "Evaluatively Incomplete States of Affairs." *Philosophical Studies* 43 (March 1983): 211–24.

211

Index

213

214

retribution, value of, 37
Ross, W. D. 3, 10, 36, 118, 133, 134; bearers of value, 20, 24, 33; conditionality, 41–6; higher goods, 48–50, 54–5

St. Thomas, 42, 88
Scheler, Max, 180, 181
Schopenhauer, Arthur, 15, 51–2, 201
semantic test of properties, 123–4; *see also* naturalism, properties
Sher, George, 59
Sidgwick, Henry, 60
Sosa, Ernest, 14, 105f, 158f, 171, 174–5, 179

states of affairs: basic assumptions, 21–2; identity criteria, 112–8; objects of ethical belief, 103–7; *see also* bearers of value, natural properties and facts, naturalism, nonnaturalism
supervenience, 5, 111, 118–20, 171
summation, principle of, 33, 48, 59, 61–6; *see also* organic unities, rank, principle of
Summerfield, Donna, 146–9, 165, 167

Tolhurst, William, 86, 180, 182–3

universality, principle of, 11, 25, 32, 40, 47; *see also* conditionality, principle of